MODERN ENGLISH STRUCTURES

FORM, FUNCTION, AND POSITION
SECOND EDITION

Workbook and Answer Key

BERNARD T. O'DWYER

broadview press

BROADVIEW PRESS

is an independent, international publishing house, incorporated in 1985. Broadview believes in shared ownership, both with its employees and with the general public; since the year 2000 Broadview shares have traded publicly on the Toronto Venture Exchange under the symbol bdp.

NORTH AMERICA

PO Box 1243
Peterborough, Ontario
Canada K9J 7H5

PO Box 1015
3576 California Road
Orchard Park, New York
USA 14127

tel (705) 743-8990
fax (705) 743-8353
customerservice
    @broadviewpress.com

UK, IRELAND, AND
CONTINENTAL EUROPE

NBN International
Estover Road, Plymouth
PL6 7PY, UK
tel 44 (0) 1752 202300
fax order line:
44 (0) 1752 202330
enquiries@nbninternational.
    com

AUSTRALIA

UNIREPS University of
New South Wales
Sydney, NSW 2052 Australia
tel: 61 2 96640999
fax: 61 2 96645420
infopress@unsw.edu.au

www.broadviewpress.com

LIBRARY AND ARCHIVES CANADA CATALOGUING IN PUBLICATION

O'Dwyer, Bernard
    Modern English structures : form, function, and position.
    Workbook and answer key / Bernard T. O'Dwyer. — 2nd ed.

13-digit ISBN: 978-1-55111-764-5
10-digit ISBN: 1-55111-764-9

1. English language—Grammar—Problems, exercises, etc.   I. Title.

PE1112.O38 2006 Suppl.   428'.2   C2006-902656-4

Broadview Press acknowledges the financial support of the Government of Canada through the Book Publishing Industry Development Program (BPIDP) for our publishing activities.

Original design by Zack Taylor, Black Eye Design, Inc. Second Edition by Liz Broes, Black Eye Design Inc. Typeset in Bembo, Agenda, and Filosofia. Cover Design by Lisa Brawn

Printed in Canada

This book has been printed on 100% post consumer waste paper, certified Eco-logo and processed chlorine free.

CONTENTS

[3]

Modifiers   151
Appositives and complements   154
Connectors   155
Grammatical functions   157
Match exercises   165
Paragraph analysis   169

EIGHT CLAUSE FUNCTIONS   172

Definitions   172
Grammatical functions of noun clauses   174
Grammatical functions of relative pronouns   175
Relative adjective and adverb clauses as modifiers   176
Grammatical functions of adverb clauses   179
Grammatical functions of dependent clauses   181
Match exercises   187
Paragraph analysis   191

NINE GRAMMATICAL POSITIONS   196

Definitions   196
Nominal positions   198
Verbal positions   201
Adjectival positions   203
Adverbial positions   207
Grammatical positions   210
Match exercises   213
Paragraph analysis   216

TEN SENTENCES   222

Definitions   222
SVO variations   223
Sentence structure variations   224
Sentence pattern variations   228
Match exercises   232
Paragraph analysis   235
Sentence analysis   237

✿ ✿ ANSWER KEY   239

INTRODUCTION

Modern English Structures, the textbook which precedes this *Workbook*, presents and discusses the theoretical points of Modern English grammar; the *Workbook* applies these theoretical points to practical exercises. Each of the ten chapters of exercises parallels chapters of theory in the textbook.

To illustrate the use of English grammar, I have selected examples from nineteenth, twentieth, and twenty-first century authors. These vary in style and include literary writers, academic authors, and newspaper journalists. I chose these examples to provide an introduction to the many styles found in written English; keep in mind that *structure plus style is the basis of understanding language in use*.

Wherever possible I have taken complete sentences from these authors; at times, however, because some authors use extremely long sentences, I have taken only dependent clausal structures to emphasize the grammatical focus. Where illustrative examples could not be found, contrived examples are used; but these are very few. All examples have been documented and precise references are available upon request.

With the exception of chapters 5 and 10 (which have 15 exercises respectively), all other chapters have 20 exercises each. These exercises become more difficult as you proceed. The more challenging exercises are those that ask you to match specific sentence structures and to find or identify grammatical features in paragraphs.

The best tool that I can recommend to assist you in these exercises is a good dictionary—not just any dictionary, but one that identifies affixes and the grammatical functions of words. You should be able to look up morphemes (affixes) and learn their meanings; you should also be able to identify many other features of the various word groups. Developing an understanding of the form of words helps in understanding grammatical functions and grammatical positions. If you have access to the internet, there are many excellent dictionaries available to you through that medium as well.

You do not need to complete all of the exercises in this book. Some students will enjoy doing them like a crossword puzzle; others will find them boring. However, they are essential and play a significant role in successfully understanding English grammar. If you find as you work through a set of exercises that you are completing them correctly, you might consider moving on to the next group. Exercises should be challenging.

HOW TO USE THE KEY

You should not look at the answer key until after you have completed a full exercise. Too many students review the keys first, or go one-on-one while completing the exercises. If you review a key before answering an exercise, then you are answering the exercise with prepared answers. By constantly referring to the key as you go along, you have no way of knowing whether you are completing the exercise correctly or not. Chances are that you are looking at the next answer while correcting the previous one. It is essential to complete the whole exercise first, and then to refer to the key. By doing so, you can be confident that you are utilizing the material correctly. The degree of success achieved in completing these exercises will reflect your progress in the course.

WHEN TO BEGIN EXERCISES

Begin the exercises when you have completed the corresponding chapter in the text. If you leave the exercises until later, you will be into new text material and this may cause further problems. On the other hand, do not go page by page; that is, do not study one page, do one exercise, and then look up the answers. A little distance from the material is helpful. Wait until most of the chapter has been completed before starting. By that time you will have an overview of all the material in that chapter, which will be very helpful.

Another good approach is to divide a chapter into sections and to complete the exercises after that section. But there is no definitive means of answering these exercises. The point here is that the best approach is to allow a little time to elapse between theory and practice.

workbook

1 MORPHEMES

DEFINITIONS

⚙ **E1-1** → Match Part A with the correct definition in Part B.

Part A

1. Morphemes are. . . . . _____
2. Morphemes create. . . . . _____
3. Listing variations of a single lexical form is. . . . . _____
4. Morphemes can consist of one or several . . . . _____
5. Free morphemes do not . . . . _____
6. Free morphemes join with. . . . . _____
7. Bound morphemes require . . . . _____
8. Lexical meaning is . . . . _____
9. Affixes are bound morphemes . . . . _____
10. Affixes create new words from. . . . . _____
11. Affixes sometimes change word categories . . . . _____
12. A base is . . . . _____
13. A stem is . . . . _____
14. Prefixes are. . . . . _____
15. An ablaut is . . . . _____
16. Derivation describes the process of . . . . _____
17. Inflectional morphemes are. . . . . _____
18. Unlike its Germanic cousins, English has . . . . _____
19. An umlaut is . . . . _____
20. Grammatical meaning has to do with . . . . _____

Part B

   A. ... a paradigm.

   B. ... lost most of its inflections, which were more commonly used in Old English.

   C. ... basic meaningful units in our grammatical system.

   D. ... pre-existing words.

   E. ... derivational morphemes added to the beginning of a base or stem to create new words from pre-existing ones.

   F. ... the lexical morpheme, with or without derivational affixes, minus all inflectional affixes.

   G. ... from one word class to another by adding affixes.

   H. ... the addition of affixes or change of stem to form new derivative words.

   I. ... require a second morpheme to express lexical meaning.

   J. ... the lexical morpheme minus all derivational and inflectional affixes.

   K. ... a dictionary meaning that a speaker attaches to actual objects and events.

   L. ... a morphological process (internal modification) in nouns.

   M. ... a second morpheme, free or bound, to form a word, to change word category or to extend grammatical meaning.

   N. ... the relationships of words within sentences.

   O. ... new words, change word category, or extend grammatical meaning.

   P. ... other free and/or bound morphemes to create words.

   Q. ... identified as prefixes and suffixes that occur before or after a base morpheme.

   R. ... syllables or parts of syllables.

   S. ... a morphological process (internal modification) in verbs.

   T. ... bound morphemes attached to a base or a stem as suffixes, or inserted into words as umlauts or ablauts.

BASE MORPHEMES

✿ E1-2 → Identify the base morphemes.

Example: nonmilitary → military

1. empower	_____	6. cannot	_____
2. happily	_____	7. annual	_____
3. guiltless	_____	8. successful	_____
4. authentication	_____	9. undesirability	_____
5. oceanography	_____	10. depersonalize	_____

✿ E1-3 → Identify the base morphemes.

Example: popularize → popular

1. uninhabitable	_____	6. irregularities	_____
2. canonization	_____	7. unenlightenment	_____
3. situation	_____	8. assimilation	_____
4. non-representational	_____	9. nonreciprocating	_____
5. broadcasting	_____	10. exemplification	_____

FREE MORPHEMES

1 While free morphemes are frequently base morphemes, base morphemes are not always free.

✿ E1-4 → Identify the free morphemes.[1]

Example: unhappiness → happy

1. architecturally	_____	6. unwillingness	_____
2. laboriousness	_____	7. mistreatment	_____
3. baseball	_____	8. nonobservance	_____
4. unperishable	_____	9. gravitational	_____
5. oversubscribe	_____	10. ventilation	_____

✿ E1-5 → Identify the free morphemes.

Example: richest → rich

1. kaleidoscope	_____	6. mythological	_____
2. undisclosed	_____	7. disproportionate	_____
3. nonconformity	_____	8. discontinuance	_____
4. infirmities	_____	9. unperishable	_____
5. disinterment	_____	10. multiformity	_____

BOUND MORPHEMES

☼ **E1-6** → Identify the bound morphemes.

Example: smarter → er

1. dropping _____
2. redevelop _____
3. waters _____
4. behold _____
5. confiscation _____

6. incline _____
7. boldness _____
8. shouted _____
9. hottest _____
10. unhappy _____

☼ **E1-7** → Identify the bound morphemes.

1. tenure _____
2. colonization _____
3. misdirections _____
4. wealthiest _____
5. emboldened _____

6. expense _____
7. lengthening _____
8. unwillingness _____
9. subject _____
10. semiskilled _____

DERIVATIONAL MORPHEMES

☼ **E1-8** → Identify the derivational morphemes.

1. lanky _____
2. stillness _____
3. neutralized _____
4. symbolism _____
5. consistency _____

6. disagreement _____
7. noncritical _____
8. illegality _____
9. thriftiness _____
10. unpardonable _____

☼ **E1-9** → Identify the derivational morphemes.

1. ungracefully _____
2. nonfulfillment _____
3. unfortunately _____
4. inaccessibility _____
5. reconsiderations _____

6. demoralization _____
7. conceptualizing _____
8. representational _____
9. unimaginatively _____
10. comprehensively _____

INFLECTIONAL MORPHEMES

⚙ **E1-10** → Identify the inflection and its grammatical meaning in the bolded words.

Example: "The tinkly piano of my youth had **disappeared**."

	INFLECTION	MEANING
	-ed	{-ed ptp}

1. "Genomics is already **having** a large influence on medical practice." _____

2. "These **folks'** religious faith was very real." _____

3. "The sounds and the technology were the **latest**." _____

4. "Since this article was **written**, Sir Andrew Lloyd Webber has been knighted by Queen Elizabeth II of England." _____

5. "Its colorful collage of musical **images**." _____

6. "She **hates** her last name, which means happy in Spanish." _____

7. "She **dropped** onto a couch next to her disabled father." _____

8. "Security say they are simply **enforcing** laws adopted in 1996." _____

9. "'The numbers are **expected** to swell', added Ms. Schmalzbauer." _____

10. "First, he **bought** a motorcycle. (Truly, it was a hog.)" _____

⚙ **E1-11** → Identify the inflectional meanings noted in the bolded words.

1. "A cabdriver with 20 **years'** residence in the United States was deported to Nigeria six hours after he reported for a green card." _____

2. "He had been **denied** his rightful victory." _____

3. "**Women** are beginning to replace men as the primary migrants." _____

4. "She could no **longer** afford to buy clothes, food and school supplies for her son." _____

5. "What Roddick did not explain at the time was that he had **felt** a twinge in his leg." _____

6. "Indeed, **Edwards's** announcement of Pennington's return was perfunctory." _____

7. "Perhaps the **most** wrongheaded policy is that of incarcerating addicts." _____

8. "That**'s** how it was under the old system." _____

9. "The PGA also stuck with its system of **awarding** points only to the top 10." _____

10. "The police are also being provided larger weapons and **more secure** police stations." _____

MORPHEME CLASSIFICATION

⚙ **E1-12** → Identify the bolded morphemes according to the classifications.

Example: cats → bound → inflectional

	BASE	BOUND	FREE	DERIVATIONAL	INFLECTIONAL
1. g**ee**se	☐	☐	☐	☐	☐
2. **mal**content	☐	☐	☐	☐	☐
3. dis**agree**ment	☐	☐	☐	☐	☐
4. elat**ed**	☐	☐	☐	☐	☐
5. cloth**ed**	☐	☐	☐	☐	☐
6. st**o**le	☐	☐	☐	☐	☐
7. **cosm**ic	☐	☐	☐	☐	☐
8. hostil**iti**es	☐	☐	☐	☐	☐
9. alumn**i**	☐	☐	☐	☐	☐
10. inter**city**	☐	☐	☐	☐	☐

⚙ **E1-13** → Identify the bolded morphemes according to the classifications.

Example: inner-**city** → base → free

	BASE	BOUND	FREE	DERIVATIONAL	INFLECTIONAL
1. brok**en**	☐	☐	☐	☐	☐
2. **steril**ize	☐	☐	☐	☐	☐
3. sky**ward**	☐	☐	☐	☐	☐
4. childr**en**	☐	☐	☐	☐	☐
5. young**est**	☐	☐	☐	☐	☐
6. **even**handedness	☐	☐	☐	☐	☐
7. play**er**	☐	☐	☐	☐	☐
8. wep**t**	☐	☐	☐	☐	☐
9. great**er**	☐	☐	☐	☐	☐
10. e**ject**	☐	☐	☐	☐	☐

MATCH EXERCISES
✿ **E1-14** → Find examples for Part A in part B, **USING EACH SENTENCE ONLY ONCE.**

Part A
1. Noun umlaut (-S PL PS) . . . . _____
2. Bound Base . . . . _____
3. 5 derivational affixes . . . . _____
4. Verb ablaut (-ED PTP) . . . . _____
5. 2 prefixes, a stem plus an inflectional suffix . . . . _____

Part B
A. "The agreement cost the fund $20 million in losses, undisclosed commissions and fees."
B. "No one has ever considered it an institution subject to independence and integrity."
C. "But we've started women's groups."
D. "Most are victims of the nationwide policy of deinstitutionalization that has dominated the mental-health field since the mid '60s."
E. "Other investigations have found this practice was to hide the prisoners from Red Cross inspectors."

✿ **E1-15** → Find examples for Part A in Part B, **USING EACH SENTENCE ONLY ONCE.**

Part A
1. Polysyllabic single morpheme word . . . . _____
2. Spelling change to accommodate a derivational affix. . _____
3. Remove a single affix and still have a stem. . . . . _____
4. A derivational suffix with the meaning of "little or like" _____
5. Derivational suffix for an adverb . . . . _____

Part B
A. "Sometimes even their brilliancy produces a sort of stupidity."
B. "The larger ones are more apt to be dirty and dangerous."
C. "Then, with the lights dimmed and the volume control turned counterclockwise, the bass soloed the finale."
D. "The body rested in a fine mahogany coffin fitted with a plate of glass."
E. "The medical encounter or patient–doctor relationship is what medicine is about."

✿ E1-16 → Match the following.

1. extreme _____   A. 2 syllables
2. dog → do _____   B. a stem
3. able _____   C. bound base
4. variable _____   D. 1 morpheme
5. cosmic _____   E. not the same lexical base

✿ E1-17 → Match the following.

1. {-ing pp} _____   A. droppings
2. {-ed ptp} _____   B. went
3. {-s 3 p sg} _____   C. going
4. {-s pl} _____   D. is
5. {-ed pt} _____   E. woken

PARAGRAPH ANALYSIS

✿ E1-18 → Find examples for the following in the paragraph below.

1. Morpheme variant past participle

_____

2. Morpheme suffix meaning "one who"

_____

3. derivational suffix

_____

4. Derivational prefix plus an inflectional suffix on a stem

_____

5. Two free morphemes forming a word

_____

"BAGHDAD—In the second major assault on Baghdad's police force in two days, two car bombs—at least one of them driven by a suicide attacker—exploded next to an Iraqi police station just outside Baghdad's Green Zone on Saturday, killing seven people and wounding 59, mostly police.

Two U.S. soldiers were killed by roadside bombs in Baghdad and north of the capital Saturday, and two other Americans died in a suicide car bombing of their post near the Jordanian border the day before, the U.S. military said.

The attacks came after a day of increased violence Friday, when 30 Iraqis—most of them policemen—and two more American troops were killed in attacks in Baghdad and to the north."

⚙ **E1-19** → Find examples for the following in the paragraph below.

1. Derivational adjective suffix

   _____

2. Inflectional morpheme superlative

   _____

3. Inflectional morpheme singular possessive

   _____

4. Inflectional morpheme past participle

   _____

5. Bound base

   _____

"Ninety-five percent of all international commerce enters the United States through its roughly 360 public and private ports. But nearly 80 percent of that trade moves through only 10 ports, with the biggest loads passing through Los Angeles, Long Beach and Oakland in California and New York. That is why the nation's biggest ports are seen as particularly attractive as terrorist targets. Severely damaging one would not only cause deaths, injuries and property damage, but could also disrupt the flow of many basic goods into and out of the country, port officials say."

MORPHEME ANALYSIS
✿ E1-20 → Break down the following words into morphemes and identify each morpheme.

Example: **randomize**

random   -ize

FREE   BOUND   DERIVATIONAL

1. **workmanship**

2. **tenability**

3. **unwashed**

4. **immortality**

5. **unconventional**

6. **nonirritating**

7. **cryptographers**

8. **unenlightened**

9. **disproportionate**

10. **mispronunciations**

2   WORDS: FORM CLASS

DEFINITIONS

✿ **E2-1** → Match Part A with the correct definition in Part B.

Part A

1. Words are free-standing forms consisting of . . . . ____
2. Words as sentence constituents are analyzed in three ways: . . . . ____
3. Form class words are . . . . ____
4. Structure class words are . . . . ____
5. Nouns generally complete the paradigm of inflections . . . . ____
6. Periphrastic possessive attributes possessiveness . . . . ____
7. Common nouns designate . . . . ____
8. Proper nouns refer to . . . . ____
9. Concrete nouns have . . . . ____
10. Countable nouns occur . . . . ____
11. Verbs are form class words having distinction for . . . . ____
12. Irregular verbs are distinctive . . . . ____
13. Finite verbs are marked for . . . . ____
14. The initial verb in a verb phrase is always . . . . ____
15. Infinitives are . . . . ____
16. Participles are non-finite forms having the inflections . . . . ____
17. Gerunds are . . . . ____
18. Adjectives complete the paradigm of inflections . . . . ____
19. Adverbs are generally noted by the derivational suffixes . . . . ____
20. For irregular adverbs . . . . ____

Part B

A. ... -s plurality, 's singular possessive and 's or s' plural possessive.

B. ... with an inflectional ablaut.

C. ... a general class of objects or concepts.

D. ... -ing for the present participle and -en or -ed for the past participle.

E. ... the finite verb.

F. ... -er/more for the comparative and -est/most for the superlative.

G. ... stem forms of the verb preceded by the particle *to*; they are not limited by person, number or tense.

H. ... nouns, verbs, adjectives and adverbs.

I. ... positive forms differ more than the comparative or superlative.

J. ... -ly, -wise, and -ward.

K. ... as singular or plural in an identifiable number.

L. ... -ing verb forms that can replace nouns.

M. ... pronouns, determiners, auxiliaries, prepositions and conjunctions.

N. ... material substance while abstract nouns refer to concepts, qualities and states.

O. ... by grammatical form, by grammatical function, and by grammatical position.

P. ... the stem, the third person singular and the present participle.

Q. ... tense.

R. ... one or more morphemes of which one is the lexical base.

S. ... specific persons, places, things, or concepts.

T. ... to inanimate objects.

NOUNS

✿ **E2-2** → Identify the nouns by form, giving inflections for the noun paradigm. Where a
form is usually not inflected write n/a (non-applicable).

Example:

"Each yellow light looked down like a golden eye."

STEM	(-S PL)	(-S SG PS)	(-S PL PS)
light	lights	light's	n/a
eye	eyes	eye's	eyes'

1. "The sun goes down in a cold pale flare of light."

_____ _____ _____ _____

_____ _____ _____ _____

_____ _____ _____ _____

2. "The practice of medicine combines both science and art."

_____ _____ _____ _____

_____ _____ _____ _____

_____ _____ _____ _____

_____ _____ _____ _____

3. "A clamor of frosty sirens mourns at the night."

_____ _____ _____ _____

_____ _____ _____ _____

_____ _____ _____ _____

4. "The tinkly piano of my youth had disappeared."

_____ _____ _____ _____

_____ _____ _____ _____

5. "The eternal asker of answers, stands in the street."

_____ _____ _____ _____

_____ _____ _____ _____

_____ _____ _____ _____

6. "Over the past two years, a peace process has been initiated in Northern Ireland."

_____ _____ _____ _____

_____ _____ _____ _____

_____ _____ _____ _____

_____ _____ _____ _____

7. "The words ring over us like vague bells of sorrow."

_____ _____ _____ _____

_____ _____ _____ _____

_____ _____ _____ _____

8. "The defence had pressed for an acquittal, arguing that a fair retrial would be impossible."

_____ _____ _____ _____

_____ _____ _____ _____

_____ _____ _____ _____

9. "Christian rock traces its roots to the Jesus movement of the early 1970s."

_____ _____ _____ _____

_____ _____ _____ _____

_____ _____ _____ _____

10. "The court's decision signaled a turning point."

_____ _____ _____ _____

_____ _____ _____ _____

_____ _____ _____ _____

✿ **E2-3** → Identify the nouns by form and their categories.

Example:

"It's a challenge."

NOUN	TYPE
challenge	common-abstract-countable

1. "My three days' experiences had begun with a death."

   _____   _____

   _____   _____

   _____   _____

2. "The Yankees would probably be content with that storyline, too."

   _____   _____

   _____   _____

3. "Genomics is already having a large influence on medical practice."

   _____   _____

   _____   _____

   _____   _____

4. "I saw a rough Michigander, with an arm blown off at the shoulder."

   _____   _____

   _____   _____

   _____   _____

5. "There was an uncanny sort of fascination in watching him."

   _____   _____

   _____   _____

6. "On Friday, the pressure mounted on the Irish athletic director."

   _____   _____

   _____   _____

   _____   _____

7. "The Bruins were more physical and undoubtedly more experienced at this level."

   _____   _____

   _____   _____

8. "The auditorium was on the second floor of the building."

_____   _____

_____   _____

_____   _____

9. "The U.S.A. holds off the chaos and evil of the world until Jesus comes back."

_____   _____

_____   _____

_____   _____

_____   _____

_____   _____

10. "Many critics seem frustrated by how difficult it is to categorize your works."

_____   _____

_____   _____

☼ **E2-4** → Identify the noun-forming derivational suffixes.

Example:

"I knew not how to appraise my **bereavement**."

WORD		DERIVATIONAL SUFFIX
bereavement	+	-ment

1. "I had a sense of comfort, but not of security."

_____   +   _____

2. "The entire countryside had the solemn stillness of a summer night."

_____   +   _____

3. "At that moment my attention was drawn to a light that suddenly streamed from an upper window of the house."

_____   +   _____

4. "Vienneau first made his mark as a justice writer covering the Supreme Court."

_____   +   _____

5. "His stories convinced the federal government to track down and prosecute war criminals from the Second World War."

 _____ + _____

6. "Ukraine legislature fails to pass electoral changes."

 _____ + _____

7. "The home-heating subsidy for the poor will be improved by more than 25 per cent."

 _____ + _____

8. "You can also search our extensive database of internships."

 _____ + _____

9. "Manager Willie Randolf said he would be satisfied with a defensive specialist at first base."

 _____ + _____

 _____ + _____

10. "They seemed to him fragmentary utterances of a monstrous conspiracy against his body and soul."

 _____ + _____

 _____ + _____

VERBS

✿ **E2-5** → Identify the lexical verbs.

Example:

"The apartment and furniture would have been nothing extraordinary."

LEXICAL VERB
been

1. "While enjoying a month of fine weather at the sea coast, I was thrown into the company of a most fascinating creature—a real goddess in my eyes, as long as she took no notice of me."

 _____ _____

2. "She understood me at last, and looked a return—the sweetest of all imaginable looks."

 _____ _____

3. "Criticism against modern medicine has led to some improvements in the curricula of medical schools, which now teach students systematically on medical ethics, holistic approaches to medicine, the biopsychosocial model and similar concepts."

    _____   _____

4. "He had been standing a long time in that position, for I saw a pair of ousels passing and repassing scarcely three feet."

    _____   _____

5. "Possibly, some people might suspect him of a degree of underbred pride; I have a sympathetic chord within that tells me it is nothing of the sort."

    _____   _____   _____

    _____

6. "My dear mother used to say I should never have a comfortable home, and only last summer I proved myself perfectly unworthy of one."

    _____   _____   _____

7. "It is astonishing how sociable I feel myself, compared with him."

    _____   _____

8. "The study of human minds and what they do in the world, accordingly, was separated sharply from the study of nature."

    _____   _____

9. "Defenders of the academic disciplines often claim that all that is needed is that the results attained in the various disciplines be added to one another and integrated."

    _____   _____   _____

    _____   _____

10. "But our most basic criticism must be directed toward ourselves and our leaders, rather than toward the economists to whom we have turned for guidance."

    _____   _____

✿ E2-6 → Identify the verb-forming derivational affixes.

Example:

"Too stupified to be curious myself, I fastened my door and glanced round for the bed."

WORD		DERIVATIONAL AFFIX
fasten	+	-en

1. "But, for all that, I was not going to sympathize with him."

   _____ + _____

2. "It was the nose of a gentleman whom he was accustomed to shave twice weekly."

   _____ + _____

3. "One of his favorite techniques is to pour a blob of melted lead onto his already ashen canvas, which serves to heighten the suggestion of incineration."

   _____ + _____

4. "How dare you? I have kept you and clothed you and fed you! You owe everything to me!"

   _____ + _____

5. "'I don't think it possible for me to get home now without a guide,' I could not help exclaiming."

   _____ + _____

6. "Officials in Yakima are investigating what caused four railroad cars to derail and crash into a warehouse Sunday afternoon."

   _____ + _____

7. "Mr. Yushchenko was buoyed by the Supreme Court's ruling to invalidate the Nov. 21 run-off."

   _____ + _____

8. "But not all tears attest to equally deep springs of sorrow."

   _____ + _____

9. "All the buildings postdate 1950."

   _____ + _____

10. "The White House on Tuesday disclosed a series of orders that Mr. Bush signed last week intended to strengthen the nation's intelligence capabilities."

    _____ + _____

✿ E2-7 → Identify the source verb for the nouns.

Example:

"I sank into a basket chair feeling distinctly glad that I had accepted John's invitation."

		SOURCE VERB
invitation	→	invite

1. "But I don't see anything to laugh at. There's nothing funny about a proposal."

   _____

2. "The labourer is worthy of his hire, you know."

   _____

3. "Her few quiet remarks heightened my first impression of her as a thoroughly fascinating woman."

   _____

4. "The entertainment was a great success, Mrs. Inglethorp's recitation receiving tremendous applause."

   _____   _____   _____

5. "She took us up to her sanctum, and introduced us to her fellow dispenser."

   _____

6. "The Pentagon also said the medical care given detainees was first-rate."

   _____

7. "The issue of whether torture at Guantánamo was condoned or encouraged has been a problem before for the Bush administration."

   _____

8. "In them, our need for God and their forgiveness becomes blatantly apparent."

   _____

9. "Repentance denies complacency to the viewer of another's passion."

   _____   _____

10. "The 2-to-1 decision relied in large part on a decision in 2000 by the United States Supreme Court to allow the Boy Scouts to exclude gay scoutmasters."

    _____

⚙ E2-8 → Identify the lexical verbs and give all inflections.

Example:

"The front ranges stopped the tide of squatters for some little time."

STEM	(S 3RD P SG)	(-ING PP)	(-ED PT)	(-ED PTP)
stop	stops	stopping	stopped	stopped

1. "Men pushed farther and farther into the mountains."

_____ _____ _____ _____ _____

2. "This second range, however, seemed to mark the extreme limits of pastoral country."

_____ _____ _____ _____ _____

3. "It is surprising how soon the eye becomes accustomed to missing twenty sheep out of two or three hundred."

_____ _____ _____ _____ _____

_____ _____ _____ _____ _____

4. "He had never seen any one who had been there."

_____ _____ _____ _____ _____

_____ _____ _____ _____ _____

5. "At last I hinted about grog, and presently he feigned consent."

_____ _____ _____ _____ _____

_____ _____ _____ _____ _____

6. "The butter makes no sign of coming, at last one tells by the sound that the cream has gone to sleep."

_____ _____ _____ _____ _____

_____ _____ _____ _____ _____

_____ _____ _____ _____ _____

7. "His mouth extended almost from ear to ear, grinning horribly and showing all his teeth."

_____ _____ _____ _____ _____

8. "I heard their ghostly chanting."

_____ _____ _____ _____ _____

9. "They rose most vividly to my recollection the moment my friend began."

   _____ _____ _____ _____ _____

   _____ _____ _____ _____ _____

10. "But over and above these thoughts came that of the great range itself."

    _____ _____ _____ _____ _____

⚙ **E2-9** → Identify the bolded verbs as finite or non-finite.

Example:

   "ALICE was **beginning** to get very tired of sitting by her sister on the bank."

   beginning   non-finite

1. "Once or twice she **had** peeped into the book her sister was **reading**."
   - ☐ finite   ☐ non-finite
   - ☐ finite   ☐ non-finite

2. "In another moment down **went** Alice after it, never once considering how in the world she **was** to get out again."
   - ☐ finite   ☐ non-finite
   - ☐ finite   ☐ non-finite

3. "Mauriac's silence **is** ambivalent; it does not **break** the word of redemption as much as it **hushes** its utterance."
   - ☐ finite   ☐ non-finite
   - ☐ finite   ☐ non-finite
   - ☐ finite   ☐ non-finite

4. "Artists in the Christian rock scene **have** a tendency to copy the styles of successful mainstream performers in order to provide godly alternatives to whatever **is** popular at the time."
   - ☐ finite   ☐ non-finite
   - ☐ finite   ☐ non-finite

5. Closer to home, a California-based band that **has** been **making** a similar musical spiritual exploration, with very little notice or fanfare, **is** The Call."
   - ☐ finite   ☐ non-finite
   - ☐ finite   ☐ non-finite
   - ☐ finite   ☐ non-finite

6. "Although I **am** interested in differences between these two great religious traditions, I do not **believe** these differences **are** important for the critique of the dominant pattern of economic thinking."

☐ finite ☐ non-finite
☐ finite ☐ non-finite
☐ finite ☐ non-finite

7. "To what extent Germany **is** fairly **represented** in Kiefer's ideological campaign, the Germans themselves **are** in a far better position than I to decide."

☐ finite ☐ non-finite
☐ finite ☐ non-finite
☐ finite ☐ non-finite

8. "The judgment could **have** ramifications for similar cases, including a massive national lawsuit **being** pressed by more than 20 lawyers across Canada."

☐ finite ☐ non-finite
☐ finite ☐ non-finite

9. "That sense of uncertainty only **deepens** when she **thinks** of her older sister's delayed reaction to the outbreak."

☐ finite ☐ non-finite
☐ finite ☐ non-finite

10. "As she couldn't **answer** either question, it **didn't** much matter which way she **put** it."

☐ finite ☐ non-finite
☐ finite ☐ non-finite
☐ finite ☐ non-finite

✿ **E2-10** → Identify the bolded verbs as transitive, intransitive or linking verb.

Example:

"Can I **trust** myself?"

TRANSITIVE verb

1. "That **is** the goal towards which all divinely endowed, noble natures **strive**."

☐ transitive ☐ intransitive ☐ linking
☐ transitive ☐ intransitive ☐ linking

2. "The Irish **lost** a one-on-one competition for the coach who **emerged** as the university's leading candidate."

   □ transitive   □ intransitive   □ linking
   □ transitive   □ intransitive   □ linking

3. "We **were** in the small southern Indiana town where I **grew up**, and a gospel concert was advertised for the auditorium of the little Christian college there."

   □ transitive   □ intransitive   □ linking
   □ transitive   □ intransitive   □ linking

4. "Like the soprano, the tenor could not **hit** the high notes, but he **made up** for that by sporting a frizzy hairdo and by ripping open his ruffled shirt front, in the process making one wonder if he **were** really bald under the curls."

   □ transitive   □ intransitive   □ linking
   □ transitive   □ intransitive   □ linking
   □ transitive   □ intransitive   □ linking

5. "Mauriac, long a poignant witness to the connection between suffering and love, **knew** well that the cornerstone of his faith **was** at stake in Wiesel's narrative."

   □ transitive   □ intransitive   □ linking
   □ transitive   □ intransitive   □ linking

6. "The IRA has not **disbanded** nor scaled down its operations and has not **ceased** planning terrorist attacks to be carried out if the ceasefire **ends**."

   □ transitive   □ intransitive   □ linking
   □ transitive   □ intransitive   □ linking
   □ transitive   □ intransitive   □ linking

7. "She had **acquired** property, to an amount that **made** that luxury just possible."

   □ transitive   □ intransitive   □ linking
   □ transitive   □ intransitive   □ linking

8. "The changing political milieu **is creating** conditions that **are** more conducive to accommodation in any new Northern Ireland-wide assembly."

   □ transitive   □ intransitive   □ linking
   □ transitive   □ intransitive   □ linking

9. "The events in Pasadena **show** that theories of racism **are** not enough to explain the events surrounding anti-busing campaigns."

   □ transitive   □ intransitive   □ linking
   □ transitive   □ intransitive   □ linking

10. "Before he **arrived** at the university, he **had spent** most of his time writing books and teaching in the Catholic theology departments of several German universities."

☐ transitive ☐ intransitive ☐ linking
☐ transitive ☐ intransitive ☐ linking

ADJECTIVES

⚙ **E2-11** → Identify form class adjectives.

Example:

"There it stood, years afterwards, above the warehouse door: Scrooge and Marley."

ADJECTIVE
warehouse

1. "A frosty rime was on his head, and on his eyebrows, and his wiry chin."

_____   _____

2. "There's no protection for that undocumented labor, and even though we speak of family values, there's also no protection for the children."

_____   _____

3. "That drew snickers from opposition benches and indignation from the government side."

_____   _____

4. "A powerful car bomb detonated outside a Shiite mosque in the capital's Adhamiya neighbourhood."

_____   _____

_____   _____

5. "The patient–doctor relationship is important to the doctor in order to obtain an accurate medical history and obtain compliance with the treatment plan."

_____   _____

_____   _____

6. "Fundamentalists in all the major world religions tend to reinforce male-dominant gender roles."

_____   _____

_____   _____

7. "According to this final group, Christ had chosen America, especially its white immigrants, as a special rod of iron to scourge his wayward world and return it to the pristine purity of capitalist Eden."

_____   _____   _____

_____   _____   _____

8. "A genre distinction is usually drawn between 'contemporary Christian music' (ccm for short) and 'modern worship music.'"

_____   _____   _____

_____   _____

9. "A class action would also allow plaintiffs to sue for cultural damage such as language loss."

_____   _____

_____

10. "Deliberately and consciously the Enlightenment thinkers reacted against the Medieval understanding of the world in which organic models played a primary role."

_____   _____

_____   _____

✿ **E2-12** → Identify the adjectives and give all inflections.

Example:

"This wise and magnanimous programme for the world had passed."

STEM	{-ER CP}	{-EST SP}
wise	wiser	wisest
magnanimous	more magnanimous	most magnanimous

1. "A green and yellow parrot, which hung in a cage outside the door, kept repeating over and over: 'Allez vous-en!'"

_____   _____   _____

_____   _____   _____

2. "He walked down the gallery and across the narrow 'bridges.'"

_____   _____

3. "Her eyebrows were a shade darker than her hair."

   _____   _____   _____

4. "All declared that Mr. Pontellier was the best husband in the world."

   _____   _____   _____

5. "One would not have wanted her white neck a mite less full or her beautiful arms more slender."

   _____   _____   _____

   _____   _____   _____

   _____   _____   _____

   _____   _____   _____

6. "They all knew each other, and felt like one large family, among whom existed the most amicable relations."

   _____   _____   _____

   _____   _____   _____

7. "When it came her turn to read it, she did so with profound astonishment."

   _____   _____   _____

8. "But twice in her life she had left the Cheniere Caminada, and then for the briefest span."

   _____   _____   _____

9. "'He found wiser use for his money, he says,' explained Madame Lebrun."

   _____   _____   _____

10. "There were only a few lines, setting forth that he would leave the city that afternoon, that he had packed his trunk in good shape."

    _____   _____   _____

    _____   _____   _____

✿ **E2-13** → Identify the adjectives with derivational suffixes.

Example:

"I have described my critique as Buddhist-Christian."

BASE		DERIVATIONAL SUFFIX
Budda	+	-ist
Christ	+	-ian

1. "'Styles is really a glorious old place,' I said to John."

   _____   _____

2. "And, with a characteristic shrug, he dismissed whatever it was that was worrying him from his mind."

   _____   _____

3. "The evening passed pleasantly enough; and I dreamed that night of that enigmatical woman, Mary Cavendish."

   _____   _____

4. "The answer brought a momentary stiffness in its train."

   _____   _____

5. "This, we trust, will effectually silence the sensational rumours which still persist."

   _____   _____

6. "No, Cynthia is a protégée of my mother's, the daughter of an old schoolfellow of hers, who married a rascally solicitor."

   _____   _____

7. "An appreciative listener is always stimulating, and I described, in a humorous manner."

   _____   _____

   _____   _____

8. "Annie was a fine, strapping girl, and was evidently labouring under intense excitement, mingled with a certain ghoulish enjoyment of the tragedy."

   _____   _____

9. "The next morning dawned bright and sunny, and I was full of the anticipation of a delightful visit."

   _____   _____

   _____   _____

10. "I felt that I was right in my opinion that Dorcas was the person most affected by the personal side of the tragedy."

_____   _____

ADVERBS

⚙ **E2-14** → Identify the single-word adverbs.

Example:

So silently had he come up the path leading from the brook that we had not heard him.

ADVERB
silently

1. "The candles threw their flickering rays upward until they danced on the high ceiling."

_____

2. "It came down instantly with a crash, so that the panes rattled again."

_____   _____

3. "These things I remember, and likewise sobbing myself to sleep in the four-poster."

_____

4. "She turned to the letter again, holding it very near to her eyes, and made a wry face of impatience."

_____   _____   _____

5. "Sometimes men stopped and talked loudly there, and again a rattle of drums would send me running to see the soldiers."

_____   _____

_____   _____

6. "But I remember chiefly my insatiable longing to escape from this prison, as the great house soon became for me."

_____   _____

7. "Catching me by the hand, she ran like a deer across the road to where her grandfather was still quarrelling violently with Hans, and pulled him backward by the skirts of his hunting shirt."

_____   _____   _____

8. "Boy-like, I was absorbed in this."

    _____

9. "Polly Ann, just you go along and pretend to be happy, and tear off a snatch of your dress now and then, if you get a chance."

    _____   _____   _____

10. "Here and there a lean-to—silent remnant of the year gone by—spoke of the little bands of emigrants which had once made their way so cheerfully to the new country."

    _____   _____   _____

    _____   _____   _____

☼ **E2-15** → Identify the adverbs, giving their inflected forms.

POSITIVE	{-ER CP}	{-EST SP}
powerfully	more powerfully	most powerfully

1. "He was spotlessly neat, apparelled in immaculate white from shoes to hat."

    _____   _____   _____

2. "'Before you tell me what you think of me,' I went on quickly, 'will you kindly tell me what it is I've said or done?'"

    _____   _____   _____

    _____   _____   _____

3. "In time, beside the original disdain there grew up slowly another sentiment."

    _____   _____   _____

4. "Nevertheless, with black ingratitude he would throw up the job suddenly and depart."

    _____   _____

5. "The old training-ship chained to her moorings quivered all over, bowing gently head to wind."

    _____   _____   _____

6. "He saw the boat, manned, drop swiftly below the rail, and rushed after her."

    _____   _____   _____

7. "A yelling voice in her reached him faintly: 'Keep stroke, you young whelps.'"

    _____   _____

8. "Every morning the sun, as if keeping pace in his revolutions with the progress of the pilgrimage, emerged with a silent burst of light exactly at the same distance astern of the ship."

_____ _____ _____

9. "After two years of training he went to sea, and entering the regions so well known to his imagination, found them strangely barren of adventure."

_____ _____ _____

10. "He lay there battened down in the midst of a small devastation, and felt secretly glad he had not to go on deck."

_____ _____ _____

MATCH EXERCISES
✿ E2-16 → Find examples for Part A in Part B, **USING EACH SENTENCE ONLY ONCE**.

Part A

1. A noun without a singular _____
2. A verb with identical forms for the base, past tense and past participle _____
3. A gerund _____
4. A disyllabic adjective _____
5. An irregular adverb _____

Part B

A. "Exact casualty figures were hard to establish because many towns were cut off by landslides."
B. "I'm very happy that NBC asked me to be a part of 'The Apprentice' finale."
C. "Others were typically much older or far younger."
D. "Finally, somebody told the king he didn't have any clothes."
E. "To understand the working of the clock we attend only to efficient causes."

⚙ **E2-17** → Find examples for Part A in Part B, **USING EACH SENTENCE ONLY ONCE.**

Part A

1. An irregular noun plural   _____

2. A non-finite verb form   _____

3. An intransitive verb   _____

4. An irregular adjective   _____

5. An adverb   _____

Part B

A. "In 1576, El Greco was hounded out of town (or so we are told) for suggesting that Michelangelo, though a great sculptor, could not paint."

B. "She was quickly clapped into handcuffs, and within hours placed on a plane to her native Honduras."

C. "By all reports Virginia Feliz had been a happy 6-year-old before her mother's expulsion."

D. "Sticky bunker oil will be difficult to clean up and could harm endangered sea lions as well as sea otters, diving sea ducks, loons and salmon."

E. "The judge put off a ruling on the matter pending further legal arguments."

PARAGRAPH ANALYSIS

⚙ **E2-18** → Find examples for the following in the paragraph below.

1. A noun whose singular and plural forms are alike   _____

2. An irregular verb (-ED PTP)   _____

3. A regular adverb   _____

4. A polysyllabic adjective (-ER CP)   _____

5. An intransitive verb   _____

"The phrase 'contemporary Christian music' evokes for many people visions of pious confection and Amy Grant; singers preaching to the converted in an extremely insular subculture. However, a few performers in recent years have brought to the industry a more substantial expression of feelings, thoughts and impressions that center on a seriously considered journey of faith."

✿ **E2-19** → Find examples for the following in the paragraph below.

1. A noun (-S SG PS) _____

2. A word used as a noun and as an adjective _____

3. A transitive verb _____

4. A series of three adjectives _____

5. An adverb _____

"Medicine is a diverse field and the provision of medical care is therefore provided in a variety of locations. Primary healthcare medical services are provided by physicians or other health professionals who have first contact with a patient seeking medical treatment or care. These occur in physician's offices, clinics, nursing homes, schools, home visits and other places close to patients. About 90% of medical visits can be treated by the primary care provider. These include treatment of acute and chronic illnesses, preventive care and health education for all ages and both sexes."

✿ **E2-20** → Identify the bolded words, giving full descriptions, in the following paragraph.

1. _____
2. _____
3. _____
4. _____
5. _____
6. _____
7. _____
8. _____
9. _____
10. _____

"The **existing**[1] local government system in **Northern Ireland**[2] was **established**[3] following the Local Government (NI) Act (1972). Under this Act 26 local government districts have three basic roles: an executive role, a representative role and a consultative role. Their executive role involves the provision of a **limited**[4] range of

services, such as **environmental**[5] health, cleansing, recreation and **latterly**[6]
economic development. Services, such as housing, education, roads and personal social
services, are the responsibility of either government departments, public agencies or
area boards. The **councils'**[7] representative role involves nominating local councillors
to **sit**[8] as members of the various statutory boards. They are consulted by
government department officials on the operation of regional services in their area.
Their relatively minor role is illustrated by a current estimated net expenditure budget
of £192m from a total public expenditure purse of £8 billion. Yet local authorities
are[9] important, **apart**[10] from the executive functions they undertake."

3   WORDS: STRUCTURE CLASS

DEFINITIONS
✿ **E3-1** → Match Part A with the correct definition in Part B.

Part A

1. Pronouns are . . . . _____
2. We inflect many pronouns noting . . . . _____
3. Number is . . . . _____
4. Gender is a grammatical category . . . . _____
5. Case is a grammatical category for . . . . _____
6. Person is a category that . . . . _____
7. Personal pronouns are . . . . _____
8. Possessive pronouns mark the distinction of . . . . _____
9. Reflexive or intensive pronouns . . . . _____
10. Relative pronouns relate to other words in sentences . . . . _____
11. Three of the five relative pronouns have inflections for . . . . _____
12. Interrogative pronouns are question-words which produce . . . . _____
13. Reciprocal pronouns . . . . _____
14. Indefinite pronouns form a large class of words . . . . _____
15. Auxiliaries are structure class words making distinctions for . . . . _____
16. Non-finite verbs need . . . . _____
17. Modal auxiliaries note . . . . _____
18. Do is often used . . . . _____
19. Prepositions are structure words . . . . _____
20. Conjunctions are structure class words . . . . _____

Part B

A. ... prenominal (coming before a noun) or substitutional (substituting for a noun).

B. ... case but not for gender or person.

C. ... with masculine, feminine and sometimes neuter genders.

D. ... often identified as specifiers, quantifiers, and determiners.

E. ... probability, possibility, and obligation.

F. ... inflected nouns and pronouns showing their relationships to other words in the sentence.

G. ... number, gender, case and some for person.

H. ... express mutual relationships.

 I. ... primary auxiliaries to express tense, aspect and voice.

 J. ... information in contrast to yes/no questions.

K. ... as a stand-in auxiliary, much in the same way as the primary auxiliaries.

 L. ... preceding a noun or its replacement and introducing a phrase.

M. ... tense, aspect, and voice in the verb phrase.

N. ... identifying subordination, coordination, and conjunctiveness.

O. ... structure class words that substitute for nouns.

P. ... distinctive in person (first, second, third), number (singular and plural), and case (subjective, objective and possessive).

Q. ... rename or intensify a previous noun or pronoun.

R. ... a grammatical category referring to singular and plural.

S. ... but they do not rename them as reflexive pronouns do.

T. ... points out and notes the speaker or hearer.

PRONOUNS

⚙ **E3-2** → Identify the personal pronouns, marking them for person, number, gender, and case where possible.

Example:

"I saw his form pass by—appealing—significant—under a cloud—perfectly silent."

PRONOUN	PERSON	NUMBER	GENDER	CASE
I	1st	Singular	n/a	Subjective
his	3rd	Singular	Masculine	Possessive

1. "We want to make sure that whatever decision is taken is one that is going to benefit our own security."

   _____   _____   _____   _____   _____

   _____   _____   _____   _____

2. "'Chad had to go through the steps to show me he could do it,' Edwards said."

   _____   _____   _____   _____   _____

   _____   _____   _____   _____   _____

   _____   _____   _____   _____   _____

3. "'I guess that's why they call him "Cat,"' Crawford said."

   _____   _____   _____   _____   _____

   _____   _____   _____   _____   _____

   _____   _____   _____   _____   _____

4. "The unsteady phantom of terror behind his glassy eyes seemed to stand still and look into mine wistfully."

   _____   _____   _____   _____   _____

   _____   _____   _____   _____   _____

5. "None of them was quick enough to see her go, but they saw that she was gone right enough, and sang out together."

   _____   _____   _____   _____   _____

   _____   _____   _____   _____   _____

   _____   _____   _____   _____   _____

   _____   _____   _____   _____

6. "I haven't opened my lips in your hearing."

_____ _____ _____ _____ _____

_____ _____ _____ _____ _____

_____ _____ _____ _____ _____

7. "*The New York Times* recently obtained a memorandum, based on the report, that quotes from it in detail and lists its major findings."

_____ _____ _____ _____ _____

_____ _____ _____ _____ _____

8. "Where you see that, they do very well."

_____ _____ _____ _____ _____

_____ _____ _____ _____ _____

9. "'It wasn't anything that would have disturbed much either of us two,' I said."

_____ _____ _____ _____ _____

_____ _____ _____ _____ _____

_____ _____ _____ _____ _____

10. "Upon my soul! I think they would have had their wish if they had only kept quiet."

_____ _____ _____ _____ _____

_____ _____ _____ _____ _____

_____ _____ _____ _____ _____

_____ _____ _____ _____ _____

_____ _____ _____ _____ _____

✿ **E3-3** → Identify the reflexive/intensive pronouns, marking them for person, number, gender where possible, and reference.

Example:

"Richard therefore found himself largely his own master."

PRONOUN	PERSON	NUMBER	GENDER	REFERENCE
himself	3rd	Sg	masculine	Richard

1. "Point Pleasant itself was then a collection of half a dozen big farms which stretched from the Manasquan River to the ocean half a mile distant."

   _____ _____ _____ _____ _____

2. "She does not take any interest in my pink wrapper, but contents herself with passing cabs and stray dogs."

   _____ _____ _____ _____ _____

3. "You will enjoy those days more to look back to when you wandered around some little town by yourselves."

   _____ _____ _____ _____ _____

4. "I have had a first rate time but I do not see that there has been much in it to interest any one but myself."

   _____ _____ _____ _____ _____

5. "Yesterday we both tried to impress her by riding down in front of the porch and showing off the horses and ourselves."

   _____ _____ _____ _____ _____

6. "He hasn't left himself anything to do when he gets old."

   _____ _____ _____ _____ _____

7. "I think you will find some great thoughts in human beings—they will help you to understand yourself and God, when you try to help them God makes you happy my darling."

   _____ _____ _____ _____ _____

8. "At this time neither of these friends of Richard, nor Richard himself, allied themselves very closely to the literary colony."

   _____ _____ _____ _____ _____

   _____ _____ _____ _____ _____

9. "There are times when it is one's duty to assert oneself."

   _____ _____ _____ _____ _____

10. "Under the circumstances, I am afraid an inquest can hardly be avoided—these formalities are necessary, but I beg that you won't distress yourselves."

   _____ _____ _____ _____ _____

☼ **E3-4** → Identify the relative and interrogative pronouns, noting the type and giving the case where applicable.

Example:

"From the avenue came the sound of rushing men who wildly shouted."

PRONOUN	TYPE	CASE
who	relative	Sj (subjective)

1. "Given that liturgical use of the piece was not likely or practical, what did you think would happen with it?"

   _____ _____ _____

2. "These were the college boys who had returned home, the ones whose individual names were known."

   _____ _____ _____

   _____ _____ _____

3. "The Downing Street Declaration, set alongside a flurry of secret discussions which included an unpublished peace plan."

   _____ _____ _____

4. "If it was not a mother's place to look after children, whose on earth was it?"

   _____ _____ _____

5. "The groups and the songs that had gone before had received enthusiastic applause."

   _____ _____ _____

6. "Which song do you choose, 'The Dying Swan' or 'The Elegy on the Death of a Mad Dog'?"

   _____ _____ _____

7. "'Whom do you now elect as Koschevoi?' asked the chiefs."

   _____   _____   _____

8. "This was not addressed to Scrooge, or to any one whom he could see, but it produced an immediate effect."

   _____   _____   _____

9. "The fight over the future of a system whose existence has not yet been officially disclosed first came to light this week."

   _____   _____   _____

10. "Who was in Goodenow's corner?"

   _____   _____   _____

⚙ **E3-5** → Identify the demonstrative and reciprocal pronouns, noting the type.

1. **for demonstratives give proximity**

Example:

   "What do we want with all these things?"

PRONOUN	TYPE	PROXIMITY
these	demonstrative	nearby

2. **for reciprocals give referent**

Example:

   "But I really think we may suit one another much better than you suppose."

PRONOUN	TYPE	REFERENT
one another	reciprocal	we

1. "He has been trying to get Hamas, Islamic Jihad and Fatah, the main Palestinian faction, to diminish their sometimes violent rivalry, which has included assassinations of one another's leaders."

   _____   _____   _____

2. "This is Sotheby's fourth sale of wines from Massandra since 1990."

   _____   _____   _____

3. "They were silent—their faces hid against each other, and washed by each other's tears."

_____   _____   _____

_____   _____   _____

4. "Does everybody at the academy dress like that?"

_____   _____   _____

5. "Where unionists or nationalists do not form the largest single grouping these are described as no-majority councils."

_____   _____   _____

6. "The church-bells, with various tones, but all in harmony, were calling out, and responding to one another."

_____   _____   _____

7. "She is one of those who continue to suffer."

_____   _____   _____

8. "'People refer to that as a Sophie's choice situation,' he said."

_____   _____   _____

9. "They were rustics, living in a constricted valley, interested only in one another and in The Building."

_____   _____   _____

10. "So I think these are steps in the right direction."

_____   _____   _____

✿ **E3-6** → Identify the indefinite pronouns, indicating whether it is a specifier or a quantifier.

Example:

"I never heard of anyone whose whole heart was set upon finding a flower."

PRONOUN anyone   ■ SPECIFIER   ☐ QUANTIFIER

1. "Even these were fenced and guarded so that no one might come near to them."

_____   ☐ SPECIFIER   ☐ QUANTIFIER

2. "After three months of nothing, the two sides in the NHL lockout are at least talking to each other."

_____   ☐ SPECIFIER   ☐ QUANTIFIER

3. "I liked the way in which he told of his adventures, with a little frank boasting, enough to season but not to spoil the story."

_____   ☐ SPECIFIER   ☐ QUANTIFIER

4. "No one could have heard this low droning of the gathering clans."

_____   ☐ SPECIFIER   ☐ QUANTIFIER

5. "Some of the contents of the annex were reported this week by The Washington Post and The Los Ángeles Times."

_____   ☐ SPECIFIER   ☐ QUANTIFIER

6. "To prevent insurgents from discovering their identities, many lie to everyone, wives and family included, about their real jobs."

_____   ☐ SPECIFIER   ☐ QUANTIFIER

_____   ☐ SPECIFIER   ☐ QUANTIFIER

7. "I promise you everything, and this is all I ask in return. Do you consent?"

_____   ☐ SPECIFIER   ☐ QUANTIFIER

_____   ☐ SPECIFIER   ☐ QUANTIFIER

8. "Something that did not belong to him had dropped away; he had returned to a former state of being."

_____   ☐ SPECIFIER   ☐ QUANTIFIER

9. "Not from Spy Rock nor from anywhere else can you see anything at Hilltop that is not honest and pure and loyal."

_____ ☐ SPECIFIER ☐ QUANTIFIER

10. "Expanding rapidly in Japan are the so-called new religions, several of which are essentially Buddhist counterparts to Protestant fundamentalism."

_____ ☐ SPECIFIER ☐ QUANTIFIER

⚙ **E3-7** → Identify the pronouns, giving the type.

Example:

"So I went back."

PRONOUN	TYPE
I	personal

1. "Say, when a cow's laying down, which end of her gets up first?"

_____ _____

_____ _____

2. "Nobody could spread himself like Tom Sawyer in such a thing as that."

_____ _____

_____ _____

_____ _____

_____ _____

3. "Who the man was the town authorities certainly did not know, neither could they apparently find out."

_____ _____

_____ _____

4. "Though many of them oppose modern culture, they do not oppose it in the same way or oppose the same aspects."

_____   _____
_____   _____
_____   _____
_____   _____

5. "You'll make such a pretty song, you're so different from each other!"

_____   _____
_____   _____
_____   _____
_____   _____

6. "The most influential German philosopher between the wars was Martin Heidegger, whose indebtedness to Nietzsche and his spiritual kinship with the expressionists were obvious."

_____   _____
_____   _____

7. "There is much to be said positively about the achievements of the Enlightenment and its children."

_____   _____
_____   _____

8. "They then become idols themselves instead of pointers to the mystery that transcends history and culture."

_____   _____
_____   _____
_____   _____

9. "He has been trying to get Hamas, Islamic Jihad and Fatah, the main Palestinian faction, to diminish their sometimes violent rivalry, which has included assassinations of one another's leaders."

_____   _____
_____   _____
_____   _____
_____   _____

10. "What now about all those long days and nights ahead before he might go, violin in hand, to meet his father in that far-away country?"

_____   _____

_____   _____

_____   _____

_____   _____

_____   _____

_____   _____

DETERMINERS

⚙ **E3-8** → Identify the determiners, giving the type.

Example:

"It was a tint rather than a shade, like ivory."

DETERMINER	TYPE
a	indefinite article

1. "You just have to lower your expectations on the timetable on when they're going to get things done."

_____   _____

_____   _____

2. Florida is expected to introduce him as its new football coach in the next few days."

_____   _____

_____   _____

3. "Doctors cannot now tell, however, which women need the chemotherapy."

_____   _____

_____   _____

4. "She had neither opportunity nor inclination to observe him closely during their interview in the vestibule."

_____   _____

_____   _____

5. "The president's position on missile defence has been known for quite some time."

_____   _____

_____   _____

_____   _____

6. "Austrians have dominated the first two days of training and will challenge for the podium in both races."

_____   _____

_____   _____

_____   _____

_____   _____

_____   _____

7. "For us a truce means that two warring parties live side-by-side in peace and security for a certain period and this period is eligible for renewal."

_____   _____

_____   _____

_____   _____

_____   _____

8. "Mr. Kuchma and Mr. Putin, whose support for Mr. Yanukovich has provoked angry protests here and abroad, mocked the idea of another runoff as impractical."

_____   _____

_____   _____

_____   _____

9. "I'm very happy that NBC asked me to be a part of 'The Apprentice' finale…. Me and the Trumpster, what a team."

_____   _____

_____   _____

_____   _____

10. "Fans will look at the box score and see eight players in double figures for only the second time in franchise history."

_____   _____

_____   _____

_____   _____

_____   _____

_____   _____

AUXILIARIES

✿ **E3-9** → Identify the primary auxiliaries, giving the form and tense where distinctive. Write n/d where the form or tense is non-distinctive.

Example:

"The station was crowded, as it always is in the afternoon."

AUXILIARY	FORM	TENSE
was	3rd pr sg	past

1. "They are Walkerton survivors, and for some, survival is proving to have long-term consequences."

_____ _____ _____

2. "Canada has been discussing the issue with the Americans for 18 months."

_____ _____ _____

_____ _____ _____

3. "He said the coastal village could not be easily reached because landslides were blocking the road."

_____ _____ _____

_____ _____ _____

4. "The horses had started, and the carriage was half-way across the street before the Bishop noticed me."

_____ _____ _____

5. "I ought to have been strapped for it."

_____ _____ _____

_____ _____ _____

6. "And the fact that pre-1917 these wines were being made for the czar gives them a special quality."

_____ _____ _____

_____ _____ _____

7. "Look here, Nance, are you going to flunk?"

_____ _____ _____

8. "Having survived the 1917 Russian Revolution, the collection was menaced during the Second World War by the threat of Nazi invasion."

_____ _____ _____

9. "She was shopping in the same department store as Donna."

_____ _____ _____

10. "Denise Rudnicki, spokeswoman for Justice Minister Irwin Cotler, said the Ontario judgment is being reviewed before the minister decides whether to appeal."

_____ _____ _____

_____ _____ _____

⚙ **E3-10** → Identify the modal auxiliaries, giving the mood/attitude.

Example:

"Internal divisions will ultimately impact upon inter-party working relationships."

AUXILIARY	MOOD/ATTITUDE
will	futurity

1. "Be that how it may, there stands the vast arched bone of the whale's jaw, so wide, a coach might almost drive beneath it."

_____ _____

_____ _____

2. "I told him that I never liked to sleep two in a bed; that if I should ever do so, it would depend upon who the harpooneer might be."

_____ _____

_____ _____

_____ _____

3. "They make the price. They say just how much the peasant shall pay for his loaf of bread. If he can't pay the price he simply starves."

_____   _____

_____   _____

4. "Whatever I said to you this evening, I must answer now—as I should have answered then—truthfully and unhesitatingly, no."

_____   _____

_____   _____

5. "Should a rational person believe that Social Security's very real financial shortfall can be reduced just by shifting from bonds into stocks?"

_____   _____

_____   _____

6. "Suppose now, he should tumble in upon me at midnight—how could I tell from what vile hole he had been coming?"

_____   _____

_____   _____

7. "They say at this rate everybody will consider me engaged, and I ought to consider myself so, because it's not fair to you."

_____   _____

_____   _____

8. "I lay there dismally calculating that sixteen entire hours must elapse before I could hope for a resurrection."

_____   _____

_____   _____

9. "Lower courts had said the former students would have to sue individually because their complaints are different."

_____   _____

10. "Some cobblers may survive by repairing factory-made shoes. But most must become part of the wage labor force."

_____   _____

_____   _____

⚙ **E3-11** → Identify the auxiliaries and the type.

Example:

"The opportunity to sue as a class means more low-income survivors of abuse will have their day in court."

AUXILIARY	TYPE
will	modal

1. "Several other less distinct breeds might have been specified."

_____ ☐ PRIMARY	☐ MODAL	☐ STAND-IN DO
_____ ☐ PRIMARY	☐ MODAL	☐ STAND-IN DO
_____ ☐ PRIMARY	☐ MODAL	☐ STAND-IN DO

2. "Canadian producers who have lost some $5 billion Cdn during the 18-month ban were disappointed Bush didn't give them a more definitive timetable when he met in Ottawa this week with Prime Minister Paul Martin."

_____ ☐ PRIMARY	☐ MODAL	☐ STAND-IN DO
_____ ☐ PRIMARY	☐ MODAL	☐ STAND-IN DO

3. "Who can tell what metals the gods use in forging the subtle bond which we call sympathy, which we might as well call love."

_____ ☐ PRIMARY	☐ MODAL	☐ STAND-IN DO
_____ ☐ PRIMARY	☐ MODAL	☐ STAND-IN DO

4. "If you can get away with a safer medication, you ought to."

_____ ☐ PRIMARY	☐ MODAL	☐ STAND-IN DO
_____ ☐ PRIMARY	☐ MODAL	☐ STAND-IN DO

5. "Who could have been imposing such a tale upon you?"

_____ ☐ PRIMARY	☐ MODAL	☐ STAND-IN DO
_____ ☐ PRIMARY	☐ MODAL	☐ STAND-IN DO
_____ ☐ PRIMARY	☐ MODAL	☐ STAND-IN DO

6. "His position must be confirmed by the Senate."

_____ ☐ PRIMARY	☐ MODAL	☐ STAND-IN DO
_____ ☐ PRIMARY	☐ MODAL	☐ STAND-IN DO

7. "Launching evaluation procedure doesn't mean that we will issue safety certification to them."

   _____   ☐ PRIMARY   ☐ MODAL   ☐ STAND-IN DO

   _____   ☐ PRIMARY   ☐ MODAL   ☐ STAND-IN DO

8. "If the Yankees no longer wanted Giambi, the union would undoubtedly maintain that the club should simply release him and pay him the remainder of his contract."

   _____   ☐ PRIMARY   ☐ MODAL   ☐ STAND-IN DO

   _____   ☐ PRIMARY   ☐ MODAL   ☐ STAND-IN DO

9. "The results of the S.E.C.'s investigation are expected soon, and enforcement actions may follow."

   _____   ☐ PRIMARY   ☐ MODAL   ☐ STAND-IN DO

   _____   ☐ PRIMARY   ☐ MODAL   ☐ STAND-IN DO

10. "Lower courts had said the former students would have to sue individually because their complaints are different."

   _____   ☐ PRIMARY   ☐ MODAL   ☐ STAND-IN DO

   _____   ☐ PRIMARY   ☐ MODAL   ☐ STAND-IN DO

PREPOSITIONS

✿ **E3-12** → Identify the prepositions, noting the type.

Example:

"It consisted in a bedroom, a kitchen and a scullery."

PREPOSITION	TYPE
in	simple

1. "When I came to Ottawa, I thought stories about leaks in plain brown envelopes were apocryphal until I saw them coming to David."

   _____   ☐ SIMPLE   ☐ -ING   ☐ PHRASAL

   _____   ☐ SIMPLE   ☐ -ING   ☐ PHRASAL

   _____   ☐ SIMPLE   ☐ -ING   ☐ PHRASAL

   _____   ☐ SIMPLE   ☐ -ING   ☐ PHRASAL

2. "We know absolutely nothing concerning the Force we call God; and, assuming such an intelligent ruling force to be in existence."

_____ ☐ SIMPLE	☐ -ING	☐ PHRASAL
_____ ☐ SIMPLE	☐ -ING	☐ PHRASAL

3. "I would love to get 20 rebounds in a close game, instead of a game that was out of reach for the other team."

_____ ☐ SIMPLE	☐ -ING	☐ PHRASAL
_____ ☐ SIMPLE	☐ -ING	☐ PHRASAL
_____ ☐ SIMPLE	☐ -ING	☐ PHRASAL
_____ ☐ SIMPLE	☐ -ING	☐ PHRASAL

4. "Three days later Fairfax received a letter from the officer charged with dispersing the group."

_____ ☐ SIMPLE	☐ -ING	☐ PHRASAL
_____ ☐ SIMPLE	☐ -ING	☐ PHRASAL

5. "As traditional department stores like Lord & Taylor and Macy's struggle to push sales slightly ahead of last year's holiday season, merchants like Bergdorf Goodman and Neiman Marcus, along with brands like *Gucci, Louis Vuitton* and *Chanel*, are prospering."

_____ ☐ SIMPLE	☐ -ING	☐ PHRASAL
_____ ☐ SIMPLE	☐ -ING	☐ PHRASAL
_____ ☐ SIMPLE	☐ -ING	☐ PHRASAL
_____ ☐ SIMPLE	☐ -ING	☐ PHRASAL
_____ ☐ SIMPLE	☐ -ING	☐ PHRASAL

6. "This kind of simple technology would enable women in villages to use their time efficiently and profitably during periods when they did not need to work in the fields."

_____ ☐ SIMPLE	☐ -ING	☐ PHRASAL
_____ ☐ SIMPLE	☐ -ING	☐ PHRASAL
_____ ☐ SIMPLE	☐ -ING	☐ PHRASAL
_____ ☐ SIMPLE	☐ -ING	☐ PHRASAL

7. "Perhaps it is more accurate to say that the focus of the liberation theologies widened to include, in addition to all oppressed human beings, all oppressed creatures as well as planet earth."

_____ ☐ SIMPLE	☐ -ING	☐ PHRASAL
_____ ☐ SIMPLE	☐ -ING	☐ PHRASAL

8. "I didn't know that there could be literature of that kind, with such subversive qualities, because up to that point I had come to begin to believe what white people said about us."

_____	☐ SIMPLE	☐ -ING	☐ PHRASAL
_____	☐ SIMPLE	☐ -ING	☐ PHRASAL
_____	☐ SIMPLE	☐ -ING	☐ PHRASAL
_____	☐ SIMPLE	☐ -ING	☐ PHRASAL

9. "He said this treatment was not only counterproductive to gaining information from high-ranking prisoners, but might also violate the Geneva Convention's protections for treating prisoners with regard to rank and stature."

_____	☐ SIMPLE	☐ -ING	☐ PHRASAL
_____	☐ SIMPLE	☐ -ING	☐ PHRASAL
_____	☐ SIMPLE	☐ -ING	☐ PHRASAL
_____	☐ SIMPLE	☐ -ING	☐ PHRASAL

10. "Following Chapter 1 of Paul's Epistle to the Romans, Christian theology has traditionally taught that revelation is present in a general sense throughout creation."

_____	☐ SIMPLE	☐ -ING	☐ PHRASAL
_____	☐ SIMPLE	☐ -ING	☐ PHRASAL
_____	☐ SIMPLE	☐ -ING	☐ PHRASAL
_____	☐ SIMPLE	☐ -ING	☐ PHRASAL
_____	☐ SIMPLE	☐ -ING	☐ PHRASAL

CONJUNCTIONS

✿ **E3-13** → Identify the conjunctions, noting the type and the structure class word group to which it belongs.

Example:

"Also, I paid for him with a bull when he was accepted."

CONJUNCTION	TYPE	GROUP
when	subordinating	relative adverb

1. "He is called the Dead Wolf as long as he lives, which is not long, as a rule."

_____	_____	_____
_____	_____	_____

2. "Christianity sometimes suggests that craving for spiritual goods is desirable, but it gives no support to craving for unneeded material possessions and consumption."

_____   _____   _____

_____   _____   _____

_____   _____   _____

3. "If neither Ferentz nor Mariucci emerges, Notre Dame will most probably sift through a hodgepodge of candidates, none of whom would make the splash that Meyer would have made."

_____   _____   _____

_____   _____   _____

_____   _____   _____

4. "There are millions of people who are illegally in the United States, and it's unfortunate, when they're caught, seeing a family split up."

_____   _____   _____

_____   _____   _____

_____   _____   _____

5. "One day, however, as he was lying half asleep in the warm water somewhere off the Island of Juan Fernandez, he felt faint and lazy all over."

_____   _____   _____

_____   _____   _____

_____   _____   _____

6. "We want to make sure that whatever decision is taken is one that is going to benefit our own security."

_____   _____   _____

_____   _____   _____

7. "I grew very uncomfortable, meanwhile, for the afternoon wore fast away, the man whom I had sent off returned from his errand."

_____   _____   _____

_____   _____   _____

_____   _____   _____

8. "Federal officials encouraged people to call, but now cite the deluge of calls to explain why they were unable to give accurate answers."

_____ _____ _____

_____ _____ _____

9. "Almost three months have passed since the players made their last proposal and we have yet to receive a counter-offer from the league."

_____ _____ _____

_____ _____ _____

10. "The kingpin, whose hair has become grey and chubby while in a Colombian prison over the past nine years, faces trial in federal courts in Miami and New York for trafficking cocaine and laundering money."

_____ _____ _____

_____ _____ _____

_____ _____ _____

_____ _____ _____

WORD TYPES

✿ **E3-14** → Identify the bolded words, noting the type.

Example:

"Babbitt could have entered his office **from** the street."

WORD	TYPE
preposition	simple

1. "Suddenly he strode across **in front of** her, barring her way."

_____ _____

2. "Before, while she **had** striven against him bitterly, she had fretted after him, **as if** he had gone astray from her."

_____ _____

_____ _____

3. "Paul **could** choose the lesser in place of the higher, she saw."

_____ _____

4. "On the Monday **following** the day of the rupture he went down to the work-room."

_____   _____

5. "One day, **however, as** he was lying half asleep in the warm water somewhere off the Island of Juan Fernandez, he felt faint **and** lazy all over."

_____   _____

_____   _____

_____   _____

6. "The figures in _The Potato Eaters_ **do** not engage **each other** in conversation."

_____   _____

_____   _____

7. "**Although** most of van Gogh's biographers view this transition as a rejection of religion, in fact, art rather than preaching became **van Gogh's** chief form of religious expression."

_____   _____

_____   _____

8. "The painting **might** seem rather discordant **but for** its one unifying element: the lamp, with its warm glow piercing the isolation."

_____   _____

_____   _____

9. "After three months of nothing, the **two** sides in the NHL lockout are at least talking to **each other**."

_____   _____

_____   _____

10. "Paul had **been** many times **up to** Willey Farm during the autumn."

_____   _____

_____   _____

MATCH EXERCISES
✿ **E3-15** → Find examples for Part A in Part B, **USING EACH SENTENCE ONLY ONCE.**

Part A

1. A reflexive pronoun/2nd person   _____

2. A phrasal preposition   _____

3. Two primary auxiliaries   _____

4. A conjunctive adverb, noting concession _____

5. A determiner plus a post-determiner   _____

Part B

A. "As traditional department stores like Lord & Taylor and Macy's struggle to push sales slightly ahead of last year's holiday season."

B. "However, on Friday morning Israeli soldiers shot and killed an Islamic Jihad leader during an arrest raid in the West Bank village of Rabba near Jenin."

C. "The assistant coach Brian Hill joined the Nets for the first time this season on Friday."

D. "'Any player coming off an injury, that's the first thing you concern yourself with,' Edwards said."

E. "Lord and his Conservative government have been feeling the heat following a series of bad-news announcements that have shaken the forest, energy and health sectors."

✿ **E3-16** → Find examples for Part A in Part B, **USING EACH SENTENCE ONLY ONCE.**

Part A

1. A personal pronoun/feminine/3rd person/prenominal   _____

2. A modal expressing futurity   _____

3. A relative pronoun/possessive   _____

4. A coordinating conjunction   _____

5. A determiner plus a pre-determiner   _____

Part B

A. "Mr. Yousef did not spell out the conditions for the renewable cease-fire nor did he say how long it would last."

B. "The kingpin, whose hair has become grey and chubby while in a Colombian prison over the past nine years, faces trial in federal courts in Miami and New York for trafficking cocaine and laundering money."

C. "Martin said no specific proposals are on the table, but as soon as his government reaches some conclusions, it will bring them before Parliament."

D. "But this month, Ms. Blanchett appears in a role that may outdo all her previous ones in nerve and ambition."

E. "She has lost one-third of her kidney function and suffers from high blood pressure."

PARAGRAPH ANALYSIS

⚙ **E3-17** → Find examples for the following in the paragraph below.

1. Primary 2 auxiliary   _____

2. Relative adverb   _____

3. Determiner plus post-determiner   _____

4. Coordinating conjunction   _____

5. Indefinite pronoun   _____

"We were in the small southern Indiana town where I grew up, and a gospel concert was advertised for the auditorium of the single Christian college there. It seemed like a grand opportunity to let my family in on a part of my cultural heritage. I could already hear the piano runs, the black and white spirituals, the gospel folk tunes from the hills, the glorious harmonies of the male quartets—it all welled up from my memories of hot, humid nights in the small, dimly lit churches of my youth."

⚙ **E3-18** → Find examples for the following in the paragraph below.

1. Stand-in auxiliary   _____

2. Determiner plus pre-determiner   _____

3. Relative pronoun/subjective   _____

4. A correlative conjunction   _____

5. A subordinating conjunction/concession   _____

"I have described my critique as Buddhist-Christian. By this I do not mean anything esoteric. Although I am interested in differences between these two great religious traditions, I do not believe these differences are important for the critique of the dominant pattern of economic thinking. It is interesting that an early critic who wrote on 'Buddhist Economics' was a conservative Catholic. I refer, of course, to Schumacher.

"A critique of neo-liberal economics can emphasize either the theory or the practice. Both critiques are important, and a Buddhist or Christian perspective can inform either one. I have chosen to emphasize the theoretical one, although I will also indicate how theory works out in practice. What is wrong, from a Buddhist or Christian point of view, with the theory of neo-liberal economics?"

⚙ **E3-19** → Identify the bolded words, giving full descriptions, in the following paragraph.

1. _____

2. _____

3. _____

4. _____

5. _____

6. _____

7. _____

8. _____

9. _____

10. _____

"For **the first**[1] time in my life I **was**[2] confronted by the phenomenon of audible silence. **When**[3] we **had**[4] climbed the first flight of stairs, I added another discovery to **my**[5] limited knowledge of natural phenomena—that of tangible darkness. A match showed us where the upward road continued. We went to the next floor and then to the next and the next **until**[6] I had lost count and then there came still another floor, and suddenly **we**[7] had plenty of light. This floor was on an even height **with**[8] the roof of the church, and it was used as a storeroom. Covered with many inches of dust, there lay the abandoned symbols of a venerable faith which had been discarded by the good people of the city many years ago. That **which**[9] had meant life and death to **our**[10] ancestors was here reduced to junk and rubbish."

WORD ANALYSIS
⚙ **E3-20** → Construct diagrams to illustrate the breakdown of the following word groups.

....

1. Nouns

   a. **churches**   b. **deer** (plural)

    c.   **Prime Minister's**   d.   **the Jones'**

    e.   **boys**   f.   **girl's**

2. Verbs
    a.   **carried**   b.   **cut** (past)

    c.   **looking**   d.   **walks**

3. Adjectives
    a.   **gentle**   b.   **further**

c.   **more powerful**   d.   **shortest**

4. Adverbs

a.   **happily**   b.   **northward**

5. Pronouns

a.   **theirs**   b.   **whom**

c.   **these**   d.   **one another's**

4   PHRASES

DEFINITIONS

✿ E4-1 → Match Part A with the correct definition in Part B.

Part A

1. Sentence constituents are . . . . _____
2. Noun phrases are cohesive word groups focusing on . . . . _____
3. Adjective phrases are cohesive word groups . . . . _____
4. Adjective phrases generally . . . . _____
5. Verb phrases are cohesive word groups . . . . _____
6. Tense is the grammatical feature of . . . . _____
7. The present tense is expressed . . . . _____
8. The past tense is expressed with . . . . _____
9. Past actions and states can also be noted by . . . . _____
10. English expresses future time by . . . . _____
11. Aspect expresses meanings concerned with . . . . _____
12. English aspects are . . . . _____
13. The perfect progressive aspect expresses . . . . _____
14. Participle phrases are cohesive word groups focusing on . . . . _____
15. Gerund phrases focus on . . . . _____
16. Gerund phrases often begin with . . . . _____
17. Infinitive phrases are cohesive word groups focusing on . . . . _____
18. Prepositional phrases are cohesive word groups forming syntactic units, consisting of . . . . _____
19. Prepositional phrases can modify both . . . . _____
20. Absolute phrases are cohesive word groups not linked . . . . _____

Part B

A. ... the continuity or distribution of events in time.

B. ... nouns and verbs.

C. ... describing or qualifying nouns or their replacements.

D. ... an -*ing* non-finite verb as their head word.

E. ... consisting of a lexical verb plus one or more auxiliaries.

F. ... the structure of a particle *to* plus a *verb stem*.

G. ... an -(e)d or -t inflectional suffix for regular verbs and generally an inflectional ablaut for irregular verbs.

H. ... simple, progressive, perfect, and perfect progressive.

I. ... to the main clause syntactically or semantically by shared elements.

J. ... words or cohesive word groups, which are phrases or clauses.

K. ... with a verb stem, which takes the inflectional -s suffix for the third person singular.

L. ... precede nouns or their substitutes, but sometimes they occur after the head noun as well.

M. ... a preposition plus a head noun or its replacement.

N. ... adverbs of time and other time references.

O. ... verbs and auxiliaries relating to time.

P. ... a possessive noun or pronoun.

Q. ... an activity or event that has continuous past action completed before another action in the past.

R. ... a head noun or its replacement.

S. ... non-finite verbs, present or past, as their head word.

T. ... adding the modals shall or will to the present tense stem.

NOUN PHRASES

☼ **E4-2** → Identify the noun phrases.

Example:

"All classes alike thus build their plans."

NOUN PHRASE
All classes
their plans

1. "The new rich of the nineteenth century were not brought up to large expenditures."

   _____   _____   _____

2. "But these thoughts lead too far from my present purpose."

   _____   _____

3. "The delicate organisation by which these peoples lived depended partly on factors internal to the system."

   _____   _____   _____

   _____

4. "Seeing the good does not preclude taking steps to discipline our children."

   _____   _____

5. "Thus this remarkable system depended for its growth on a double bluff or deception."

   _____   _____   _____

6. "Entertainment Weekly has named 15 rising stars to its annual 'Breakouts' issue."

   _____   _____   _____

7. "He is a legend in the business and I personally invited him to join me in hosting 'The Apprentice' 3-hour finale."

   _____   _____   _____

8. "But the greater part of the money interest accruing on these foreign investments was reinvested and allowed to accumulate, as a reserve."

   _____   _____   _____

   _____

9. "Bridges TV, billed as the first American Muslim TV network, has agreed with Comcast to launch in the Arab-population-rich metro Detroit area."

_____   _____

_____

10. "His walk, his hand, and his voice were not lacking in vigour, but he bore nevertheless, especially after the attempt upon him, the aspect of a very old man conserving his strength for important occasions."

_____   _____   _____

_____   _____   _____

VERB PHRASES

⚙ **E4-3** → Identify the verb phrases.[1]

Example:

"And I very much enjoy writing for the sound of the Latin language."

VERB PHRASE
very much enjoy

1. "Or it would have been nice if he could have been taken with fever all alone at his hotel."

_____   _____

2. "He was really almost reaching out in imagination—as against time—for something that would do."

_____   _____

3. "To tell her what he had told her—what had it been but to ask something of her?"

_____   _____

4. "Nothing for a long time had made him easier than the thought that the aching must have been much soothed by Miss Bartram's now finding herself able to set up a small home in London."

_____   _____

5. "You've mentioned that you never really intended the Requiem to be a theater piece as such."

_____   _____

1 Where adverbs are embedded into the verb phrase, include them as part of the phrase.

6. "'The cornerstone, the bedrock of immigration law is family unity,' said Jeffrey A. Feinbloom, an immigration lawyer who has been working for Mrs. Feliz's return since her deportation and has been frustrated by delays in processing."

_____   _____

7. "If neither Ferentz nor Mariucci emerges, Notre Dame will most probably sift through a hodgepodge of candidates, none of whom would make the splash that Meyer would have made."

_____   _____

_____

8. "A serosurvey for measles, mumps and rubella was conducted in Italy; incidence based on statutory notifications over the last three decades was also calculated."

_____   _____

9. "If he could have done that moment as he wanted he would simply have stretched himself on the slab that was ready to take him, treating it as a place prepared to receive his last sleep."

_____   _____

10. "Indeed, if OPEC does not control production with somewhat longer-term concerns in view, market forces will probably lead to that outcome."

_____   _____

⚙ **E4-4** → Identify the verb phrases, noting their tenses.

Example:

"Often loud and brash, D.C. Talk can also be soulful and sensitive."

VERB PHRASE	TENSE
can also be	present

1. "A moment earlier it had seemed quite deserted, this church set by the roadside on the high bank of the Peribonka."

_____   ☐ PRESENT   ☐ PAST   ☐ FUTURE

_____   ☐ PRESENT   ☐ PAST   ☐ FUTURE

2. "Well, Mr. Larouche, do things go pretty well across the water?"

_____   ☐ PRESENT   ☐ PAST   ☐ FUTURE

3. "I am glad that I saw you, for I shall be passing up the river near your place in two or three weeks, when the ice goes out."

_____ ☐ PRESENT ☐ PAST ☐ FUTURE

_____ ☐ PRESENT ☐ PAST ☐ FUTURE

4. "If hung councils are seen as long-lasting the duration of the council term, for example then stability is more likely."

_____ ☐ PRESENT ☐ PAST ☐ FUTURE

5. "Twenty years before great forest fires had swept through, and the new growth was only pushing its way amid the standing skeletons and the charred-down timber."

_____ ☐ PRESENT ☐ PAST ☐ FUTURE

_____ ☐ PRESENT ☐ PAST ☐ FUTURE

6. "'They will be glad to see you again, Maria,' said her father. 'They have been lonesome for you, every one of them.'"

_____ ☐ PRESENT ☐ PAST ☐ FUTURE

_____ ☐ PRESENT ☐ PAST ☐ FUTURE

7. "'There! You are forever saying that we are buried in the woods and see no company,' triumphed her husband."

_____ ☐ PRESENT ☐ PAST ☐ FUTURE

_____ ☐ PRESENT ☐ PAST ☐ FUTURE

8. "When the boys are back from the woods we shall set to work, they two, Tit'Bé, and I, and presently we shall have our land cleared."

_____ ☐ PRESENT ☐ PAST ☐ FUTURE

_____ ☐ PRESENT ☐ PAST ☐ FUTURE

9. "'Did you picture it to yourselves as you have found it,' Chapdelaine persisted, 'the country here, the life?'"

_____ ☐ PRESENT ☐ PAST ☐ FUTURE

_____ ☐ PRESENT ☐ PAST ☐ FUTURE

10. "I wish other unionists would have the sense to play the game because we are essentially playing the game in Newry and Mourne and to the best of our belief we haven't been caught at it, certainly we haven't been caught by the electorate."

_____ ☐ PRESENT	☐ PAST	☐ FUTURE
_____ ☐ PRESENT	☐ PAST	☐ FUTURE
_____ ☐ PRESENT	☐ PAST	☐ FUTURE
_____ ☐ PRESENT	☐ PAST	☐ FUTURE

✪ **E4-5** → Identify the verb phrases, noting aspect.

Example:

"The reader may perhaps choose to assign an actual locality to the imaginary events of this narrative."

PHRASE	ASPECT
may ... choose	simple

1. "There may be some cause for hope in Ulster's new councils."

_____ ☐ SIMPLE ☐ PROGRESSIVE ☐ PERFECT ☐ PERFECT PROGRESSIVE

2. "We have been lucky because we haven't been caught ... some people misunderstand that."

_____ ☐ SIMPLE ☐ PROGRESSIVE ☐ PERFECT ☐ PERFECT PROGRESSIVE

_____ ☐ SIMPLE ☐ PROGRESSIVE ☐ PERFECT ☐ PERFECT PROGRESSIVE

3. "Genomics is already having a large influence on medical practice, as most monogenic genetic disorders have now been linked to causative genes."

_____ ☐ SIMPLE ☐ PROGRESSIVE ☐ PERFECT ☐ PERFECT PROGRESSIVE

_____ ☐ SIMPLE ☐ PROGRESSIVE ☐ PERFECT ☐ PERFECT PROGRESSIVE

4. "Canada has been discussing the issue with the Americans for 18 months, Conservative Leader Stephen Harper said."

_____ ☐ SIMPLE ☐ PROGRESSIVE ☐ PERFECT ☐ PERFECT PROGRESSIVE

5. "Melanie Turgeon of Quebec City, the 2003 world downhill champion who is slowly returning to form after missing all last season with a back injury, had planned to skip Thursday's training anyway."

_____ ☐ SIMPLE ☐ PROGRESSIVE ☐ PERFECT ☐ PERFECT PROGRESSIVE

_____ ☐ SIMPLE ☐ PROGRESSIVE ☐ PERFECT ☐ PERFECT PROGRESSIVE

6. "One player who didn't make the team but certainly would have if the new system had been in effect was Todd Hamilton, who won the Honda Classic last spring and then won the British Open in a playoff with Ernie Els."

_____ ☐ SIMPLE ☐ PROGRESSIVE ☐ PERFECT ☐ PERFECT PROGRESSIVE

_____ ☐ SIMPLE ☐ PROGRESSIVE ☐ PERFECT ☐ PERFECT PROGRESSIVE

_____ ☐ SIMPLE ☐ PROGRESSIVE ☐ PERFECT ☐ PERFECT PROGRESSIVE

7. "Bush last week said he would instruct federal officials to speed up the process of lifting the ban on Canadian cattle and said new regulations could be ready by early next year."

_____ ☐ SIMPLE ☐ PROGRESSIVE ☐ PERFECT ☐ PERFECT PROGRESSIVE

_____ ☐ SIMPLE ☐ PROGRESSIVE ☐ PERFECT ☐ PERFECT PROGRESSIVE

8. "'The cornerstone, the bedrock of immigration law is family unity,' said Jeffrey A. Feinbloom, an immigration lawyer who has been working for Mrs. Feliz's return since her deportation and has been frustrated by delays in processing."

_____ ☐ SIMPLE ☐ PROGRESSIVE ☐ PERFECT ☐ PERFECT PROGRESSIVE

_____ ☐ SIMPLE ☐ PROGRESSIVE ☐ PERFECT ☐ PERFECT PROGRESSIVE

9. "Palestinian officials suggest that Mr. Abbas himself might meet with Mr. Meshaal, the Hamas political chief, while in Damascus, as well as with the leaders of Islamic Jihad who are based in Syria."

_____ ☐ SIMPLE ☐ PROGRESSIVE ☐ PERFECT ☐ PERFECT PROGRESSIVE

_____ ☐ SIMPLE ☐ PROGRESSIVE ☐ PERFECT ☐ PERFECT PROGRESSIVE

10. "Lord and his Conservative government have been feeling the heat following a series of bad-news announcements that have shaken the forest, energy and health sectors, but the throne speech says better times are ahead."

_____ ☐ SIMPLE ☐ PROGRESSIVE ☐ PERFECT ☐ PERFECT PROGRESSIVE

_____ ☐ SIMPLE ☐ PROGRESSIVE ☐ PERFECT ☐ PERFECT PROGRESSIVE

⚙ **E4-6** → Identify the verb phrases, noting tense and aspect.

Example:

"Then you will have to practise it every day."

VERB PHRASE	TENSE	ASPECT
will have	future	simple

1. "Meyer will face high expectations at Florida even though he is succeeding Zook rather than Spurrier."

_____ _____ _____

_____ _____ _____

2. "The four were returning to camp in an unarmored Humvee that their unit had rigged with scrap metal."

_____ _____ _____

_____ _____ _____

3. "While this question was being discussed neither of the pair noticed, in their preoccupation, that little Abraham had crept into the room, and was awaiting an opportunity of asking them to return."

_____ _____ _____

_____ _____ _____

_____ _____ _____

4. "The marines, based at Camp Pendleton in southern California, had been asked to rid the provincial capital of one of the most persistent insurgencies."

_____ _____ _____

5. "The latter so far forgot himself as to look up with an appearance of no small astonishment; whomever he may have been expecting, he had evidently not counted on meeting anyone like this."

_____ _____ _____

_____ _____ _____

6. "'On the twenty-eighth of August, at the hour of midnight, and if the moon is shining—the moon must be shining—a spirit that has haunted these shores for ages rises up from the Gulf."

_____ _____ _____

_____ _____ _____

_____ _____ _____

7. "'The church clock struck, when suddenly the student said that he must leave—he had been forgetting himself—he had to join his companions."

_____ _____ _____

_____ _____ _____

8. "'The lantern hanging at her waggon had gone out, but another was shining in her face—much brighter than her own had been."

_____ _____ _____

_____ _____ _____

_____ _____

9. "No doubt errors will have crept in, though I hope I have always been cautious in trusting to good authorities alone."

_____ _____ _____

_____ _____ _____

10. "Who doesn't want to see him foaming at the mouth—yes, it will be hard to tell—at the Cuban delegate over Castro's imaginary W.M.D.?"

_____ _____ _____

_____ _____ _____

ADJECTIVE AND ADVERB PHRASES

✪ **E4-7** → Identify the adjective and adverb phrases, noting the type.

Example:

"She did her wedding gown, not for a fine glossy surface, but such qualities as would wear well."

PHRASE	TYPE
her wedding	adjective
a fine glossy	adjective

1. "One of the most distinctive and innovative features of the Requiem is the major emphasis on a child to proclaim a message of death."

_____ ☐ ADJECTIVE ☐ ADVERB

2. "But this was now too late: I therefore made directly homewards, resolving to get the draft changed into money at my friend's as fast as possible."

_____ ☐ ADJECTIVE ☐ ADVERB

_____ ☐ ADJECTIVE ☐ ADVERB

_____ ☐ ADJECTIVE ☐ ADVERB

3. "The councils' representative role involves nominating local councillors to sit as members of the various statutory boards."

_____ ☐ ADJECTIVE ☐ ADVERB

4. "The most highly developed systems of medicine outside of the Western or Hippocratic tradition are the Ayurvedic school (of India) and traditional Chinese medicine."

_____ ☐ ADJECTIVE ☐ ADVERB

_____ ☐ ADJECTIVE ☐ ADVERB

_____ ☐ ADJECTIVE ☐ ADVERB

5. "The patient-doctor relationship is important to the doctor in order to obtain an accurate medical history and obtain compliance with the treatment plan; respect, understanding, and trust is important."

_____ ☐ ADJECTIVE ☐ ADVERB

_____ ☐ ADJECTIVE ☐ ADVERB

6. "'And how could you,' said I, 'so basely, so ungratefully presume to write this letter?'"

_____ ☐ ADJECTIVE ☐ ADVERB

7. "'We take everything the Red Cross gives us and study it very carefully to look for ways to do our job better,' he said in his Guantánamo headquarters."

_____ ☐ ADJECTIVE ☐ ADVERB

8. "'What!' cried he again, 'not have Mr. Jenkinson, your benefactor, a handsome young fellow with five hundred pounds and good expectations.'"

_____ ☐ ADJECTIVE ☐ ADVERB

_____ ☐ ADJECTIVE ☐ ADVERB

9. "The shafts of sunshine fell more obliquely across the eastern end of the gallery."

_____ ☐ ADJECTIVE ☐ ADVERB

10. "Another town, a little further off, with five or six millions of inhabitants, was also, through its newspapers, aware of Miss Winwood."

_____ ☐ ADJECTIVE ☐ ADVERB

_____ ☐ ADJECTIVE ☐ ADVERB

PARTICIPLE AND GERUND PHRASES
⚙ **E4-8** → Identify the participle and gerund phrases, noting the type.

Example:

"The weeds growing rankly by the roadside showed it in blots and splashes on their big, broad leaves."

PHRASE | TYPE
growing rankly | present participle

1. "That faith was then new to me, and all Moxon's expounding had failed to make me a convert."

_____ ☐ P-PARTICIPLE ☐ PT-PARTICIPLE ☐ GERUND

2. "When imparting shocking intelligence to the sick he was affable enough."

_____ ☐ P-PARTICIPLE ☐ PT-PARTICIPLE ☐ GERUND

3. "Second-Lieutenant Brainerd Byring was a brave and efficient officer, young and comparatively inexperienced as he was in the business of killing his fellow-men."

_____ ☐ P-PARTICIPLE ☐ PT-PARTICIPLE ☐ GERUND

_____ ☐ P-PARTICIPLE ☐ PT-PARTICIPLE ☐ GERUND

4. "In the pauses between I now became conscious of a low humming or buzzing which, like the thunder, grew momentarily louder."

_____ ☐ P-PARTICIPLE ☐ PT-PARTICIPLE ☐ GERUND

5. "A strongly defined shadow passed across the face of the dead, left it luminous, passed back upon it and left it half obscured."

   _____   ☐ P-PARTICIPLE   ☐ PT-PARTICIPLE   ☐ GERUND

   _____   ☐ P-PARTICIPLE   ☐ PT-PARTICIPLE   ☐ GERUND

6. "It seemed to come from the body of the automaton, and was unmistakably a whirring of wheels."

   _____   ☐ P-PARTICIPLE   ☐ PT-PARTICIPLE   ☐ GERUND

7. "Since Direct Rule began in 1972, a series of failed initiatives provide evidence of the immense difficulty facing the government in trying to juggle the demands of restoring devolution to Northern Ireland, giving constitutional guarantees to unionists of their position within the United Kingdom and delivering some sort of power arrangements between Catholics and Protestants within an all-Ireland framework."

   _____   ☐ P-PARTICIPLE   ☐ PT-PARTICIPLE   ☐ GERUND

   _____   ☐ P-PARTICIPLE   ☐ PT-PARTICIPLE   ☐ GERUND

   _____   ☐ P-PARTICIPLE   ☐ PT-PARTICIPLE   ☐ GERUND

   _____   ☐ P-PARTICIPLE   ☐ PT-PARTICIPLE   ☐ GERUND

   _____   ☐ P-PARTICIPLE   ☐ PT-PARTICIPLE   ☐ GERUND

   _____   ☐ P-PARTICIPLE   ☐ PT-PARTICIPLE   ☐ GERUND

8. "My father was, in fact, a singularly good-natured man, and I think quietly enjoyed Nature's practical joke."

   _____   ☐ P-PARTICIPLE   ☐ PT-PARTICIPLE   ☐ GERUND

9. "The doctor nodded civilly, half thinking that the stranger's uncommon greeting was perhaps in deference to the historic surroundings."

   _____   ☐ P-PARTICIPLE   ☐ PT-PARTICIPLE   ☐ GERUND

   _____   ☐ P-PARTICIPLE   ☐ PT-PARTICIPLE   ☐ GERUND

   _____   ☐ P-PARTICIPLE   ☐ PT-PARTICIPLE   ☐ GERUND

10. "A single policeman, with upturned collar, was leaning against a gatepost, quietly smoking a cigar."

   _____   ☐ P-PARTICIPLE   ☐ PT-PARTICIPLE   ☐ GERUND

   _____   ☐ P-PARTICIPLE   ☐ PT-PARTICIPLE   ☐ GERUND

INFINITIVE AND PREPOSITIONAL PHRASES

⚙ **E4-9** → Identify the phrases as infinitive or prepositional.

Example:

"I should not allow any one to inconvenience me."

PHRASE	TYPE
to inconvenience	infinitive

1. "Success on television can be as brutal as failure; the job of a network anchor, and particularly a morning anchor who must banter for hours on end, is more harmful to the ego than almost any other kind of public performance."

   _____ ☐ INFINITIVE   ☐ PREPOSITIONAL

   _____ ☐ INFINITIVE   ☐ PREPOSITIONAL

   _____ ☐ INFINITIVE   ☐ PREPOSITIONAL

   _____ ☐ INFINITIVE   ☐ PREPOSITIONAL

   _____ ☐ INFINITIVE   ☐ PREPOSITIONAL

   _____ ☐ INFINITIVE   ☐ PREPOSITIONAL

2. "Saddam Hussein appeared in a Baghdad courtroom to hear the charges he will face when he goes to trial as a war criminal."

   _____ ☐ INFINITIVE   ☐ PREPOSITIONAL

   _____ ☐ INFINITIVE   ☐ PREPOSITIONAL

   _____ ☐ INFINITIVE   ☐ PREPOSITIONAL

   _____ ☐ INFINITIVE   ☐ PREPOSITIONAL

3. "I don't think it possible for me to get home now without a guide."

   _____ ☐ INFINITIVE   ☐ PREPOSITIONAL

   _____ ☐ INFINITIVE   ☐ PREPOSITIONAL

4. "I warn you to refrain from provoking me, or I'll ask your abduction as a special favour."

   _____ ☐ INFINITIVE   ☐ PREPOSITIONAL

   _____ ☐ INFINITIVE   ☐ PREPOSITIONAL

   _____ ☐ INFINITIVE   ☐ PREPOSITIONAL

5. "His first intention was to hire a horse there and ride home forthwith, for to walk many miles without a gun in his hand and along an ordinary road, was as much out of the question to him as to other spirited young men of his kind."

   _____ ☐ INFINITIVE   ☐ PREPOSITIONAL

   _____ ☐ INFINITIVE   ☐ PREPOSITIONAL

_____ ☐ INFINITIVE   ☐ PREPOSITIONAL

_____ ☐ INFINITIVE   ☐ PREPOSITIONAL

_____ ☐ INFINITIVE   ☐ PREPOSITIONAL

_____ ☐ INFINITIVE   ☐ PREPOSITIONAL

_____ ☐ INFINITIVE   ☐ PREPOSITIONAL

_____ ☐ INFINITIVE   ☐ PREPOSITIONAL

_____ ☐ INFINITIVE   ☐ PREPOSITIONAL

6. "Too stupefied to be curious myself, I fastened my door and glanced round for the bed."

_____ ☐ INFINITIVE   ☐ PREPOSITIONAL

_____ ☐ INFINITIVE   ☐ PREPOSITIONAL

7. "His growing reputation was enhanced by the prominent role he was said to have played at the Second Vatican Council called by Pope John XXIII in 1962 to formulate doctrines for the church in the modern world."

_____ ☐ INFINITIVE   ☐ PREPOSITIONAL

_____ ☐ INFINITIVE   ☐ PREPOSITIONAL

_____ ☐ INFINITIVE   ☐ PREPOSITIONAL

_____ ☐ INFINITIVE   ☐ PREPOSITIONAL

_____ ☐ INFINITIVE   ☐ PREPOSITIONAL

_____ ☐ INFINITIVE   ☐ PREPOSITIONAL

_____ ☐ INFINITIVE   ☐ PREPOSITIONAL

_____ ☐ INFINITIVE   ☐ PREPOSITIONAL

8. "If she was to forsake him it was surely for her to take leave."

_____ ☐ INFINITIVE   ☐ PREPOSITIONAL

_____ ☐ INFINITIVE   ☐ PREPOSITIONAL

9. "The Red Cross committee was considering whether to bring more senior officials to Washington and whether to make public its criticisms."

_____ ☐ INFINITIVE   ☐ PREPOSITIONAL

_____ ☐ INFINITIVE   ☐ PREPOSITIONAL

_____ ☐ INFINITIVE   ☐ PREPOSITIONAL

10. "Federal officials said they leave time for parents to make arrangements for their children, and refer them to a social service agency if necessary; others, especially those who have no one to assume responsibility for a child, take the children along when they are expelled."

	☐ INFINITIVE	☐ PREPOSITIONAL
_____	☐ INFINITIVE	☐ PREPOSITIONAL
_____	☐ INFINITIVE	☐ PREPOSITIONAL
_____	☐ INFINITIVE	☐ PREPOSITIONAL
_____	☐ INFINITIVE	☐ PREPOSITIONAL
_____	☐ INFINITIVE	☐ PREPOSITIONAL

PHRASE TYPES

⚙ **E4-10** → Identify the bolded phrases by type.

Example:

"I reached **my destination** in one of the last months of 1868."

PHRASE TYPE
noun phrase

1. "**Starting with early dawn**, it would be night before I could complete my round."

   _____

2. "The interest of the government in removing this woman pales in comparison with **her suffering** and her family's."

   _____

3. "His eyes glared, though they remained **quite fixed**, and his forehead was contracted with a most malevolent scowl."

   _____

4. "When the water boiled we threw in **two or three large pinches** of tea and let them brew."

   _____

5. "Thus, a day or two later my arrival at the Nosnibors', one of the many ladies who called on me made excuses for **her husband's only sending** his card."

   _____

6. "Alice had got so much into the way of expecting nothing but out-of-the-way things to happen, that it seemed quite dull and stupid **for life to go on** in the common way."

   _____

7. "'And who is Dinah, if I **might venture to ask** the question?' said the Lory."

   _____

8. "**The door being opened**, the child addressed him as grandfather, and told him the little story of our companionship."

   _____

9. "'Yes, it is his business!' said Five, 'and I'll tell him—it was for bringing the cook tulip-roots **instead of onions.**'"

   _____

10. "She was **a good deal frightened** by this very sudden change."

    _____

⚙ **E4-11** → Identify the bolded phrases by type.

Example:

"You are **a clever, extraordinary** man."

PHRASE TYPE
adjective phrase

1. "**Very opportunely** a long letter came from Tanya Pesotsky, who asked him to come and stay with them at Borissovka."

   _____

2. "When he came back to Kovrin, his face looked **exhausted and mortified**."

   _____

3. "They reached Sevastopol in the evening and stopped at an hotel **to rest and go** on the next day to Yalta."

   _____

4. "The flowers, **having just been watered**, gave forth a damp, irritating fragrance."

   _____

5. "There was a long silence after **the brute's wailing and whining** died away on the desolate shore."

   _____

6. "It may have been only embarrassment, for he would also fidget with his cravat and his tie-pin, which were at once **handsome and unusual**, like himself."

   _____

7. "The moment Nox saw that man, the dog **dashed forward and stood** in the middle of the path barking at him madly."

8. "Dr. Valentine is a curious man. His appearance is **rather striking** but very foreign."

   _____

9. "The Colonel was **a very wealthy man**, and his will was important."

   _____

10. "Of course it was his demeanor **during these days** that made Druce's daughter so wild with him."

    _____

MATCH EXERCISES

✿ **E4-12** → Find examples for Part A in Part B, **USING EACH SENTENCE ONLY ONCE.**

Part A

1. Participle phrase _____

2. Adjective phrase _____

3. Adverb phrase _____

4. Gerund phrase _____

5. Infinitive phrase _____

Part B

A. "Seeing that the hand was not withdrawn, she clasped it firmly and warmly."

B. "Montel was a middle aged gentleman whose vain ambition and desire for the past twenty years had been to fill the void which Monsieur Lebrun's taking off had left in the Lebrun household."

C. "Mr. Pontellier finally lit a cigar and began to smoke, letting the paper drag idly from his hand."

D. "'Nice thing for a woman to say to her husband!' exclaimed Mr. Pontellier."

E. "Woman is a very peculiar and delicate organism—a sensitive and highly organized woman, such as I know Mrs. Pontellier to be, is especially peculiar."

✿ **E4-13** → Find examples for Part A in Part B, **USING EACH SENTENCE ONLY ONCE.**

Part A

1. Noun phrase _____

2. Past participle phrase _____

3. Present participle phrase _____

4. Prepositional phrase   _____

5. Verb phrase in past perfect aspect   _____

Part B

A. "He had been seated before the door of the main house."

B. "She played very well, keeping excellent waltz time and infusing an expression into the strains which was indeed inspiring."

C. "Her hair, artificially crimped, stood out like fluffy black plumes over her head."

D. "Her little ones ran to meet her."

E. "Early modern thinkers rightly saw that teleology had misdirected much thought and research."

In the following four exercises, the features of the requested phrase are identified in brackets.

⚙ **E4-14** → Find examples for Part A in Part B, **USING EACH SENTENCE ONLY ONCE**.

Part A

1. Noun phrase [NOUN (HN) + CONJUNCTION + PRONOUN].   _____

2. Adjective phrase [ADJECTIVE + PRESENT PARTICIPLE (HAJ)].   _____

3. Verb phrase [FINITE/PRIMARY + NON-FINITE LEXICAL VERB (HV)].   _____

4. Verb phrase [PRESENT TENSE + PROGRESSIVE ASPECT].   _____

5. Verb phrase [PAST TENSE + PERFECT ASPECT].   _____

Part B

A. "But the mater cottoned to him at once, took him on as secretary—you know how she's always running a hundred societies?"

B. "He thought he was walking along a dusty road."

C. "Lawrence, the younger, had been a delicate youth."

D. "Scrooge and he were partners for I don't know how many years."

E. "There was the man in the middle, with a kind of black sneering coolness—frightened to."

✿ E4-15 → Find examples for Part A in Part B, **USING EACH SENTENCE ONLY ONCE.**

Part A

1. Present participle phrase [PRESENT PARTICIPLE (HPP)].   _____

2. Gerund phrase [GERUND PHRASE (HG)].   _____

3. Prepositional phrase [NOUN OBJECT (HP)].   _____

4. Verb phrase [FINITE/MODAL + PRIMARY + NON-FINITE LEXICAL VERB (HV)].   _____

5. Absolute phrase [GERUND PHRASE (HG)].   _____

Part B

A. "She was quite mistress of herself when the instant came for her to speak."

B. "But talking of books, there is Southey's 'Peninsular War.'"

C. "Scrooge was a squeezing, wrenching, grasping, scraping, clutching, covetous old sinner."

D. "There was a long silence after the brute's wailing and whining died away on the desolate shore."

E. "The additional price will be paid when we are forced to make a change."

✿ E4-16 → Find examples for Part A in Part B, **USING EACH SENTENCE ONLY ONCE.**

Part A

1. Noun phrase [DETERMINER + ADJECTIVE + POSSESSIVE NOUN + NOUN (HN)].   _____

2. Adjective phrase [PAST PARTICIPLE (HAJ) + PREPOSITIONAL PHRASES].   _____

3. Verb phrase [FINITE/PRIMARY + ADVERB + NON-FINITE LEXICAL VERB (HV)].   _____

4. Verb phrase [PAST TENSE + SIMPLE ASPECT].   _____

5. Participle phrase [PRESENT PARTICIPLE (HPP) + ADVERB + PARTICLE].   _____

Part B

A. "Along the darkening road he hurried alone, with his eyes cast down."

B. "Frayser had already attained the age of thirty-two."

C. "He was spotlessly neat, apparelled in immaculate white from shoes to hat."

D. "A few gobblers on the far side began the flight, running swiftly off."

E. "Even the blind men's dogs appeared to know him."

✿ **E4-17** → Find examples for Part A in Part B, **USING EACH SENTENCE ONLY ONCE**.

Part A

1. Past participle phrase [PAST PARTICIPLE (HPP) + INFINITIVE]. _____

2. Infinitive phrase [INFINITIVE PHRASE (HI)]. _____

3. Present participle phrase [PRESENT PARTICIPLE + NOUN]. _____

4. Verb phrase [PRESENT TENSE + PERFECT PROGRESSIVE ASPECT]. _____

5. Noun phrase [DETERMINER + PRESENT PARTICIPLE + NOUN (HN)]. _____

Part B

A. "The first time I ever saw a man (it was in Australia when I was a three-year-old) I ran for half a day, and if I'd seen a camel I should have been running still."

B. "The fireplace was an old one, built by some Dutch merchant long ago, and paved all round with quaint Dutch tiles, designed to illustrate the Scriptures."

C. "When you got to the table you couldn't go right to eating, but you had to wait for the widow to tuck down her head and grumble a little over the victuals."

D. "This coming child was too much for her."

E. "It was while living with a fellow survivor near the town of St. Helena, awaiting news and remittances from home, that he had gone gunning and dreaming."

PARAGRAPH ANALYSIS

✿ **E4-18** → Find examples for the following in the paragraph below.

1. past participle phrase _____

2. infinitive phrase _____

3. -ing prepositional phrase _____

4. determiner + adjective phrase _____

5. gerund phrase _____

"But by a combination of events almost to be called a coincidence, it appears that both the path and the entrance were watched during the crucial time, and there is a chain of witnesses who confirm each other where there is no exit or entrance of any kind. The central garden path is a lane between two ranks of tall delphiniums, planted so close that any stray step off the path would leave its traces; and both path and plants run right up to the very mouth of the summer-house, so that no straying from that straight path could fail to be observed, and no other mode of entrance can be imagined."

☼ **E4-19** → Identify the bolded words, giving full descriptions, in the paragraph below.

1. _____
2. _____
3. _____
4. _____
5. _____
6. _____
7. _____
8. _____
9. _____
10. _____

"My father did not answer. It was **late indeed**[1] when we lay down **to rest**,[2] and the night I spent between **waking and dreaming**[3] of the wonderland **beyond the mountains**,[4] **hoping against hope**[5] that my father would go. The sun **was just flooding**[6] the slopes when our guest arose to leave, and my father bade him **God-speed**[7] with a heartiness that was rare to him. But, to my bitter regret, neither spoke of **my father's going**.[8] **Being a man of understanding**,[9] Mr. Boone knew it were little use to press. He patted me on the head. 'You're **a wise**[10] lad, Davy,' said he. 'I hope we shall meet again.'"

PHRASE ANALYSIS

✿ **E4-20** → Construct diagrams to illustrate the breakdown of the following phrases.

1. Noun

   a.   **the overly excited young boys and girls**

   b.   **golfing every day of the week**

2. Adjective

   a.   **the crazy little black furry**

   b.   **the successful and long sought-after**

....

 3. Verb

   a.   **should have called**

   b.   **might have been going**

....

4. Adverb

a. **rather quietly and very quickly**

b. **noticeably in a hurry**

··

5. Participle

a. **the quiet and gently falling**

b.   **rather unusually discouraged**

6. Gerund

   a.   **his keen understanding**

   b.   **Friday's most decisive ruling**

7. Infinitive

   a.   **for you to think that way**

   b.   **to do so gently**

8. Prepositional

   a.   **during the ball game**

b. **in spite of the time**

---

9. Absolute

a. **space obviously available**

b. **given the situation**

5   CLAUSES

DEFINITIONS
✿ E5-1 → Match Part A with the correct definition in Part B.

Part A

1. Independent clauses are. . . . . ____
2. Independent clauses are also called . . . . ; ____
3. The basis of a clause is that it contains . . . . ____
4. Dependent clauses are. . . . . ____
5. Four types of clauses are . . . . ____
6. Conjunctions signal . . . . ____
7. Noun clauses are . . . . ____
8. Noun clauses parallel. . . . . ____
9. Many frontal noun clauses . . . . ____
10. While some sentences are simple in structure and are independent clauses . . . ____
11. Relative clauses are. . . . . ____
12. Relative adjective clauses are introduced by . . . . ____
13. While relative conjunctions introduce clauses . . . . ____
14. The subject can be expressed in a number of ways . . . . ____
15. Like the relative pronoun conjunctions, relative adverb conjunctions also have . ____
16. Phrases frequently contain verb forms that are non-finite . . . . ____
17. Relative adverb clauses are introduced by . . . . ____
18. Relative adverb clauses express meanings pertaining to . . . . ____
19. It is generally *the completed* meaning of a structure that signals . . . . ____
20. Perhaps the most common cause of sentence fragments . . . . ____

Part B

A. ... are extra-posed to a position after the predicate.

B. ... but the verb phrase must always show tense.

C. ... that the clause is dependent and that it must rely upon a second clause to give it full meaning.

D. ... whether it is a sentence or not.

E. ... is the use of a non-finite verb instead of a finite one.

F. ... a dual role, as connector and as an adverb within their own clause.

G. ... subject and finite verb structures carrying out the grammatical functions attributed to a modifier.

H. ... but clauses must always contain a finite verb.

I. ... noun words and noun phrases by form, function, and position.

J. ... main or matrix clauses.

K. ... noun, relative adjective, relative adverb and adverb clauses.

L. ... the relative adverbs *when*, *where*, and *why*.

M. ... subject and finite verb structures that stand alone with completed meaning.

N. ... as time, place, condition and so forth.

O. ... subject and finite verb structures needing a second clause structure for completed meaning.

P. ... they also carry out particular grammatical functions within that clause.

Q. ... most sentences consist of more than one clause, usually a combination of independent and/or dependent clauses.

R. ... the relative pronouns *who*, *whom*, *whose*, *which*, and *that*.

S. ... subject and finite verb structures carrying out the grammatical functions attributed to a noun, noun phrase, or its replacement.

T. ... a noun phrase (subject) and a verb phrase (predicate).

CLAUSE TYPES

✿ **E5-2** → Identify the clauses as independent or dependent.

Example:

"But for Company E, it was the first reality check on the constraints that would mark their tour."

CLAUSE	TYPE
But for Company E, it was the first reality check on the constraints	independent
that would mark their tour.	dependent

1. "I am free to confess that I had a realizing sense of the fact that my hospital bed was not a bed of roses just then."

_____

☐ INDEPENDENT   ☐ DEPENDENT

_____

☐ INDEPENDENT   ☐ DEPENDENT

_____

☐ INDEPENDENT   ☐ DEPENDENT

2. "Bioethics is a field of study which concerns the relationship between biology, science, medicine and ethics, philosophy and theology."

_____

☐ INDEPENDENT   ☐ DEPENDENT

_____

☐ INDEPENDENT   ☐ DEPENDENT

3. "But when I peeped into the dusky street lined with what I at first had innocently called market carts, now unloading their sad freight at our door, I recalled sundry reminiscences I had heard from nurses of longer standing."

_____

☐ INDEPENDENT   ☐ DEPENDENT

_____

☐ INDEPENDENT   ☐ DEPENDENT

_____

☐ INDEPENDENT   ☐ DEPENDENT

_____

☐ INDEPENDENT   ☐ DEPENDENT

4. "I progressed by slow stages up stairs and down, till the main hall was reached, and I paused to take breath and a survey."

_____

☐ INDEPENDENT   ☐ DEPENDENT

_____

☐ INDEPENDENT   ☐ DEPENDENT

_____

☐ INDEPENDENT   ☐ DEPENDENT

5. "Tell them to take off socks, coats and shirts, scrub them well, put on clean shirts, and the attendants will finish them off, and lay them in bed."

_____

☐ INDEPENDENT   ☐ DEPENDENT

_____

☐ INDEPENDENT   ☐ DEPENDENT

_____

☐ INDEPENDENT   ☐ DEPENDENT

_____

☐ INDEPENDENT   ☐ DEPENDENT

_____

☐ INDEPENDENT   ☐ DEPENDENT

6. "He thought it odd, and with a little perfunctory shiver, as if in deference to a seasonal presumption that the night was chill, he lay down again and went to sleep."

_____

☐ INDEPENDENT   ☐ DEPENDENT

_____

☐ INDEPENDENT   ☐ DEPENDENT

_____

☐ INDEPENDENT   ☐ DEPENDENT

_____

☐ INDEPENDENT   ☐ DEPENDENT

7. "He thought he was walking along a dusty road that showed white in the gathering darkness of a summer night."

_____

☐ INDEPENDENT   ☐ DEPENDENT

_____

☐ INDEPENDENT   ☐ DEPENDENT

_____

☐ INDEPENDENT   ☐ DEPENDENT

8. "Their children had the social and educational opportunities of their time and place, and had responded to good associations and instruction with agreeable manners and cultivated minds."

_____

☐ INDEPENDENT   ☐ DEPENDENT

_____

☐ INDEPENDENT   ☐ DEPENDENT

9. "As he grew to such manhood as is attainable by a Southerner who does not care which way elections go, the attachment between him and his beautiful mother—whom from early childhood he had called Katy—became yearly stronger and more tender."

_____

☐ INDEPENDENT   ☐ DEPENDENT

_____

☐ INDEPENDENT   ☐ DEPENDENT

_____

☐ INDEPENDENT   ☐ DEPENDENT

_____

☐ INDEPENDENT   ☐ DEPENDENT

_____

☐ INDEPENDENT   ☐ DEPENDENT

_____

☐ INDEPENDENT   ☐ DEPENDENT

10. "The dust in the road was laid; trees were adrip with moisture; birds sat silent in their coverts; the morning light was wan and ghastly, with neither colour nor fire."

☐ INDEPENDENT   ☐ DEPENDENT

☐ INDEPENDENT   ☐ DEPENDENT

☐ INDEPENDENT   ☐ DEPENDENT

☐ INDEPENDENT   ☐ DEPENDENT

NOUN CLAUSES

✿ **E5-3** → Identify the noun clauses.

Example:

"The SDLP have engaged in what they prefer to call 'partnership' government."

NOUN CLAUSE
what they prefer to call 'partnership' government

1. "Indeed it is not certain whether the DUP would agree to participate in such a forum with Sinn Fein members."

---

2. "To begin with, whoever else might benefit by Mrs. Inglethorp's death, her husband would benefit the most."

---

3. "The farmer explained that he was too old to work, and his only son had been killed in Vietnam, so now there was nothing to do but sit."

---

4. "He said he wanted everyone to know how important their support was in his final battle."

---

5. "We want to make sure that whatever decision is taken is one that is going to benefit our own security."

   _____

6. "The research shows the emotional impacts are huge, whether they're separated from parents on this side or on the other side of the border."

   _____

7. "The SDLP have engaged in what they prefer to call 'partnership' government."

   _____

8. "Mr. Hunter, whose son has served in Iraq, argues that the current bill would endanger troops by interfering with the Pentagon's ability to share intelligence with battlefield commanders."

   _____

9. "Those on the right of the party opposed it on the basis that it was undemocratic and that the government was surreptitiously setting this agenda."

   _____

   _____

10. "I told father that in the Bible itself maxims can be found by which we may test our convictions to see whether they are reasonable and just."

    _____

    _____

RELATIVE ADJECTIVE CLAUSES

☼ **E5-4** → Identify the relative adjective clauses.

Example:

"The difference is that it is the discipline that has succeeded most brilliantly."

RELATIVE ADJECTIVE CLAUSE
that has succeeded most brilliantly

1. "For example, people value unspoiled landscapes, which are not for sale in the market."

   _____

2. "If neither Ferentz nor Mariucci emerges, Notre Dame will most probably sift through a hodgepodge of candidates, none of whom would make the splash that Meyer would have made."

_____

_____

3. "If you take me, Hilton, you will take a woman who has nothing that she need be personally ashamed of; but you will have to be content with my word for it, and to allow me to be silent as to all that passed up to the time when I became yours."

_____

_____

_____

4. "This was the woman who had warned me so earnestly, and to whose warning I had, alas, paid no heed!"

_____

_____

5. "The chairman of the court's 18 justices called for another election on Dec. 26, news that brought a boost of optimism to the Yushchenko supporters who have been in the streets of Kiev since the original vote."

_____

_____

6. "Other names that may surface are California Coach Jeff Tedford, whom White knows from his Pac-10 days as the athletic director at Arizona State, and Boise State Coach Dan Hawkins, who has led the Broncos on a 22-game-winning streak, the longest current streak in N.C.A.A. Division I-A."

_____

_____

_____

7. "Phoebe wondered whose care and toil it could have been that had planted these vegetables, and kept the soil so clean and orderly."

_____

_____

8. "Laura, for whom this opera night had been an event, a thing desired and anticipated with all the eagerness of a girl who had lived for twenty-two years in a second-class town of central Massachusetts, was in great distress."

_____

_____

9. "The cold wave that was ushered in that December morning was the beginning of a long series of days that vied with each other as to which could induce the mercury to drop the lowest."

_____

_____

10. "The personnel that work in these medical laboratory departments are technically trained staff, each of whom usually hold a medical technology degree, who actually perform the tests, assays, and procedures needed for providing the specific services."

_____

_____

_____

RELATIVE ADVERB CLAUSES

☼ **E5-5** → Identify the relative adverb clauses.

Example:

"Acrimony heightened in 1985 when Sinn Fein councillors were elected to local authorities."

RELATIVE ADVERB CLAUSE
when Sinn Fein councillors were elected to local authorities

1. "In those councils where unionists have a slim hold on the largest party title, power sharing has featured prominently on their agenda."

_____

2. "Edna tapped her foot impatiently, and wondered why the children persisted in playing in the sun when they might be under the trees"

_____

_____

3. "Once graduated from medical school most physicians begin their residency training, where skills in a speciality of medicine are learned, supervised by more experienced doctors."

_____

4. "He stopped to talk, and asked the old farmer why he sat alone when the farm work needed to be done."

_____

_____

5. "Where the Bible was 'opened,' flowers spelled out the words to John 3:16— 'For God so loved the U.S.A.'"

_____

6. "There are millions of people who are illegally in the United States, and it's unfortunate, when they're caught, seeing a family split up."

_____

7. "The visiting NATO commander expressed surprise Friday that Iraq's insurgency had proven so resilient by comparison with Afghanistan, where he said security has improved significantly."

_____

8. "To those who weren't here when the water went bad in May, 2000, Walkerton is now an aging media drama."

_____

9. "Federal officials encouraged people to call, but now cite the deluge of calls to explain why they were unable to give accurate answers."

_____

10. "I remained standing on the spot where he had left me, unwilling to depart, and yet unknowing why I should loiter there."

_____

_____

ADVERB CLAUSES
☼ **E5-6** → Identify the adverb clauses.

Example:

"Although 21 councils can be described as hung, there are obvious political coalitions that form, based on either the unionist or nationalist cleavages."

ADVERB CLAUSE
Although 21 councils can be described as hung

1. "Firstly, political history and culture are seen as important in that if the ideological gap between the sharing parties is narrow, chances of a successful partnership are high."

_____

_____

2. "Prince also stood firm and motionless as long as he could; till he suddenly sank down in a heap."

_____

_____

3. "Thus, as soon as this view of the world is adopted and the other discarded, a demand for a Carthaginian peace is inevitable, to the full extent of the momentary power to impose it."

_____

_____

4. "The skipper presented an unmoved breadth of back: it was the renegade's trick to appear pointedly unaware of your existence unless it suited his purpose to turn at you with a devouring glare before he let loose a torrent of foamy, abusive jargon that came like a gush from a sewer."

_____

_____

5. "If we are to criticize economists, it is to point out that they have been all too willing to agree that wealth is the supreme goal and that, therefore, they are the best counselors of national and global policy."

_____

6. "Or that a joke current during the Nazi period was that Hitler walked on water because he could not swim."

_____

7. "The science of medicine is the body of knowledge about body systems and diseases, while the profession of medicine refers to the social structure of the group of people formally trained to apply that knowledge to treat disease."

_____

8. "Since Oct. 1, U.S. authorities have intercepted 639 migrants trying to enter Puerto Rico, while another 337 have been detained on shore, Lieut. Willis said."

_____

9. "These years, during which he awaited a papal pardon so that he could return to Rome, were a period of exile, but they were also a liberating experience."

_____

10. "As soon as he was warm he began to think it would be a long while to wait till after supper before he drew out his guineas, and it would be pleasant to see them on the table before him as he ate his unwonted feast."

_____

_____

_____

DEPENDENT CLAUSE TYPES

✿ **E5-7** → Identify the dependent clauses, noting the type.

Example:

"The country was the grandest that can be imagined."

CLAUSE	TYPE
that can be imagined	relative adjective

1. "I knew that there was a range still farther back; but except from one place near the very top of my own mountain, no part of it was visible."

_____

☐ NOUN ☐ REL-ADJ ☐ REL-ADV ☐ ADVERB

2. "There was no one in the whole world who had the smallest idea, save those who were themselves on the other side of it—if, indeed, there was any one at all."

_____

☐ NOUN ☐ REL-ADJ ☐ REL-ADV ☐ ADVERB

_____

☐ NOUN ☐ REL-ADJ ☐ REL-ADV ☐ ADVERB

_____

☐ NOUN ☐ REL-ADJ ☐ REL-ADV ☐ ADVERB

3. "I kept aloof from Chowbok for the next few days, and showed no desire to question him further; when I spoke to him I called him Kahabuka, which gratified him greatly."

_____

☐ NOUN   ☐ REL-ADJ   ☐ REL-ADV   ☐ ADVERB

_____

☐ NOUN   ☐ REL-ADJ   ☐ REL-ADV   ☐ ADVERB

4. "Having therefore made up my mind that I would begin exploring as soon as shearing was over, I thought it would be a good thing to take Chowbok with me; so I told him that I meant going to the nearer ranges for a few days' prospecting, and that he was to come too."

_____

☐ NOUN   ☐ REL-ADJ   ☐ REL-ADV   ☐ ADVERB

_____

☐ NOUN   ☐ REL-ADJ   ☐ REL-ADV   ☐ ADVERB

_____

☐ NOUN   ☐ REL-ADJ   ☐ REL-ADV   ☐ ADVERB

_____

☐ NOUN   ☐ REL-ADJ   ☐ REL-ADV   ☐ ADVERB

_____

☐ NOUN   ☐ REL-ADJ   ☐ REL-ADV   ☐ ADVERB

5. "And then, in answer to my asking why this should be so, he gave me a long story of which with my imperfect knowledge of the language I could make nothing whatever, except that it was a very heinous offence."

_____

☐ NOUN   ☐ REL-ADJ   ☐ REL-ADV   ☐ ADVERB

_____

☐ NOUN   ☐ REL-ADJ   ☐ REL-ADV   ☐ ADVERB

_____

☐ NOUN   ☐ REL-ADJ   ☐ REL-ADV   ☐ ADVERB

6. "Alice started to her feet, for it flashed across her mind that she had never before seen a rabbit with either a waist-coat pocket or a watch to take out of it."

_____

☐ NOUN   ☐ REL-ADJ   ☐ REL-ADV   ☐ ADVERB

7. "And she began thinking over all the children _she knew_ that were of the same age as herself, to see if she could have been changed for any of them."

_____

☐ NOUN   ☐ REL-ADJ   ☐ REL-ADV   ☐ ADVERB

_____

☐ NOUN   ☐ REL-ADJ   ☐ REL-ADV   ☐ ADVERB

_____

☐ NOUN   ☐ REL-ADJ   ☐ REL-ADV   ☐ ADVERB

8. "While she was looking at the place _where it had been_, it suddenly appeared again."

_____

☐ NOUN   ☐ REL-ADJ   ☐ REL-ADV   ☐ ADVERB

_____

☐ NOUN   ☐ REL-ADJ   ☐ REL-ADV   ☐ ADVERB

9. "Those whom she sentenced were taken into custody by the soldiers, who of course had to leave off being arches to do this."

_____

☐ NOUN   ☐ REL-ADJ   ☐ REL-ADV   ☐ ADVERB

_____

☐ NOUN   ☐ REL-ADJ   ☐ REL-ADV   ☐ ADVERB

10. "'If the Israelis stop their aggression against our people, I think through the negotiations ... we can reach a final agreement,' he said."

_____

☐ NOUN   ☐ REL-ADJ   ☐ REL-ADV   ☐ ADVERB

_____

☐ NOUN   ☐ REL-ADJ   ☐ REL-ADV   ☐ ADVERB

⚙ **E5-8** → Identify the dependent clauses, noting the type.

Example:

> "According to Isid. Geoffroy there is no doubt that Goethe was an extreme partisan of similar views."

CLAUSE	TYPE
that Goethe was an extreme partisan of similar views	noun

1. "Development workers often found that the people they worked with were very loath to leave the villages in which they lived."

_____

☐ NOUN   ☐ REL-ADJ   ☐ REL-ADV   ☐ ADVERB

_____

☐ NOUN   ☐ REL-ADJ   ☐ REL-ADV   ☐ ADVERB

_____

☐ NOUN   ☐ REL-ADJ   ☐ REL-ADV   ☐ ADVERB

2. "To say that Kiefer is a modern German artist is tantamount to saying that he is an expressionist, for German art in the 20th century has been overwhelmingly expressionistic and existentialistic."

_____

☐ NOUN   ☐ REL-ADJ   ☐ REL-ADV   ☐ ADVERB

_____

☐ NOUN   ☐ REL-ADJ   ☐ REL-ADV   ☐ ADVERB

3. "I cannot here enter on the copious details which I have collected on this curious subject; but to show how singular the laws are which determine the reproduction of animals under confinement, I may just mention that carnivorous animals, even from the tropics, breed in this country pretty freely under confinement, with the exception of the plantigrades or bear family; whereas, carnivorous birds, with the rarest exceptions, hardly ever lay fertile eggs."

_____

☐ NOUN   ☐ REL-ADJ   ☐ REL-ADV   ☐ ADVERB

_____

☐ NOUN   ☐ REL-ADJ   ☐ REL-ADV   ☐ ADVERB

☐ NOUN ☐ REL-ADJ ☐ REL-ADV ☐ ADVERB

☐ NOUN ☐ REL-ADJ ☐ REL-ADV ☐ ADVERB

4. "When we look to the hereditary varieties or races of our domestic animals and plants, and compare them with species closely allied together, we generally perceive in each domestic race, as already remarked, less uniformity of character than in true species."

☐ NOUN ☐ REL-ADJ ☐ REL-ADV ☐ ADVERB

☐ NOUN ☐ REL-ADJ ☐ REL-ADV ☐ ADVERB

5. "In regard to ducks and rabbits, the breeds of which differ considerably from each other in structure, I do not doubt that they all have descended from the common wild duck and rabbit."

☐ NOUN ☐ REL-ADJ ☐ REL-ADV ☐ ADVERB

☐ NOUN ☐ REL-ADJ ☐ REL-ADV ☐ ADVERB

6. "One circumstance has struck me much; namely, that all the breeders of the various domestic animals and the cultivators of plants, with whom I have ever conversed, or whose treatises I have read, are firmly convinced that the several breeds to which each has attended, are descended from so many aboriginally distinct species."

☐ NOUN ☐ REL-ADJ ☐ REL-ADV ☐ ADVERB

☐ NOUN ☐ REL-ADJ ☐ REL-ADV ☐ ADVERB

☐ NOUN ☐ REL-ADJ ☐ REL-ADV ☐ ADVERB

☐ NOUN ☐ REL-ADJ ☐ REL-ADV ☐ ADVERB

☐ NOUN   ☐ REL-ADJ   ☐ REL-ADV   ☐ ADVERB

7. "On the other hand, if we look at each species as a special act of creation, there is no apparent reason why more varieties should occur in a group having many species, than in one having few."

☐ NOUN   ☐ REL-ADJ   ☐ REL-ADV   ☐ ADVERB

☐ NOUN   ☐ REL-ADJ   ☐ REL-ADV   ☐ ADVERB

8. "And this certainly is the case, if varieties be looked at as incipient species; for my tables clearly show as a general rule that, wherever many species of a genus have been formed, the species of that genus present a number of varieties, that is of incipient species, beyond the average."

☐ NOUN   ☐ REL-ADJ   ☐ REL-ADV   ☐ ADVERB

☐ NOUN   ☐ REL-ADJ   ☐ REL-ADV   ☐ ADVERB

☐ NOUN   ☐ REL-ADJ   ☐ REL-ADV   ☐ ADVERB

9. "Now the number of mice is largely dependent, as every one knows, on the number of cats; and Mr. Newman says, 'Near villages and small towns I have found the nests of bumble-bees more numerous than elsewhere, which I attribute to the number of cats that destroy the mice.'"

☐ NOUN   ☐ REL-ADJ   ☐ REL-ADV   ☐ ADVERB

☐ NOUN   ☐ REL-ADJ   ☐ REL-ADV   ☐ ADVERB

☐ NOUN   ☐ REL-ADJ   ☐ REL-ADV   ☐ ADVERB

☐ NOUN   ☐ REL-ADJ   ☐ REL-ADV   ☐ ADVERB

10. "'If we assume from the start that we cannot learn anything from others because our own position has no room for growth, then entering into dialogue would be dishonest.'"

_____

☐ NOUN   ☐ REL-ADJ   ☐ REL-ADV   ☐ ADVERB

_____

☐ NOUN   ☐ REL-ADJ   ☐ REL-ADV   ☐ ADVERB

_____

☐ NOUN   ☐ REL-ADJ   ☐ REL-ADV   ☐ ADVERB

MATCH EXERCISES
⚙ **E5-9** → Find examples for Part A in Part B, **USING EACH SENTENCE ONLY ONCE**.

Part A

1. 1 independent + 1 dependent clause   _____

2. 2 independent + 1 dependent clause   _____

3. 2 independent + 2 dependent clauses   _____

4. 1 independent clause + 3 dependent clauses _____

5. 3 independent clauses   _____

Part B

A. "Now, medical records show, she takes antidepressant drugs and sees a therapist, but the problems persist."

B. "But such an eclipse could not be expected to last, and at present Germany is experiencing a Nietzschian revival, Kiefer is plainly indebted to it.'"

C. "Although a large number of alternative approaches to health await scientific validation, many report improvement of symptoms after obtaining alternative therapies."

D. "We were in the small southern Indiana town where I grew up, and a gospel concert was advertised for the auditorium of the little Christian college there."

E. "Nevertheless, when it resumes as most observers believe it will the political challenge will be to find a model in which all parties play a legitimate role in the future government of Northern Ireland."

✿ **E5-10** → Find examples for Part A in Part B, **USING EACH SENTENCE ONLY ONCE**.

Part A

1. Noun clause   _____

2. Relative adjective clause   _____

3. Relative adverb clause   _____

4. Adverb clause [CONTRAST]   _____

5. Adverb clause [TIME]   _____

Part B

A. "Those who knew him at that time can easily understand why Richard attracted men and women so much older than himself."

B. "This analysis should proceed until we arrive at those parts that are indivisible and therefore not further analyzable."

C. "Whereas other techniques, like those of science and engineering, can remove more mundane obstacles, religions attend to the most irremovable limits on life: fate, guilt, meaninglessness, and death."

D. "Johnson could then display all the dignity of a man whose duty it was to protect Jimmie from a splashing."

E. "We want to make sure that whatever decision is taken is one that is going to benefit our own security."

PARAGRAPH ANALYSIS

✿ **E5-11** → Find the following clauses in the paragraph below.

1. Adverb clause [reason]   _____

2. Relative/possessive adjective clause   _____

3. Noun clause   _____

4. Adverb clause [concession]   _____

5. Relative/non-personal adjective clause _____

"All having eaten, drank, and rested, the surgeons began their rounds; and I took my first lesson in the art of dressing wounds. It wasn't a festive scene, by any means, because Dr. P. ... fell to work with a vigor which soon convinced me that I was a weaker vessel, though nothing would have induced me to confess it then. He had served in the Crimea, and seemed to regard a dilapidated body very much as I should have regarded a damaged garment; and, turning up his cuffs, whipped out a very unpleasant looking houseknife, cutting, sawing, patching and piecing, with the enthusiasm of an accomplished surgical seamstress; explaining the process, in scientific terms, to the patient, meantime; ... . There was an uncanny sort of fascination in watching him, as he peered and probed into the mechanism of those wonderful bodies, whose mysteries he understood so well. The more intricate the wound, the better he liked it. A poor private, with both legs off, and shot through the lungs, possessed more attractions for him than a dozen generals, slightly scratched in some 'masterly retreat'; and had any one appeared in small pieces, requesting to be put together again, he would have considered it a special dispensation."

⚙ **E5-12** → Find the following clauses in the paragraph below.

1. Relative/personal-adjective clause _____
2. Adverb clause/time _____
3. Relative adverb clause _____
4. Adverb clause/concession _____
5. Relative/non-personal-adjective clause _____

"On an evening in the latter part of May a middle-aged man was walking homeward from Shaston to the village of Marlott, in the adjoining Vale of Blakemore or Blackmoor. The pair of legs that carried him were rickety, and there was a bias in his gait which inclined him somewhat to the left of a straight line. He occasionally gave a smart nod, as if in confirmation of some opinion, though he was not thinking of anything in particular. An empty egg-basket was slung upon his arm, the nap of his hat was ruffled, a patch being quite worn away at its brim where his thumb came in taking it off. Presently he was met by an elderly parson astride on a gray mare, who, as he rode, hummed a wandering tune."

⚙ **E5-13** → Identify the bolded clauses, giving full descriptions, in the following paragraph.

1. _____

2. _____

3. _____

4. _____

5. _____

6. _____

7. _____

8. _____

9. _____

10. _____

"'It is true,' he said; 'but these men have made wells close by the river, and they say **that these wells fill themselves**;[1] and they have digged channels through their gardens, and they say that these channels would always have water in them **even though the spring should cease to flow**.[2] Some of them say also **that it is an unworthy thing to drink from a source**[3] that another has opened, and **that every man ought to find a new spring for himself**;[4] so they spend the hour of the visitation, and many more, in searching among the mountains **where there is no path**.[5]"

"**While I wondered over this**,[6] we kept on in the way. There was already quite a throng of people all going in the same direction. And **when we came to the Source**,[7] **which flowed from an opening in a cliff**,[8] almost like a chamber hewn in the rock, and made a little garden of wild-flowers around it **as it fell**,[9] I heard the music of many voices and the beautiful name of him **who had given his life to find the forgotten spring**.[10]"

⚙ **E5-14** → Identify the bolded clauses, giving full descriptions, in the following paragraph.

1. _____

2. _____

3. _____

4. _____

5. _____

6. _____

7. _____

8. _____

9. _____

10. _____

"For two good reasons, I will not enter deeply into this scientific branch of my confession. First, **because I have been made to learn**[1] **that the doom and burthen of our life is bound for ever on man's shoulders,**[2] and **when the attempt is made to cast it off,**[3] it but returns upon us with more unfamiliar and more awful pressure. Second, because, **as my narrative will make, alas! too evident,**[4] my discoveries were incomplete. Enough then, **that I not only recognised my natural body from the mere aura and effulgence of certain of the powers**[5] **that made up my spirit,**[6] but managed to compound a drug **by which these powers should be dethroned from their supremacy,**[7] and a second form and countenance substituted, none the less natural to me because they were the expression, and bore the stamp of lower elements in my soul.

"I hesitated long **before I put this theory to the test of practice.**[8] I knew well that I risked death; for any drug **that so potently controlled and shook the very fortress of identity,**[9] might, by the least scruple of an overdose or at the least in opportunity in the moment of exhibition, utterly blot out that immaterial tabernacle **which I looked to it to change.**[10] But the temptation of a discovery so singular and profound at last overcame the suggestions of alarm."

CLAUSE ANALYSIS

✿ **E5-15** → Analyze the following clauses, using tree diagrams.

1.   **that he knew the answer**

2.   **who quickly swam the cold lake**

3.   **after they came to visit**

6   MAJOR GRAMMATICAL FUNCTIONS

DEFINITIONS

✿ **E6-1** → Match Part A with the correct definition in Part B.

Part A

1. Grammatical functions are the roles . . . . _____

2. Identifying words by grammatical function . . . . _____

3. Subject has the grammatical meaning . . . . _____

4. To express the grammatical meaning of the subject receiving the action . . . . . . _____

5. Predicate has the grammatical meaning . . . . _____

6. To express the grammatical meaning of a predicate asserting an action . . . . . . _____

7. Agreement is the relationship that exists . . . . _____

8. The expletives *it* and *there* . . . . _____

9. Mood (mode) . . . . _____

10. Indicative mood expresses . . . . _____

11. Imperative mood expresses . . . . _____

12. Subjunctive mood expresses . . . . _____

13. Voice is a syntactic construction indicating . . . . _____

14. Active voice describes a verbal category . . . . _____

15. Passive voice is a feature of transitive sentences . . . . _____

16. Direct object has the grammatical meaning of . . . . _____

17. The direct object can be any word, phrase or clause that can replace a noun . . _____

18. For grammatical meaning, the direct object has . . . . _____

19. Indirect object has the grammatical meaning . . . . _____

20. Indirect objects do not occur as frequently as direct objects, possibly because . . _____

Part B

A. ... is the grammatical distinction in a verb form that expresses a fact (indicative), a command (imperative), a condition contrary to fact (subjunctive), probability or possibility (conditional).

B. .... the hypothetical, doubtful, desirable or obligatory.

C. ... that which asserts, describes, or identifies.

D. ... noting the relationship between the subject and the object; the action is expressed by transitive verbs.

E. ... many semantic and logical relationships.

F. ... in which the grammatical subject of the predicate becomes the goal of the expressed action.

G. ... we use transitive, intransitive or linking verbs.

H. ... that which undergoes the action of the predicate, or is affected by it.

I. ... a command or requires/forbids an action to be carried out.

J. ... by, to or for whom the action is performed.

K. ... that is, a pronoun, a gerund or an infinitive; it can also be a noun, gerund or infinitive phrase, or a noun clause.

L. ... between two or more sentence constituents.

M. ... that which performs, describes, identifies or asserts.

N. ... are dummy words that have structural rather than grammatical functions.

O. ... relationships between the subject and direct object of the verb.

P. ... we use either an intransitive or a transitive verb.

Q. ... sentence constituents have in relationship to other sentence constituents.

R. ... we can convey the same meaning with a prepositional phrase after the direct object.

S. ... a fact or asks a question.

T. ... reveals the ongoing and often changing relationships sentence constituents have to one another.

SUBJECTS

⚙ **E6-2** → Identify the subjects of the independent and dependent clauses.

Example:

"John will show you your room."

SUBJECT
John

1. "In most countries, it is prohibited to practice medicine without a proper degree in that field and doctors must be licensed by a medical board or some other equivalent organization."

   _____   _____

2. "Notre Dame is expected to look at Iowa Coach Kirk Ferentz, whom White hired as the head coach of Maine in 1990."

   _____   _____

3. "Although a large number of alternative approaches to health await scientific validation, many report improvement of symptoms after obtaining alternative therapies."

   _____   _____

4. "Procedural disputes between the British Government and Sinn Fein have stalled the process, and the recent resumption of IRA bombings in London has called its future into doubt."

   _____   _____

5. "The village of Styles St. Mary was situated about two miles from the little station, and Styles Court lay a mile the other side of it."

   _____   _____

6. "When Joseph Ratzinger arrived at Tübingen in southern Germany in 1966, he was widely viewed as a church reformer."

   _____   _____

7. "When does the prime minister intend to tell Parliament and tell Canadians about these things and about where the government's at in this program?"

   _____   _____

8. "But Justices Michael Moldaver, Robert Sharpe and Eilleen Gillese ruled a new trial would give both sides an opportunity to deal with fresh evidence."

_____   _____

9. "Government lawyer Sylvain Lussier argued that Gomery is entitled only to the part of the information that falls within his legal mandate dealing with sponsorship."

_____   _____

_____

10. "With night at hand and a rain-storm brewing, he did not head for his own camp, some miles distant, but directed his steps toward an old log cabin."

_____   _____

PREDICATES

✿ **E6-3** → Identify the predicates of the independent and dependent clauses.

Example:

"I have focused this discussion on neo-liberal economics because this is now the dominant form."

PREDICATE
have focused
this

1. "And towards night I would often sit watching the deep blue of the mountain wall and dream of the mysteries of the land that lay beyond."

_____

_____

_____

2. "'We're confident that in the near future we're going to be able to do this again with Robert Baltovich beside us actually having been found an innocent man,' Lockyer said."

_____

_____

_____

3. "Political leaders on both sides will be watching for disaffected members who might cross the floor and tip the balance of power."

_____

_____

_____

4. "Major League Baseball did not test for steroids before 2003 and did not penalize for positive tests before last season."

_____

_____

5. "In the 'triangle of death,' the area south of Baghdad named for its lawlessness, the police have been the targets of constant attacks and are now absent from the streets entirely, even though Marine bases in the area give police training courses."

_____

_____

_____

6. "He had let go my bridle, folded his whip in his hand, and with a shout of 'Come on, Davy,' he ran for the coach, which was going slowly, caught hold of the footman's platform, and pulled himself up."

_____

_____

_____

_____

_____

_____

7. "Given the weak performance of Iraqi forces, any major withdrawal of American troops for at least a decade would invite chaos, a senior Interior Ministry official, whose name could not be used, said in an interview last week."

_____

_____

_____

8. "It just seems if you're the fifth-best American that week, you ought to get some credit."

_____

_____

_____

9. "Had he not determined that I should go, all would have been well."

_____

_____

_____

10. "As a boy of fourteen he had run off from his school and home in Iowa and, joining a wagon-train of pioneers, he was one of the first to see log cabins built on the slopes of the White Mountains."

_____

_____

✿ **E6-4** → Identify the mood of the bolded predicates.

Example:

"This **was** their criticism on his exquisite sensibility."

MOOD
indicative

1. "He **had** an extremely preoccupied air; he was always hurrying somewhere, with an expression that suggested that if he **were** one minute late all would be ruined!"

_____

_____

2. "He refused to relieve the school district of the federal order which **was forcing** them to insure that there **be** no 'majority of any minority' in a Pasadena school."

_____

_____

3. "Yet in the end he insisted on perishing with his cause by demanding that his jurors: '**Be** true to the pride of the Resistance as I **am** true to the pride of the Collaborators....'"

_____

_____

4. "In the first place it was necessary that man **clothe** himself lest he **freeze** to death."

_____

_____

5. "He **screwed up** his cherub-like face, and puffed comically enough—'**blow** them away!'"

_____

_____

6. "Very little **is known** about Winstanley's life prior to the Digger movement, other than what **can be gathered** from his own writings."

_____

_____

7. "**Come** on then, you've done enough gardening for to-day. 'The labourer is worthy of his hire,' you know. **Come and be refreshed**."

_____

_____

8. "If his account of Heathcliff's conduct **be** true, you **would** never **think** of desiring such a husband, would you?"

_____

_____

9. "If councils **had** real powers it **would be** harder to work with those parties."

_____

_____

10. "If little credence **can be given** to the stated distances of the voyage, the known route is perhaps even more vague."

_____

⚙ **E6-5** → Identify the voice of the predicates, giving the active or passive transition of the sentence as shown.

Example:

"Our conversation was interrupted by a rumbling sound."

VOICE	TRANSITION
passive	A rumbling sound interrupted our conversation.

1. "Catherine took a hand of each of the children."

   ☐ ACTIVE   ☐ PASSIVE _____

2. "Our pleasure was increased by the arrival of the Gimmerton band."

   ☐ ACTIVE   ☐ PASSIVE _____

3. "About the middle of the night I was wakened from my first nap by Mrs. Linton."

   ☐ ACTIVE   ☐ PASSIVE _____

4. "His health and strength were being sacrificed."

   ☐ ACTIVE   ☐ PASSIVE _____

5. "He may have done a little in all these vocations."

   ☐ ACTIVE   ☐ PASSIVE _____

6. "I was sweeping the hearth."

   ☐ ACTIVE   ☐ PASSIVE _____

7. "The bird was not shot."

   ☐ ACTIVE   ☐ PASSIVE _____

8. "Next time you may gather intelligence for yourself."

   ☐ ACTIVE   ☐ PASSIVE _____

9. "The latter, soon beginning to mingle in the sports, got pillaged by the young brigands most ruthlessly."

   ☐ ACTIVE   ☐ PASSIVE _____

10. "Supplemental Security Income (SSI) has been declared ineligible."

    ☐ ACTIVE   ☐ PASSIVE _____

✿ E6-6 → Identify the voice of the predicates; give the active or passive transition of the sentence as shown.

Example:

"Dorothea quite despises Sir James Chettam."

VOICE	OPPOSITE TRANSITION
active	Sir James Chettam is quite despised by Dorothea.

1. "Dorothea was altogether captivated by the wide embrace of this conception."

    ☐ ACTIVE   ☐ PASSIVE   _____

2. To them pain and mishap present a far wider range of possibilities than gladness and enjoyment."

    ☐ ACTIVE   ☐ PASSIVE   _____

3. "He was undertaking a remarkable feat of bodily exertion."

    ☐ ACTIVE   ☐ PASSIVE   _____

4. "He may pursue the gentilities of a profession."

    ☐ ACTIVE   ☐ PASSIVE   _____

5. "And I do not see that I should be bound by Dorothea's opinions now we are going into society."

    ☐ ACTIVE   ☐ PASSIVE   _____

6. "The practical unanimity of Nicaea was secured by threats."

    ☐ ACTIVE   ☐ PASSIVE   _____

7. "Her whole soul was possessed by the fact that a fuller life was opening before her."

    ☐ ACTIVE   ☐ PASSIVE   _____

8. "Lord Palmerston formally opened the company's first mine at Spinney Park, on the edge of Sherwood Forest."

    ☐ ACTIVE   ☐ PASSIVE   _____

9. "It's making life jolly difficult for us."

    ☐ ACTIVE   ☐ PASSIVE   _____

10. "Your mother very suddenly and hurriedly makes a new will."

    ☐ ACTIVE   ☐ PASSIVE   _____

⚙ E6-7 → For the bolded predicates give the tense, aspect, mood and voice.

Example:

"Marner **was** highly **thought of** in that little hidden world."

TENSE	ASPECT	MOOD	VOICE
past	simple	indicative	passive

1. "It **is** not surprising that Mr. Macey observed, later on in the evening at the Rainbow, that Marner's head **was** 'all of a muddle.'"

   _____ _____ _____ _____

   _____ _____ _____ _____

2. "She **was being lifted** from the pillion by strong arms which **seemed** to find her ridiculously small."

   _____ _____ _____ _____

   _____ _____ _____ _____

3. "Miss Lammeters' bandboxes **had been deposited** on their arrival in the morning."

   _____ _____ _____ _____

4. "'**Don't talk** so, Priscy,' said Nancy, blushing. 'You **know** I don't mean ever to be married.'"

   _____ _____ _____ _____

   _____ _____ _____ _____

5. "'Well,' returned I, 'if what you tell me **be** true and if I am to be a beggar, it **shall never make** me a rascal, or induce me to disavow my principles.'"

   _____ _____ _____ _____

   _____ _____ _____ _____

6. "**Take** from me the same horse that **was given** him by the good bishop jewel, this staff."

   _____ _____ _____ _____

   _____ _____ _____ _____

7. "The wrinkled note-shaver **will have taken** his railroad trip in vain."

   _____ _____ _____ _____

8. "There **will be** intercrossing with the other individuals of the same species on the confines of each."

   _____   _____   _____   _____

9. "But, if you **be** ashamed of your touchiness, you must ask pardon, mind, when she comes in."

   _____   _____   _____   _____

10. "Here and there **is born** a Saint Theresa, foundress of nothing, whose loving heart beats and sobs after an unattained goodness."

   _____   _____   _____   _____

DIRECT OBJECTS

⚙ **E6-8** → Identify the direct objects of the independent and dependent clauses.

Example:

"Dorothea knew many passages of Pascal's _Pensées_."

DIRECT OBJECT
many passages (of Pascal's _Pensées_)

1. "The Irish lost a one-on-one competition for the coach who emerged as the university's leading candidate."

   _____

2. "The present volume and those projected in the same series represent a major step forward in our understanding of the contemporary religious world."

   _____

3. "As a social scientist, I also question the assertion that fundamentalism arises or gains prominence in times of crisis, actual or perceived."

   _____

   _____

4. "The officer reported his meeting with a 'Mr. Winstanlie and Mr. Everard,' the 'chief men' that have persuaded these people to do what they have done."

   _____

   _____

   _____

5. "Is the artist helping us to understand the ways in which our society has, in fact, lost the personal dimension?"

_____

_____

6. "She was opening some ring-boxes and just then the sun passing beyond a cloud sent a bright gleam over the table."

_____

_____

7. "'When you read his books, you can see that he writes at the highest level of theology,' said Karl-Joseph Hummel, director of research at the Commission for Contemporary History in Bonn."

_____

_____

8. "Federal officials said they leave time for parents to make arrangements for their children, and refer them to a social service agency if necessary."

_____

_____

_____

_____

_____

9. "The serpent of selfishness found its way into the heart of Adam but, Winstanley argued, God could not destroy Adam, for 'God would suffer dishonor because his work is spoiled.'"

_____

_____

_____

10. "The prisoner thanked the judge, and said that as he had no one to look after his children if he was sent to prison, he would embrace the option mercifully permitted him by his lordship, and pay the sum he had named."

_____

_____

_____

_____

INDIRECT OBJECTS

✿ **E6-9** → Identify the indirect objects of the independent and dependent clauses.

Example:

"His words gave me keen pleasure."

INDIRECT OBJECT
me

1. "She called Chanticleer, his two wives, and the venerable chicken, and threw them some crumbs of bread from the breakfast-table."

   _____

2. "What prompted the change was the Americans' worst loss in the 77-year history of the Ryder Cup—18 1/2–9 1/2—which gave Europe the cup for the seventh time in the last 10 meetings."

   _____

3. "But the Jews forced their way into the valleys and built themselves cities and constructed a mighty temple."

   _____

4. "I can give your question a direct answer easily enough."

   _____

5. "In the course of their wartime friendship, he taught Breton detachment and sarcasm, to see life as absurd and to live for the moment."

   _____

6. "Aunt Isabella sent papa a beautiful lock of his hair."

   _____

7. "So saying, I threw him his pocket-book, which he took up with a smile."

   _____

8. "Surrender can be a wrenching adjustment for people who have lived their whole lives in the intimate embrace of an instrument and whose talent brought them glory at a young age."

   _____

9. "In the big orchard, which was called the commercial garden, and which brought Yegor Semyonitch several thousand clear profit, a thick, black, acrid smoke was creeping over the ground and, curling around the trees, was saving those thousands from the frost."

   _____

10. "What was the decorative part of the garden, and what Pesotsky contemptuously spoke of as rubbish, had at one time in his childhood given Kovrin an impression of fairyland."

   _____

GRAMMATICAL FUNCTIONS

⚙ **E6-10** → Identify the grammatical function of the bolded word(s), and where the function is a predicate also give the tense and the aspect.

Example:

"They sat on the floor and drank **their soup** out of tea-cups."

FUNCTION
direct object

1. "With such a mind, active as phosphorus, biting everything that **came** near into the form that suited it, how could Mrs. Cadwallader feel that the **Miss Brookes** and their matrimonial prospects were alien to her?"

   _____

   _____

2. "Here Mrs. Wiggs tipped **an imaginary bottle** to her lips, and gave **Lucy** a significant wink."

   _____

   _____

3. "As the debate over immigration policy heats up, such broken families **are troubling** people on all sides, and challenging **schools and mental health clinics in immigrant neighborhoods**."

   _____

   _____

4. "It wasn't the man upstairs who gave **us** this schedule; it **was** the man below."

    _____

    _____

5. "Always ready to take the children on his knee and sing **them** hymns, or those endless old songs he taught them one by one, they loved **him** with a rare affection."

    _____

    _____

6. "They know **what their image is in Manhattan and Hollywood**, and they know **they**'re not all that different from the Democrats in those places."

    _____

    _____

7. "**His face** was still smooth as a child's, with immature features and guileless eyes, and one not knowing him **would probably have been surprised** to hear him speak with all the deliberation of an older and experienced man."

    _____

    _____

8. "**Frequent changes** of wind brought **an alternation of mild rainy days and frosty mornings**."

    _____

    _____

9. "About the time when the leaves of birches and aspens **were turning, the oats and the wheat** were cut and carried to the barn under a cloudless sky, but without rejoicing."

    _____

    _____

10. "It was reported on Friday **that a Las Vegas woman was arrested last week on attempted-larceny charges**."

    _____

⚙ **E6-11** → Identify the grammatical function of the bolded word(s), and where the function is a predicate give the tense and the aspect.

Example:

"She **was** a most generous woman."

FUNCTION
predicate   past   simple

1. "An appreciative listener **is** always stimulating, and I described, in a humorous manner, **certain incidents** of my Convalescent Home, in a way which, I flatter myself, greatly amused my hostess."

   _____

   _____

2. "**Come**, breakfast's not cleared away yet, and they'll make **you** some fresh tea."

   _____

   _____

3. "**This anniversary** had fallen on a Sunday, at a season of thick fog and general outward gloom; but he had brought **her** his customary offering, having known her long enough to have established a hundred small traditions."

   _____

   _____

4. "**The perfection of household care, of high polish and finish**, always reigned in her rooms, but they now **looked** most as if everything had been wound up, tucked in, put away, so that she might sit with folded hands and with nothing more to do."

   _____

   _____

5. "Only, you know, **the form and the way in your case** were to have been—well, something so exceptional and, as one may say, so particularly your own."

   _____

6. "It is obvious **that the Yankees do not want Giambi any longer**, and they **would love** it if his admission about using steroids allowed them to escape the four seasons and $82 million left on his contract."

   _____

   _____

7. "With this latter idea in my mind, I examined all the coffee-cups most carefully, remembering that it was Mrs. Cavendish who had brought **Mademoiselle Cynthia** her coffee the night before."

   _____

8. "She did not return with us, having been asked to a supper party, and to remain the night with some friends who **had been acting** with her in the tableaux."

   _____

9. "I set **a bad example**—married a poor clergyman, and made **myself** a pitiable object among the De Bracys—obliged to get my coals by stratagem, and pray to heaven for my salad oil."

   _____

   _____

10. "I'd talk to him about whatever he should say publicly, admit **whatever he did and let the court of opinion deal with most of it**."

    _____

MATCH EXERCISES
✿ **E6-12** → Find examples for Part A in Part B, **USING EACH SENTENCE ONLY ONCE**.
Part A

1. Extra-posed (delayed) subject   _____
2. Predicate phrase   _____
3. Indirect object   _____
4. Compound subject   _____
5. Compound predicate   _____

Part B

A. "Cynthia took the bottle and examined it with the severity of a judge."

B. "It was Mrs. Cavendish who had brought Mademoiselle Cynthia her coffee the night before."

C. "It was a still, warm day in early July."

D. "It may have been my fancy, but she, too, was looking odd and disturbed."

E. "When some of the ministers that had been outed for non-conformity holding conventicles in Northamptonshire, Benjamin and Josiah adhered to them, and so continued all their lives."

✿ **E6-13** → Find examples for Part A in Part B, **USING EACH SENTENCE ONLY ONCE**.

Part A

1. Delayed object   _____

2. Indirect object phrase   _____

3. Subject noun phrase   _____

4. Predicate phrase   _____

5. Direct object phrase   _____

Part B

A. "I related the whole story, keeping back nothing, and omitting no circumstance, however insignificant, whilst he himself made a careful and deliberate toilet."

B. "He may be seen leaving the room—he may be searched."

C. "Poirot seized his hat, gave his moustache a ferocious twist and, carefully brushing an imaginary speck of dust from his sleeve, motioned me to precede him down the stairs."

D. "The Scotland Yard men were the cynosure of all eyes."

E. "I thought it right and necessary to solicit his assistance for obtaining it."

In the following four exercises, the features of the requested function are identified in brackets.

✿ **E6-14** → Find examples for Part A in Part B, **USING EACH SENTENCE ONLY ONCE**.

Part A

1. Subject [NOUN PHRASE]   _____

2. Subject [INFINITIVE PHRASE]   _____

3. Predicate [PAST TENSE + PERFECT PROGRESSIVE ASPECT]   _____

4. Predicate [QUESTION IN THE INDICATIVE MOOD]   _____

5. Predicate [SUBJUNCTIVE MOOD]   _____

Part B

A. "Then you'll write to the Princess after tea, Alfred? ... Or shall we wait until we hear from the Princess?"

B. "The whole neighborhood was alive, and this, though it was close upon one o'clock in the morning!"

C. "The lawyer who had the hardihood to move that he be 'admonished' was solemnly informed that the Court regarded the proposal with 'surprise.'"

D. "In the west, France had been fighting for a hundred years."

E. "To complete his written appeal to the benign powers, traversing the haunted wood, might sometime rescue him if he should be denied the blessing of annihilation."

✿ **E6-15** → Find examples for Part A in Part B, **USING EACH SENTENCE ONLY ONCE**.

Part A

1. Predicate [PASSIVE VOICE] _____

2. Direct object [PRONOUN] _____

3. Direct object [DELAYED OBJECT] _____

4. Indirect object [PROPER NOUN] _____

5. Predicate [PASSIVE VOICE WITH PROGRESSIVE ASPECT] _____

Part B

A. "I thought it right and necessary to solicit his assistance for obtaining it."

B. "Mr. Brooke was detained by a message, but when he re-entered the library, he found Dorothea seated and already deep in one of the pamphlets."

C. "A pale anxious youth stepping softly on long legs was being chaffed by a strutting and rubicund globe-trotter about his purchases in the bazaar."

D. "His classical training disposes him to a realistic exaggeration of individual difference."

E. "Something certainly gave Celia unusual courage; and she was not sparing the sister of whom she was occasionally in awe."

⚙ **E6-16** → Find examples for Part A in Part B, **USING EACH SENTENCE ONLY ONCE.**

Part A

1. Subject [GERUND PHRASE] _____

2. Subject [DELAYED INFINITIVE PHRASE] _____

3. Predicate [INTRANSITIVE VERB + COMPLEMENT] asserting an action _____

4. Predicate [IMPERATIVE MOOD] _____

5. Predicate [ACTIVE VOICE] _____

Part B

A. "It was time for her to dress for the early dinner."

B. "The old gentleman took a step back."

C. "O powerful Goodness! bountiful Father! merciful Guide! increase in me that wisdom which discovers my truest interest."

D. "The clock on the wall ticked loudly and lazily."

E. "The brute's wailing and whining died away on the desolate shore."

⚙ **E6-17** → Find examples for Part A in Part B, **USING EACH SENTENCE ONLY ONCE.**

Part A

1. Predicate [PASSIVE VOICE WITH A MODAL] _____

2. Direct object [GERUND PHRASE] _____

3. Indirect object [PROPER NOUN] _____

4. Direct object [INFINITIVE PHRASE] _____

5. Predicate [INTRANSITIVE VERB WITH A MODAL] _____

Part B

A. "Things cannot continue as they are."

B. "Vainly he sought, by tracing life backward in memory, to reproduce the moment of his sin."

C. "After opening the forepeak hatch I heard splashing in there."

D. "Perchance my own pages may be colored by gratitude and love for the pioneers amongst whom I found myself, and thankfulness to God that we had reached them alive."

E. "Polly, give Mis' McChesney some salt."

PARAGRAPH ANALYSIS

✿ **E6-18** → Find the following functions in the paragraph below.

1. Direct object [NOUN CLAUSE] _____

2. Predicate [PRESENT PERFECT] _____

3. Direct object [PRONOUN] _____

4. Subject [NOUN + PREPOSITIONAL PHRASE] _____

5. Predicate [PRESENT PROGRESSIVE] _____

"In England the outward aspect of life does not yet teach us to feel or realise in the least that an age is over. We are busy picking up the threads of our life where we dropped them, with this difference only, that many of us seem a good deal richer than we were before. Where we spent millions before the war, we have now learnt that we can spend hundreds of millions and apparently not suffer for it. Evidently we did not exploit to the utmost the possibilities of our economic life. We look, therefore, not only to a return to the comforts of 1914, but to an immense broadening and intensification of them. All classes alike thus build their plans, the rich to spend more and save less, the poor to spend more and work less."

✿ **E6-19** → Identify the grammatical functions of the bolded word(s) in the following paragraph.

1. _____

2. _____

3. _____

4. _____

5. _____

6. _____

7. _____

8. _____

9. _____

10. _____

"**The elder, Ostap,**[1] began his scholastic career by running away in the course of the first year. They brought him back, whipped him well, and set him down to his books. Four times did he bury **his primer in the earth,**[2] and four times, after giving him a sound thrashing, did they buy **him**[3] a new one. But he **would** no doubt **have repeated**[4] this feat for the fifth time, had not his father given him a solemn assurance that he would keep him at monastic work for twenty years, and sworn in advance **that he should never behold Zaporozhe all his life long,**[5] unless he learned all the sciences taught in the academy. It was odd **that the man who said this was that very Taras Bulba**[6] who condemned all learning, and counselled his children, as we **have seen,**[7] not to trouble themselves at all about it. From that moment, Ostap began **to pore over his tiresome books with exemplary diligence,**[8] and quickly stood on a level with the best. The style of education in that age differed widely from the manner of life. **The scholastic, grammatical, rhetorical, and logical subtilties in vogue**[9] were decidedly out of consonance with the times, never having any connection with, and never being encountered in, actual life. Those who studied them, even the least scholastic, **could not apply**[10] their knowledge to anything whatever."

☼ **E6-20** → Identify the grammatical functions of the bolded word(s) in the following paragraph.

1. _____

2. _____

3. _____

4. _____

5. _____

6. _____

7. _____

8. _____

9. _____

10. _____

The Phoenicians,[1] who were the neighbours of the Jews, were a Semitic tribe which at a very early age had settled along the shores of the Mediterranean. They **had built**[2] themselves two well-fortified towns, Tyre and Sidon, and within a short time they had gained a monopoly of the trade of the western seas. Their ships went regularly to Greece and Italy and Spain and they even ventured beyond the straits of Gibraltar to visit the Scilly islands where they could buy tin. Wherever they went, they built **themselves**[3] small trading stations, which they called colonies. Many of these were the origin of modern cities, such as Cadiz and Marseilles.

"They bought and sold **whatever promised to bring them a good profit**.[4] They were not troubled by a conscience. If we are to believe all their neighbours they did not know what the words honesty or integrity meant. They regarded **a well-filled treasure chest**[5] the highest ideal of all good citizens. Indeed they were very unpleasant people and did not have a single friend. Nevertheless they have rendered all coming generations one service of the greatest possible value. They gave **us**[6] our alphabet.

"The Phoenicians **had been**[7] familiar with the art of writing, invented by the Sumerians. But they **regarded**[8] these pothooks as a clumsy waste of time. They were practical business men and could not spend hours engraving two or three letters. They set to work and invented **a new system of writing**[9] which was greatly superior to the old one. They borrowed a few pictures from the Egyptians and they simplified a number of the wedge-shaped figures of the Sumerians. They sacrificed the pretty looks of the older system for the advantage of speed and **they**[10] reduced the thousands of different images to a short and handy alphabet of twenty-two letters."

7 MINOR GRAMMATICAL FUNCTIONS

DEFINITIONS

✿ **E7-1** → Match Part A with the correct definition in Part B.

Part A

1. An object of preposition has the grammatical meaning . . . . ____

2. A modifier has the grammatical meaning. . . . . ____

3. Compound nouns are often mistaken . . . . ____

4. Adverbs as modifiers express . . . . ____

5. Adjective modifiers may occur . . . . ____

6. Adverb nouns occupy . . . . ____

7. Appositive has the grammatical meaning. . . . . ____

8. Appositives have several qualifications:. . . . . ____

9. Appositives are also . . . . ____

10. A complement has the grammatical meaning. . . . . ____

11. Subjective complement has the grammatical meaning. . . . . ____

12. Linking verbs require a . . . . ____

13. An objective complement has the grammatical meaning . . . . ____

14. Not all transitive verbs allow . . . . ____

15. Prepositional phrase modifiers . . . . ____

16. Adverb complements occur after. . . . . ____

17. Conjunctive adverbs join . . . . ____

18. The grammatical function of modifier can be carried out. . . . . ____

19. Connectors are form class conjunctions . . . . ____

20. The grammatical function of connectors is carried out . . . . ____

Part B

A. ... of that which identifies or completes.

B. ... used to note subordination, coordination, and conjunctiveness.

C. ... of that which renames; it is a referent to the noun it qualifies.

D. ... comparison, concession, condition, contrast, degree, direction, duration, frequency, intensity, manner, place, reason, and time.

E. ... of that which follows a linking verb and has the same referent as the subject.

F. ... by adjectives, adverbs, prepositional phrases, participles, and some nouns.

G. ... their direct objects to take objective complements.

H. ... linking and intransitive verbs.

I. ... restrictive or non-restrictive regarding the information they rename.

J. ... in a pre- or post-position modifying nouns, pronouns, and other adjectives.

K. ... subjective complement, which is a predicate noun or predicate adjective, or an adverb complement.

L. ... for an adjective modifier plus noun combination.

M. ... by coordinating conjunctions, subordinating conjunctions, correlative conjunctions, conjunctive adverbs, prepositions, and relatives.

N. ... an adverbial position and carry out the grammatical function attributed to adverbs.

O. ... units of equal value, but they do so with adverb emphasis.

P. ... of that which describes or identifies a direct object.

Q. ... of that which adds or limits the meaning of sentence constituents.

R. ... occupy adjective and adverb post-modifying positions.

S. ... post-modification, additional information, or description by way of identification.

T. ... of that which relates to a noun or its replacement by means of a preposition.

OBJECTS OF PREPOSITIONS

⚙ **E7-2** → Identify the objects of prepositions in the independent and dependent clauses.

Example:

"This is a religious book written by a believer."

PREPOSITION	OBJECT
by	believer

1. "Christianity drifted into the consciousness of the Roman world."

   _____   _____

   _____   _____

2. "Upon these matters there has been much pregnant writing during the last half century."

   _____   _____

   _____   _____

3. "Whatever claim Caesar may make to rule men's lives and direct their destinies outside the will of God, is a usurpation."

   _____   _____

   _____   _____

4. "We cannot escape as easily as these brave men dreamed from the grip of the blind powers beneath the threshold."

   _____   _____

   _____   _____

   _____   _____

5. "The Christians would neither admit that they worshipped more gods than one because of the Greeks, nor deny the divinity of Christ because of the Jews."

   _____   _____

   _____   _____

   _____   _____

6. "There is no act altogether without significance, no power so humble that it may not be used for or against God, no life but can orient itself to him."

   _____   _____

   _____   _____

   _____   _____

7. "Nevertheless it is well to prepare the prospective reader for statements that may jar harshly against deeply rooted mental habits."

_____   _____

_____   _____

8. "A handful of other states impose a range of penalties, including jail time, for such actions."

_____   _____

_____   _____

_____   _____

_____   _____

9. "From its very opening proposition modern religion sweeps past and far ahead of the old Arminian teachings of Wesleyans and Methodists."

_____   _____

_____   _____

_____   _____

10. "But he has no special concern and no special preferences or commandments regarding sexual things."

_____   _____

MODIFIERS

☼ **E7-3** → Identify the modifiers in the independent and dependent clauses, noting the type. (Treat prepositional phrases as single modifiers.)

Example:

"The group has killed hundreds of Israelis in attacks during the past four years."

MODIFIER	TYPE
during the past four years	prepositional/adverb

1. "The industrious rat had built his nest among the carved images."

_____   _____

_____   _____

2. "Once outside of the water, these animals gradually adapted themselves more and more to life on land."

_____   _____

_____   _____

_____   _____

_____   _____

_____   _____

3. "Enormous open windows with heavy iron bars made the high and barren room the roosting place of hundreds of pigeons."

_____   _____

_____   _____

_____   _____

_____   _____

4. "Originally these graves had been dug into the rocks of the western mountains but as the Egyptians moved northward they were obliged to build their cemeteries in the desert."

_____   _____

_____   _____

_____   _____

_____   _____

5. "The river Nile was a kind friend but occasionally it was a hard taskmaster."

_____   _____

_____   _____

_____   _____

6. "Meanwhile a certain Venetian by the name of Barbero had explored the ruins of western Asia and had brought back reports of a most curious language."

_____   _____

_____   _____

_____   _____

_____   _____

_____   _____

_____   _____

7. "A thousand years later, the Akkadians were forced to submit to the rule of the Amorites."

_____   _____

_____   _____

_____   _____

8. "This God, one of the many divinities who were widely worshipped in western Asia, was called Jehovah."

_____   _____

_____   _____

_____   _____

9. "One day, Moses disappeared from the camp of the Jews."

_____   _____

_____   _____

_____   _____

10. "Unfortunately, the mainland, Palestine, was already inhabited by another Semitic race, called the Canaanites."

_____   _____

_____   _____

_____   _____

APPOSITIVES AND COMPLEMENTS

☼ **E7-4** → Identify the appositives and complements in the independent and dependent clauses, distinguishing one from the other.

Example:

"None of them is taken from other books."

PHRASE	FUNCTION
from other books	adverb complement

1. "Only one of them—the story of Winifried and the Thunder-Oak—has the slightest wisp of a foundation in fact or legend."

   _____   _____

2. "One of Baltovich's lawyers, James Lockyer, said he was disappointed the Appeal Court didn't declare Baltovich an innocent man."

   _____   _____

   _____   _____

3. "Many critics seem frustrated by how difficult it is to categorize your works, and yet that seems to be a large part of your appeal to the general public."

   _____   _____

   _____   _____

4. "'My son,' he answered, 'this is the city which was called Ablis, that is to say, Forsaken.'"

   _____   _____

   _____   _____

5. "Then the spring would rise to an outpouring, and the water would run down plentifully to make the gardens blossom and the city rejoice."

   _____   _____

6. "'How can that be?' I said; 'do they not drink of the water, and does it not make their fields green?'"

   _____   _____

   _____   _____

7. "On a walk, food is a hindrance, a delay."

   _____   _____

8. "But there were many people who remained working in their fields or in their houses, or stayed talking on the corners of the streets."

_____   _____

_____   _____

9. "We call it the River Carita. And the name of the city is no more Ablis, but Saloma, which is Peace."

_____   _____

_____   _____

10. "After a long voyage upon stormy seas, we came into a quiet haven, and there the friend who was dearest to me, said good-by, for he was going back to his own country and his father's house, but I was still journeying onward."

_____   _____

_____   _____

_____   _____

CONNECTORS

✿ **E7-5** → Identify the grammatical functions of connectors, noting their type.

Example:

"The street was small and what is called quiet."

CONNECTOR	TYPE
and	coordinating

1. "Yet this is where the real challenge lies."

_____   _____

_____   _____

2. "But Americans are curiously unwilling to learn from Europe, even though almost all member-states of the European Union have better policies and lower rates of addiction than the U.S."

_____   _____

_____   _____

_____   _____

3. "The court's ruling—announced just before 6 p.m. after a day of suspense that halted Parliament's deliberations as well as talks aimed at a resolution of the impasse—was a surprising and decisive victory for Viktor A. Yushchenko, the opposition leader who asserted that he had been denied his rightful victory."

_____   _____

_____   _____

_____   _____

_____   _____

_____

4. "A wave of consternation invaded the vestibule for those who had not come in carriages, or whose carriages had not arrived."

_____   _____

_____   _____

_____   _____

5. "We did want to try it in London first, however—not only because I live there, but also, I am afraid, because the enormous expense of launching a new show in America is a major factor for avoiding it as an initial testing ground."

_____   _____

_____   _____

_____   _____

_____

6. "Whatever transcends these limits, whether it be an emptiness, an abyss of nothingness, or a plenitude of being, is what we are calling mystery."

_____   _____

_____   _____

_____   _____

7. "They show that rational behavior leads to greater wealth not only on the part of those individuals who practice it but also in society as a whole."

_____   _____

_____   _____

_____   _____

8. "Since the demise of the ill-fated Northern Ireland Assembly, which was boycotted by the SDLP and Sinn Fein, the only platform shared by all the political parties (including Sinn Fein) has been local government."

   _____   _____

   _____   _____

9. "Whichever way it was, there was always sure to be something waiting at the end for him and his violin to discover, if it was nothing more than a big white rose in bloom, or a squirrel sitting by the roadside."

   _____   _____

   _____   _____

   _____   _____

   _____   _____

10. "Any theory of Cabot's coasting voyage must thus include a convincing reason why upon returning he would have run into land beyond that which he had just discovered when sailing south."

    _____   _____

    _____   _____

    _____   _____

GRAMMATICAL FUNCTIONS

✿ **E7-6** → Identify the minor grammatical functions of the bolded word(s).

Example:

> "However, medicine often refers **more specifically** to matters dealt with by physicians and surgeons."

> **FUNCTION**
> adverb modifier

1. "One of van Gogh's first successful lithographs, ***At Eternity's Gate*** (1882), depicts an old man seated by a fire, his head buried in his hands."

   _____

2. "'They call it **buying and selling**,' he went on, 'down there in La Salle Street.'"

   _____

3. "But Mrs. Wessels, **a lean, middle-aged little lady**, with a flat, pointed nose, had no suggestions to offer."

_____

4. "With every instant the number **of people** increased; progress became impossible, except an inch at a time."

_____

5. "Then Landry Court with **his exuberance and extravagance and boyishness**, and now—unexpectedly—behold, a new element had appeared."

_____

6. "No one seemed **ready** to act upon Laura's suggestion, and again the minutes passed."

_____

7. "We have sent unto you our Brother Bonifice, and appointed him **your bishop**, that he may teach you the only true faith, and baptise you."

_____

8. "Kiefer is a self-conscious, deliberately 'German' artist. As such, he is engaged in profound dialogue with **his heritage**."

_____

9. "A great, slow-moving press of men and women in evening dress filled the vestibule **from one wall to another**."

_____

10. "Hargus had become **a sort of creature of legends**, mythical, heroic, transfigured in the glory of his millions."

_____

⚙ **E7-7** → Identify the grammatical structure and function of the bolded word(s).

Example:

"Mrs. Button, **a viperous Londoner**, yearned for noise."

STRUCTURE   FUNCTION
noun phrase   appositive

1. "The periods, therefore, **of his mother's martyrdom** were those of Paul's enfranchisement."

   _____   _____

2. "Who and what Kegworthy had been **neither Paul nor any inhabitant of Bludston** knew."

   _____   _____

3. "She had appeared in the town when Paul was a year old, **giving herself out as a widow**."

   _____   _____

4. "He **very soon** shattered any such illusion by appropriating the remainder of her fortune."

   _____   _____

5. "If Paul Kegworthy had been of the same fibre as the little Buttons, he **would have felt**, thought and acted as they."

   _____   _____

6. "The discomforts affected Paul but little, he had never had experience of luxuries, and the life itself was silken ease compared with what it would have been but for **Barney Bill's kidnapping**."

   _____   _____

7. "Paul was peacock born; it was for him **to strut about** in iridescent plumage."

   _____   _____

8. "He had **a soul-reaching** contempt for Billy Goodge, a passionate envy of him."

   _____   _____

9. "The vicarage party took **a few moments' rest** in the shade of a clump of firs some distance away from the marquee."

   _____   _____

10. "Miss Ursula Winwood knew herself to be a notable person, and the knowledge did not make her **vain or crotchety or imperious**."

    _____   _____

⚙ **E7-8** → Identify the grammatical functions of the bolded word(s).

Example:

"**Luckily**, my back was toward him."

FUNCTION
adverb sentence modifier

1. "And me, **Nance Olden**, with that fat man's watch in my waist and **some girl's beautiful long** coat and hat on, all covered with chinchilla!"

   _____

   _____

2. "It was **a big, smooth face**, with **accordion-plaited chins**."

   _____

   _____

3. "She **had been sent** to help me undress, she said, and make me **comfortable**."

   _____

   _____

4. "At that time to think of the Lambeth Conference as a possible source **of enlightenment** appeared **theologically ridiculous**."

   _____

   _____

5. "**Anyhow**, it was my one chance, and I took it as unhesitatingly as a rat takes **a leap** into a trap to escape a terrier."

   _____

   _____

6. "But **the fare** was of the most substantial kind—**not only** meat and potatoes, **but** dumplings; good heavens! dumplings for supper!"

   _____

   _____

7. "I tore **myself** out of it in such a hurry that I gave **myself** a kink in the neck."

   _____

   _____

8. "I find it **ironic that the most radical change of my mind over the years has been a keener grasp of its own inadequacy when dealing with ultimacy**." [deal with "ironic" first]

   _____

   _____

9. "An example **of this type** of painting might be one of the famous clowns of Georges Rouault, **the recent contemporary French painter**."

   _____

   _____

10. "**Moreover**, Kiefer's bleak perspective **is rendered** in such massive, extremely well-crafted, grandiloquent dimensions!"

    _____

    _____

⚙ **E7-9** → Identify the grammatical functions of the bolded word(s).

Example:

"It seemed **good** to one Denzil Calmady, esquire, to build himself a stately red-brick and freestone house."

FUNCTION
subjective complement/predicate adjective

1. "And Julius March, too, found the singing **somewhat agitating**, though to him the personality of the singer was **of small account**."

   _____

   _____

2. "He took **St. Augustine's *De Civitate Dei*** from its place in the bookshelves **lining one side** of the room."

_____

_____

3. "**Pacing slowly** down the centre of the terrace came Richard and Katherine Calmady, **hand in hand**."

_____

_____

4. "Commencing his labours at Brockhurst during the closing years of the reign of Queen Elizabeth, **Denzil Calmady** completed them in 1611 **with a royal house-warming**."

_____

_____

5. "But his thought was **tumultuous**, words refused to come in proper order and sequence; and Julius abhorred that erasures should mar **the symmetry of his pages**."

_____

_____

6. "To the Church, at once **his mother and his mistress**, he had wholly given **his first love** happiness."

_____

_____

7. "The vow, **therefore**, remained **unwitnessed and unratified**, but he held it inviolable nevertheless."

_____

_____

8. "The science of medicine is the body of knowledge about body systems and diseases, while **the profession of medicine** refers to **the social structure** of the group of people formally trained to apply that knowledge to treat disease."

_____

_____

9. "In his inaugural sermon, '**Music and Worship in the Liberal Church**,' he spoke of the responsibilities **of the arts** to the church, saying that only the best is good enough."

   _____

   _____

10. "Separated from the imperiled villagers by only his apparent passivity, Chagall's Messiah, **this Jew of the cross**, is no rescuer, but himself hangs **powerless before the chaotic fire**."

    _____

    _____

⚙ **E7-10** → Identify the grammatical functions of the bolded clauses.

1. "It was agreed **that the position of the chair would be rotated**, on a six monthly basis."

   _____

2. "**What is of particular interest here**, of course, is the power sharing cohort."

   _____

3. "Mr. Chapman led a drill for about 40 recruits, many **of whom drifted away into the shade for a smoke or giggled during a drill**."

   _____

4. "Yet there is a precedent for this at local government level **where both parties recognize unbridgeable political positions**."

   _____

5. "The doctor was shaving this lawn **as if it were a priest's chin**."

   _____

6. "Immunology is the study of the immune system, **which includes the innate and adaptive immune system in human**."

   _____

7. "He could not be sad, **because his son had died for America**."

   _____

8. "There are various versions of how tumultuous these years were in Tübingen, a quaint, gingerbready town, some **of whose university buildings date from the 15th century.**"

_____

9. "A cow is worth **whatever price it brings** in the market."

_____

10. "One of the things **that does not pass away** is the Something on High and the belief in God."

_____

✿ **E7-11** → Identify the grammatical functions of the bolded clauses.

1. "**After he 'converted' to art**, van Gogh rejected the religion of his parents for what he thought was true piety, which he called 'the white ray of light.'"

_____

2. "Few findings add to the evidence that genetic tests can help predict **whether breast cancer will recur.**"

_____

3. "It really had nothing to do with **what I was doing before.**"

_____

4. "That is the best advice **which I can give you, Mr. Hilton Cubitt.**"

_____

5. "The Maules had continued to inhabit the town **where their progenitor had suffered so unjust a death.**"

_____

6. "The medical encounter or patient–doctor relationship is **what medicine is about.**"

_____

7. "**That he was a desultory tentative student of something and everything** might only have been predicted of him."

_____

8. "Kegworthy, **whoever he might have been**, was wrapt in mystery."

   _____

9. "It was she herself **whose loss would be irreparable**."

   _____

10. "He chose Reason **because he perceived God as 'that living powerfull light'** and not simply as words."

    _____

MATCH EXERCISES

⚙ **E7-12** → Find examples for Part A in Part B, **USING EACH SENTENCE ONLY ONCE**.

Part A

1. Subject complement/predicate adjectives   _____

2. Extra-posed direct object   _____

3. Objective complement   _____

4. Indirect object   _____

5. Adverb modifier   _____

Part B

A. "To my intense surprise, Cynthia burst out laughing, and called me a 'funny dear.'"

B. "Now you will begin to see hospital life in earnest, for you won't probably find time to sit down all day."

C. "He seemed prosperous, extremely married and unromantic."

D. "I thought it right and necessary to solicit his assistance for obtaining it."

E. "Polly, give Mis' McChesney some salt."

✿ E7-13 → Find examples for Part A in Part B, **USING EACH SENTENCE ONLY ONCE.**

Part A

1. Prepositional phrase sentence modifier   _____

2. Prepositional phrase adverb complement   _____

3. Coordinating conjunction as a connector   _____

4. Predicate in the negative   _____

5. Extra-posed subject   _____

Part B

A. "Thus living plants and animals are not separated from the extinct by new creations, but are to be regarded as their descendants through continued reproduction."

B. "You don't seem to know anything."

C. "He succeeded in protecting the acre or two of earth."

D. "It occurred to him that the fact was fortunate."

E. "During the preparations for the wedding, I need not describe the busy importance of my wife, nor the sly looks of my daughters."

In the following exercises, the features of the requested function are identified in brackets.

✿ E7-14 → Find examples for Part A in Part B, **USING EACH SENTENCE ONLY ONCE.**

Part A

1. Adverb complement [PREPOSITIONAL PHRASE]   _____

2. Adjective modifier [PREPOSITIONAL PHRASES]   _____

3. Adjective modifier [PAST PARTICIPLE PHRASE]   _____

4. Adverb modifier [PHRASE]   _____

5. Adverb phrase modifier [PRESENT PARTICIPLE PHRASE]   _____

Part B

A. "Nature has very evidently given him up."

B. "She smoothed with a comb their carelessly tangled locks and moistened them with her tears."

C. "'You know what there is in the house,' she said, so coldly, it sounded impersonal."

D. "'It is Mr. Jadwin,' murmured Page, looking quickly away."

E. "The moon from the summit of the heavens had long since lit up the whole courtyard filled with sleepers."

✿ **E7-15** → Find examples for Part A in Part B, **USING EACH SENTENCE ONLY ONCE.**

Part A

1. Adverb phrase modifier [OF A SENTENCE] _____

2. Adjective modifier [SUBJECTIVE COMPLEMENT + PREPOSITIONAL PHRASE] _____

3. Adverb complement [PREPOSITIONAL PHRASE] _____

4. Non-restrictive appositive _____

5. Objective complement [ADJECTIVE PHRASE] _____

Part B

A. "Thomas was bred a smith under his father."

B. "I thought, notwithstanding all his ease, that he seemed perfectly sensible of the distance between us."

C. "His most notable service in home politics was his reform of the postal system."

D. "I had thought to find him elated with victory."

E. "To Jim that gossiping crowd, viewed as seamen, seemed at first more unsubstantial than so many shadows."

✿ **E7-16** → Find examples for Part A in Part B, **USING EACH SENTENCE ONLY ONCE.**

Part A

1. Adjective modifier [ADJECTIVE PHRASE] _____

2. Adjective modifier [PRESENT PARTICIPLE PHRASE] _____

3. Adjective modifier [OF ANOTHER ADJECTIVE MODIFIER] _____

4. Adverb phrase modifier [OF A SENTENCE] _____

5. Adverb phrase modifier [OF A PREDICATE] _____

Part B

  A. "Now, what was unquestionably important, a portion of these popular rumors could be traced, though rather doubtfully and indistinctly, to chance words and obscure hints of the executed wizard's son, and the father of this present Matthew Maule."

  B. "It was very roughly yet warmly built."

  C. "Old Taras's thoughts were far away: before him passed his youth, his years—the swift-flying years, over which the Cossack always weeps."

  D. "Above his head he saw a sky-like canopy of blue carrying fleecy clouds on which floated little pink-and-white children with wings."

  E. "The haggard aspect of the little old man was wonderfully suited to the place."

⚙ **E7-17** → Find examples for Part A in Part B, **USING EACH SENTENCE ONLY ONCE**.

Part A

1. Adverbial noun   _____

2. Adverb phrase modifier [PREDICATE + INFINITIVE PHRASE]   _____

3. Restrictive appositive   _____

4. Adverb complement [PREPOSITIONAL PHRASE]   _____

5. Adverb modifier [OF A SENTENCE]   _____

Part B

  A. "Clearly, he believes that a sizable residue of Hitler's spirit still resides in the German soul."

  B. "The story goes that a boat of Her Majesty's ship Wolverine found him kneeling on the kelp, naked as the day he was born, and chanting some psalm-tune or other."

  C. "He had heard long before from his professor, of a certain portrait by the renowned Leonardo da Vinci, upon which the great master laboured several years."

  D. "I was commonly allowed to govern, especially in any case of difficulty."

  E. "The rural opinion about the new young ladies, even among the cottagers, was generally in favor of Celia."

PARAGRAPH ANALYSIS

✿ **E7-18** → Find the following in the paragraph below.

1. an appositive _____

2. a direct object [NOUN CLAUSE] _____

3. a subjective complement [PREDICATE NOUN] _____

4. modifier [RELATIVE ADVERB CLAUSE/TIME] _____

5. direct object [INFINITIVE] _____

"Charles, commonly known as Carolus Magnus or Charlemagne, succeeded Pepin in the year 768. He had conquered the land of the Saxons in eastern Germany and had built towns and monasteries all over the greater part of northern Europe. At the request of certain enemies of Abd-ar-Rahman, he had invaded Spain to fight the Moors. But in the Pyrenees he had been attacked by the wild Basques and had been forced to retire. It was this occasion that Roland ... showed what a Frankish chieftain of those early days meant when he promised to be faithful to his King, and gave his life and that of his trusted followers to safeguard the retreat of the royal army."

✿ **E7-19** → Identify the grammatical functions of the bolded word(s) in the following paragraph.

1. _____

2. _____

3. _____

4. _____

5. _____

6. _____

7. _____

8. _____

9. _____

10. _____

"But **Paul and Arthur and Annie**[1] hated it. To Paul it became almost a demoniacal noise. The winter of their first year in the new house their father was **very bad**.[2] The children played **in the street**,[3] on the brim of the wide, dark valley, until eight o'clock. Then they went to bed. Their mother sat sewing below. Having such a great space in front of the house gave **the children**[4] a feeling of night, of vastness, and of terror. This terror came in from **the shrieking**[5] of the tree and the anguish of the home discord. Often Paul would wake up, after he **had been**[6] asleep a long time, aware of thuds downstairs. Instantly he was wide awake. Then he heard the booming shouts of his father, come home nearly drunk, then the sharp replies of his mother, then the bang, bang of his father's fist on the table, and **the nasty snarling**[7] shout as the man's voice got higher. And then the whole was drowned in a piercing medley of shrieks and cries from the great, wind-swept ash-tree. The children lay silent in suspense, waiting for a lull in the wind to hear what their father was doing. He might hit **their mother**[8] again. There was a feeling of horror, **a kind of bristling in the darkness**,[9] and a sense of blood. They lay with their hearts in the grip of an intense anguish. The wind came through the tree fiercer and fiercer. All the chords of the great harp hummed, whistled, and shrieked. And then came the horror of the sudden silence, silence everywhere, **outside and downstairs**[10]. What was it? Was it a silence of blood? What had he done?"

✿ **E7-20** → Identify the grammatical functions of the bolded word(s) in the following paragraph.

1. _____
2. _____
3. _____
4. _____
5. _____
6. _____
7. _____
8. _____
9. _____
10. _____

"The Law of the Jungle lays down **very clearly**[1] that any wolf may, when he marries, withdraw from the Pack he belongs to; but as soon as his cubs are old enough to stand on their feet he must bring them to the Pack Council, which is generally held once a month at full moon, **in order that**[2] the other wolves may identify them. After that inspection the cubs are free to run where they please, and until they have killed **their first buck**[3] no excuse is accepted if a grown wolf **of the Pack**[4] kills one of them. The punishment is **death**[5] where the murderer can be found; and if you think for a minute you will see that this must be so.

"Father Wolf waited till his cubs could run a **little**,[6] and then on the night of the Pack Meeting took them and Mowgli and Mother Wolf to the Council Rock—**a hilltop covered with stones and boulders where a hundred wolves could hide**.[7] Akela, **the great gray Lone Wolf**,[8] who led all the Pack by strength and cunning, lay out at full length on his rock, and below him sat forty or more wolves of every size and colour, from badger-coloured veterans who could handle a buck alone, to young black three-year-olds who thought they could. The Lone Wolf had led them **for a year now**.[9] He had fallen twice into **a wolf-trap**[10] in his youth, and once he had been beaten and left for dead; so he knew the manners and customs of men."

8   CLAUSE FUNCTIONS

DEFINITIONS
✿ E8-1 → Match Part A with the correct definition in Part B.

Part A

1. Noun clauses carry out the grammatical functions . . . . ____

2. Relative adjective clauses carry out the grammatical functions . . . . ____

3. Relative adverb clauses carry out the grammatical functions . . . . ____

4. Adverb clauses carry out the grammatical functions . . . . ____

5. Noun clauses as direct objects can also be . . . . ____

6. Relative clauses require special consideration . . . . ____

7. Restrictive clauses give ...; non-restrictive clauses give . . . . ____

8. Appositives can be . . . . ____

9. Unlike noun clause conjunctions . . . . ____

10. Complements of nouns or adjectives are restricted to a small group of
    English words . . . . ____

11. Extra-posed direct objects can often be overlooked . . . . ____

12. Although relative conjunctions generally introduce their clauses . . . . ____

13. Relative connectors can sometimes be omitted . . . . ____

14. Relative adverb clauses begin with *when, where* and *why*; whereas . . . . ____

15. Unlike relative adverb conjunctions . . . . ____

16. Deletions or ellipses are common in sentence structures . . . . ____

17. Adjective modifiers can actually be subjective complements . . . . ____

18. For extra-posed subjects . . . . ____

19. When the subject or direct object is not extra-posed . . . . ____

20. Potentially, noun clauses can carry out all of the functions . . . . ____

Part B

A. .... extra-posed to the end of the sentence.

B. ... since the expletive is so embedded into the structure that little attention is drawn to it.

C. ... relative pronouns always have grammatical functions within their clauses.

D. ... adverb clauses begin with a variety of adverbs.

E. ... essential information ... additional information.

F. ... of a noun; however, some of them do not occur.

G. ... attributed to a relative adverb, as a complement or modifier.

H. ... derived from verbs and taking a noun clause.

I. ... they are not restricted to a particular grammatical function.

J. ... subject, direct object, indirect object, object of preposition, subjective complement, objective complement and appositive.

K. ... the phrase *the fact* can be used before the conjunction *that*.

L. ... but only when they carry out the grammatical functions of objects.

M. ... attributed to an adverb, as a complement or modifier.

N. ... the expletive is placed at the beginning of the sentence.

O. ... restrictive (essential information), or non-restrictive (non-essential information).

P. ... since that is a grammatical function for adjectives–predicate adjectives.

Q. ... attributed to an adjective, as a complement or modifier.

R. ... and this often causes a problem in identifying a relative adverb clause when it is the antecedent.

S. ... adverb connectors do not have grammatical functions within the clauses they introduce.

T. ... because of the dual role that their connectors have within the sentence.

GRAMMATICAL FUNCTIONS OF NOUN CLAUSES

⚙ **E8-2** → Identify the noun clauses, giving their grammatical functions.

Example:

"Each was interested in what the other said."

CLAUSE	FUNCTION
what the other said	object of the preposition

1. "The British Government has hinted that such arrangements may be rewarded with increased powers to local government."

   _____   _____

2. "Artists in the Christian rock scene have a tendency to copy the styles of successful mainstream performers in order to provide godly alternatives to whatever is popular at the time."

   _____   _____

3. "Whether or not Winstanley was intentionally dialectical is impossible to determine with certainty."

   _____   _____

4. "It was understood that he had often spoken words of love to Madame Ratignolle, without any thought of being taken seriously."

   _____   _____

5. "Edna was what she herself called very fond of music."

   _____   _____

6. "But Kidd made it clear that he had kept up with everything said about him in his absence."

   _____   _____

7. "This 'framework of peace,' as it was described, included the assertion that the ultimate decision on governing Northern Ireland would be made by the majority of its citizens."

   _____   _____

8. "The name of the eclipsing girl, whatever it was, has not been handed down."

   _____   _____

9. "It is perhaps ironic that local government in Northern Ireland has now become the focus of research in power sharing."

_____   _____

10. "'I reckon I don't know much about what the Rebels is fighting for,' said John Duff."

_____   _____

GRAMMATICAL FUNCTIONS OF RELATIVE PRONOUNS

☼ **E8-3** → Identify the relative pronouns, giving the grammatical functions of the pronouns within their own clauses.

Example:

"This is my old friend, Monsieur Poirot, whom I have not seen for years."

PRONOUN	FUNCTION
whom	direct object

1. "Then he went across to his mother whilst I unbolted the door that gave on the corridor."

_____   _____

2. "Mr. Hunter, whose son has served in Iraq, argues that the current bill would endanger troops by interfering with the Pentagon's ability to share intelligence with battlefield commanders."

_____   _____

3. "Mary Cavendish was standing where the staircase branched, staring down into the hall in the direction in which he had disappeared."

_____   _____

_____   _____

4. "'You remember Branscom?' said Jaralson, treating his companion's wit with the inattention that it deserved."

_____   _____

5. "There are many addicts who do not want to get off drugs, for whom the drug-induced high is the whole focus of living."

_____   _____

_____   _____

6. "The fifth gentleman took a position halfway between the two, and, opening the leather case, laid it down on the grass, where its contents glistened."

   _____   _____

7. "That sense of uncertainty only deepens when she thinks of her older sister's delayed reaction to the outbreak, and whenever something goes wrong in her own body, as it did two weeks ago."

   _____   _____

8. "George Webb, an Oxford scholar, whose time for four years he had likewise bought, intending him for a compositor, of whom more presently; and David Harry, a country boy, whom he had taken apprentice."

   _____   _____

   _____   _____

   _____   _____

9. "This was the woman who had warned me so earnestly, and to whose warning I had, alas, paid no heed!"

   _____   _____

   _____   _____

10. "In his _Entretiens_ (1952), Breton explained why the Surrealists had adopted communism even though the two ideologies seemed an unlikely pair."

    _____   _____

RELATIVE ADJECTIVE AND ADVERB CLAUSES AS MODIFIERS

✿ **E8-4** → Relative clauses are modifiers (adjective or adverb). Identify the relative clauses, noting the grammatical function of the word(s) they modify.

Example:

"'All I heard of it were a few words that sounded like 'confounded steam!'"

RELATIVE CLAUSE
that sounded like 'confounded steam'

FUNCTION MODIFIED
subjective complement/
predicate noun

1. "Down below I met one of the resident surgeons who was crossing the courtyard and _stopped me_."

   _____   _____

   _____   _____

2. "The most influential German philosopher between the wars was Martin Heidegger, whose indebtedness to Nietzsche and his spiritual kinship with the expressionists were obvious."

   _____   _____

3. "The other three chaps that had landed with him made a little groups waiting at some distance."

   _____   _____

4. "A new name that emerged on Friday is Detroit Lions Coach Steve Mariucci, whom an agent in college football said had been approached by Notre Dame."

   _____   _____

   _____   _____

5. "Finally he handed a note to the boy, with directions to put it into the hands of the person to whom it was addressed, and especially to answer no questions of any sort which might be put to him."

   _____   _____

   _____   _____

6. "He had been scanning my features as though looking for a place where he would plant his fist."

   _____   _____

7. "I was in a great city in a foreign land—a city whose people were of my own race, with minor differences of speech and costume."

   _____   _____

8. "I therefore cabled to my friend, Wilson Hargreave, of the New York Police Bureau, who has more than once made use of my knowledge of London crime."

   _____   _____

9. "I obeyed, and hemmed, and called the villain Juno, who deigned, at this second interview, to move the extreme tip of her tail, in token of owning my acquaintance."

   _____   _____

10. "Every sort of experience that has ever come to a human being is in the self that he brings to God, and there is no reason why a knowledge of evil ways should not determine the path of duty."

    _____   _____

    _____   _____

⚙ **E8-5** → Identify the relative clauses, noting them as restrictive or non-restrictive.

Example:

"The only wine they didn't take was the 1941 vintage, which was still in vats."

CLAUSE	TYPE
which was still in vats	non-restrictive

1. "Mr. Mould, who tasted the wines being auctioned, said their state of preservation—thanks to their high sugar content—is 'astonishing.'"

_____

☐ RESTRICTIVE   ☐ NON-RESTRICTIVE

2. "'My mind was set last week,' Edwards said after practice Friday, when he named Pennington to start."

_____

☐ RESTRICTIVE   ☐ NON-RESTRICTIVE

3. "The band played a waltz which involved a gift of prominence to the bass horn."

_____

☐ RESTRICTIVE   ☐ NON-RESTRICTIVE

4. "In fact, as one of the seniors said, I've made five friends where I had one before."

_____

☐ RESTRICTIVE   ☐ NON-RESTRICTIVE

5. "Zubair, who was pregnant at the time, worried that her child would grow up watching Muslims mainly portrayed as terrorists or insurgents."

_____

☐ RESTRICTIVE   ☐ NON-RESTRICTIVE

6. "First, Judge Thomas L. Ambro wrote, the schools are entitled not to associate with groups whose policies they oppose."

_____

☐ RESTRICTIVE   ☐ NON-RESTRICTIVE

7. "Human anthrax vaccines date from the 1950's and 1960's, when the United States and other governments started to experiment with anthrax as a weapon."

_____

☐ RESTRICTIVE   ☐ NON-RESTRICTIVE

8. "It was not natural for a population, of whom so few enjoyed the comforts of life, to accumulate so hugely."

_____

☐ RESTRICTIVE   ☐ NON-RESTRICTIVE

9. "Furthermore, it is difficult to see why Cabot would have followed the coast on his east—that is, Newfoundland—rather than the mainland on his west."

_____

☐ RESTRICTIVE   ☐ NON-RESTRICTIVEE

10. "Hence, too, might be drawn a weighty lesson from the little-regarded truth, that the act of the passing generation is the germ which may and must produce good or evil fruit, in a far distant time."

_____

☐ RESTRICTIVE   ☐ NON-RESTRICTIVE

GRAMMATICAL FUNCTIONS OF ADVERB CLAUSES

⚙ **E8-6** → Identify the adverb clauses, noting their grammatical functions.

Example:

"We had talks with the leadership before we endorsed this policy (responsibility sharing)."

CLAUSE	FUNCTION
before we endorsed this policy (responsibility sharing)	adverb clause as a predicate modifier/time

1. "Its colorful collage of musical images coheres largely because of the work's persistent overall theme of death."

_____

_____

2. "Although compromises were now necessary, he remained a man of principle and the Fourteen Points a contract absolutely binding upon him."

_____

_____

3. "Both sides have promised to abide by Friday's ruling, but Mr. MacKinnon, the Globe reporter in Kiev, noted that a new vote cannot go ahead unless the parliament passes a slate of laws allowing another election."

_____

_____

4. "He could not be sad because his son had died for America, died for freedom."

_____

_____

5. "It's not unthinkable, even if it's not likely."

_____

_____

6. "We believe we responded as well as we reasonably could given the unique and demanding circumstances."

_____

_____

7. "The finding of a new writer gave him as much pleasure as if he had been the fiction editor who had accepted the first story by the embryo genius."

_____

_____

8. "Since this article was written, Sir Andrew Lloyd Webber has been knighted by Queen Elizabeth II of England and has released a compact disc of music composed by his late father."

_____

_____

9. "Such lies are commonplace as shaken parents try to shield young children from the reality of deportation, counselors said."

_____

_____

10. "Lower courts had said the former students would have to sue individually because their complaints are different."

_____

_____

GRAMMATICAL FUNCTIONS OF DEPENDENT CLAUSES

✿ **E8-7** → Identify the type and function of the bolded dependent clauses.

Example:

"The Army's procurement system, **which also supplies the Marines**, has come under fierce criticism for underperforming in the war."

TYPE	GRAMMATICAL FUNCTION
relative adjective/non-restrictive	modifier

1. "Mauriac, long a poignant witness to the connection between suffering and love, knew well **that the cornerstone of his faith was at stake in Wiesel's narrative**."

_____   _____

2. "We are busy picking up the threads of our life **where we dropped them**, with this difference only, **that many of us seem a good deal richer than we were before**."

_____   _____

_____   _____

3. "'Ratzinger told me this **after I hadn't seen him in a long time** and he felt the need to explain to me **why he is so strict**,' Professor Seckler continued."

_____   _____

_____   _____

4. "I remember **how I used to prize this flower**—long ago, I suppose, very long ago!—or was it only yesterday?"

_____   _____

5. "Very clearly, resentment was growing against Rome and against the Curia, **which appeared to be the real enemy of everything _that was new and progressive_**."

_____   _____

_____   _____

6. "He had influence, was well known to all Chicago people, **what he said** carried weight, financiers consulted him, promoters sought his friendship, his name on the board of directors of a company was an all-sufficing endorsement; in a word, a 'strong' man."

_____   _____

7. "**Whereas in Greece all the good harbours faced eastward and enjoyed a full view of the busy islands of the Ægean**, the west coast of Italy contemplated nothing more exciting than the desolate waves of the Mediterranean."

_____   _____

8. "That's **why I want to sift the matter to the bottom**."

_____   _____

9. "But it seemed **as if these important things came of themselves**, independent of time and place, like birth and death."

_____   _____

10. "Evidently fearful **that Richard was writing too much and with a view to pecuniary gain**, my mother wrote the following note of warning."

_____   _____

✿ **E8-8** → Identify the type and function of the dependent clauses.

Example:

"The second category concerns a person who has a mixed track record."

CLAUSE
who has a mixed track record
TYPE   relative adjective/restrictive
FUNCTION   modifier

1. "It was agreed that the position of the chair would be rotated, on a six monthly basis, between council members 'who deplore violence and seek to pursue political progress by political means.'"

_____

_____   _____

_____

_____   _____

2. "The doctor–patient relationship is important to the patient because the doctor has been given a monopoly on access to the prescription pad."

_____

_____   _____

3. "Much time must elapse before the plant and the skilled labour could be developed within France, and even so she could hardly deal with the ore unless she could rely on receiving the coal from Germany."

_____

_____   _____

_____

_____   _____

4. "Positive judgment does not preclude taking action that will help the child to remember not to steal in the future."

_____

_____   _____

5. "Different interpretations are part of a lack of information; perhaps that is why Day seems to have used both."

_____

_____   _____

6. "They acknowledge that there are other ways of studying human beings that also throw light on what policies should be pursued."

_____

_____   _____

_____

_____   _____

_____

_____   _____

7. "Since the world operates mechanically, apparent wholes can be understood by analysis into their parts."

_____

_____   _____

8. "Our whole economy is built on the basis of ever-increasing consumption, which in turn adds endlessly to the stress upon the environment."

_____

_____   _____

9. "'It seems fitting that Detroit is the first cable market to carry Bridges TV since it is here where the idea was born and initial research was done,' Hassan said."

_____

_____   _____

_____

_____   _____

_____

_____   _____

10. "Part of the problem, the audit found, is that the annual grants were given out based on applications submitted by individual ports and then awarded even when department staff members found that many of the submissions lacked merit."

_____

_____   _____

_____

_____   _____

_____

_____   _____

_____

_____   _____

⚙ **E8-9** → Identify the type and function of the dependent clauses.

Example:

"She gives it cheerfully as you see."

CLAUSE	as you see	
TYPE	adverb/comparison	
FUNCTION	modifier	(cheerfully)

1. "If we do so, we will recognize needs before market prices reflect them."

_____

_____   _____

_____

_____   _____

2. "There's more of gravy than of grave about you, whatever you are!"

_____   _____

3. "For they are each the product of a winnowing process which sometimes only over the course of many generations establishes clearly the constraints within which they assume distinctive shapes."

_____

_____   _____

_____

_____   _____

4. "Mr. Brooke, seeing Mrs. Cadwallader's merits from a different point of view, winced a little when her name was announced in the library, where he was sitting alone."

_____

_____   _____

_____

_____   _____

5. "You know that Mrs. Gold is a very polite, quiet woman who never raises her voice."

_____

_____   _____

_____

_____   _____

6. "I presume Mrs. Inglethorp took the coffee after dinner about eight o'clock, whereas the symptoms did not manifest themselves until the early hours of the morning, which, on the face of it, points to the drug having been taken much later in the evening."

_____

_____   _____

_____

_____   _____

_____   _____

_____   _____

7. "Sherlock Holmes preserved his calm professional manner until our visitor had left us, although it was easy for me, who knew him so well, to see that he was profoundly excited."

_____

_____   _____

_____   _____

_____   _____

_____   _____

_____   _____

_____   _____

8. "Here was a man who could understand the higher inward life, and with whom there could be some spiritual communion; nay, who could illuminate principle with the widest knowledge a man whose learning almost amounted to a proof of whatever he believed!"

_____   _____

_____   _____

_____   _____

_____   _____

_____   _____

_____   _____

_____   _____

9. "Further, it is difficult to apply on a contractual basis those passages which deal with spirit, purpose, and intention; every man must judge for himself whether, in view of them, deception or hypocrisy has been practised."

_____   _____

_____   _____

_____   _____

_____   _____

10. "I was stepping leisurely across the court after breakfast, drinking the chill of the air with pleasure, when I was seized again with those indescribable sensations that heralded the change; and I had but the time to gain the shelter of my cabinet, before I was once again raging and freezing with the passions of Hyde."

_____   _____

_____   _____

_____   _____

_____   _____

MATCH EXERCISES

In the following exercises, the features of the requested function are identified in brackets.

⚙ **E8-10** → Find examples for Part A in Part B, **USING EACH SENTENCE ONLY ONCE.**

Part A

1. Noun clause as [SUBJECT] _____

2. Noun clause as [SUBJECTIVE COMPLEMENT] _____

3. Noun clause as [DIRECT OBJECT] _____

4. Noun clause as [INDIRECT OBJECT] _____

5. Noun clause as [NON-RESTRICTIVE APPOSITIVE] _____

Part B

A. "She cried that he was gay and valiant, that she would wait for him, that they would sail."

B. "That she had not been an impalpable creature of his fancy was proven by the precious cornelian heart."

C. She brought whomever she met happiness.[1]

D. "From 1988 onwards, open reference was being made to 'responsibility sharing' on councils, a term attributed to Ken Maginnis (MP for Fermanagh and South Tyrone)."

E. "Well, Fred, I don't mind telling you that the secret is that I'm one of a noble race."

1 Contrived example.

✿ E8-11 → Find examples for Part A in Part B, **USING EACH SENTENCE ONLY ONCE.**

Part A

1. Noun clause as [NON-RESTRICTIVE APPOSITIVE] _____

2. Noun clause as [OBJECT OF PREPOSITION] _____

3. Noun clause as [OBJECTIVE COMPLEMENT] _____

4. Noun clause as [COMPLEMENT OF AN ADJECTIVE] _____

5. Noun clause as [A DELAYED SUBJECT] _____

Part B

A. "'But are you not fearful,' said I, 'that you may misunderstand a charge so tender?'"

B. "He saw the master first, and made a hasty motion that she should be silent."

C. "Say it is thus with what you show me!"

D. "There was a general impression, however, that Lydgate was not altogether a common country doctor."

E. "'It's dead, whatever it is,' said Holmes."

✿ E8-12 → Find examples for Part A in Part B, **USING EACH SENTENCE ONLY ONCE.**

Part A

1. Relative conjunction as [SUBJECT] _____

2. Relative conjunction as [DIRECT OBJECT] _____

3. Relative conjunction as [OBJECT OF PREPOSITION] _____

4. Relative adjective clause as [MODIFYING A SUBJECT] _____

5. Relative adjective clause as [MODIFYING A DIRECT OBJECT] _____

Part B

A. "Those whom she sentenced were taken into custody by the soldiers."

B. "It was I who told him to be off."

C. "He was the first boy with whom I had ever had any intimacy."

D. "As he pressed forward he became conscious that his way was haunted by invisible existences whom he could not definitely figure to his mind."

E. "He gave her a momentary sharp glance, which seemed to react on him like a draught of cold air and set him coughing."

✿ **E8-13** → Find examples for Part A in Part B, **USING EACH SENTENCE ONLY ONCE.**

Part A

1. Relative adjective clause as [MODIFYING A SUBJECTIVE COMPLEMENT] _____

2. Relative adjective clause as [MODIFYING AN OBJECTIVE COMPLEMENT] _____

3. Relative adjective clause as [MODIFYING A DIRECT OBJECT] _____

4. Relative adjective clause as [MODIFYING AN INDIRECT OBJECT] _____

5. Relative adjective clause as [MODIFYING AN APPOSITIVE] _____

Part B

A. "I thought it odd that anyone else should be in there."

B. "The family sent Mary whom we missed a Christmas package."

C. "Mrs. Cavendish, however, was a lady who liked to make her own plans, and expected other people to fall in with them."

D. "And I remember a battle with one of these urchins in the briers, an affair which did not add to the love of their family for ours."

E. "He took a great liking to Richard in those days, sent him a church-warden's pipe that he had used as Corporal Brewster."

✿ **E8-14** → Find examples for Part A in Part B, **USING EACH SENTENCE ONLY ONCE.**

Part A

1. Relative conjunction [ADVERB COMPLEMENT IN ITS CLAUSE] _____

2. Relative conjunction [ADVERB MODIFIER WITHIN ITS CLAUSE] _____

3. Relative adverb clause [TIME] _____

4. Relative adverb clause [PLACE] _____

5. Relative adverb clause [REASON] _____

Part B

A. "When he felt the pangs of hunger he ate raw leaves and the roots of plants."

B. "Finally the hour came when the sun broke through the clouds."

C. "Since no practical good could result from it, but with you there is no reason why I should not be perfectly frank."

D. "On the second floor he entered a room where Dr. Trescott was working about the bedside of Henry Johnson."

E. "Kovrin remembered the raptures of the previous summer when there had been the same scent of the marvel of Peru and the moon had shone in at the window."

⚙ **E8-15** → Find examples for Part A in Part B, **USING EACH SENTENCE ONLY ONCE.**

Part A

1. Relative adverb clause [MODIFYING A COMPLEMENT] _____

2. Relative adverb clause [MODIFYING AN ADJECTIVE] _____

3. Relative adverb clause [AS A COMPLEMENT] _____

4. Relative adverb clause [MODIFYING AN ADVERB] _____

5. Relative adverb clause [MODIFYING A SENTENCE] _____

Part B

A. "When soldiers form lines, or hollow squares, you call it reason."

B. "For I never heard any one more sprightly than he was to-day when he conversed with you."

C. "You'll be where you can't stop me."

D. "You were four when I brought you here."

E. "His mother is back where she began, without a job or her children."

⚙ **E8-16** → Find examples for Part A in Part B, **USING EACH SENTENCE ONLY ONCE.**

Part A

1. Noun clause [DIRECT OBJECT] _____

2. Noun clause [NON-RESTRICTIVE APPOSITIVE] _____

3. Noun clause [OBJECT OF PREPOSITION] _____

4. Relative conjunction [DIRECT OBJECT] _____

5. Relative adjective clause [SUBJECTIVE COMPLEMENT] _____

Part B

A. "'I reckon I don't know much about what the Rebels is fighting for,' said John Duff."

B. "But we could not have told what the unfavourable conditions were which checked its increase."

C. "My second boy Moses, whom I designed for business, received a sort of miscellaneous education at home."

D. "For the Zaporozhtzi never cared for bargaining, and paid whatever money their hand chanced to grasp in their pocket."

E. "There was an old native, whom they had nicknamed Chowbok."

✿ **E8-17** → Find examples for Part A in Part B, **USING EACH SENTENCE ONLY ONCE.**

Part A

1. Relative adjective clause [OBJECTIVE COMPLEMENT]   _____

2. Relative adverb clause [MODIFYING A PREDICATE]   _____

3. Relative adverb clause [A COMPLEMENT]   _____

4. Adverb clause [MODIFYING AN ADVERB]   _____

5. Adverb clause [MODIFYING AN INFINITIVE]   _____

Part B

A. "It was that dull kind of a regular sound that comes from oars working in rowlocks when it's a still night."

B. "'I shall not ride any more,' said Dorothea, urged to this brusque resolution by a little annoyance that Sir James would be soliciting her attention when she wanted to give it all to Mr. Casaubon."

C. "He ruled that dissenters must not try to sway public opinion because open criticism hurts the church."

D. "I shall relate my wrongs the persecutions that I endure."

E. "They're not moving for the churches, and they don't vote for Mr. Bush simply because he reads the Bible every day."

PARAGRAPH ANALYSIS

✿ **E8-18** → Identify the bolded clauses by type and function in the following paragraph.

1. _____

2. _____

3. _____

4. _____

5. _____

6. _____

7. _____

8. _____

9. _____

10. _____

"Old Matthew Maule, in a word, was executed for the crime of witchcraft. He was one of the martyrs to that terrible delusion, **which should teach us**,[1] among its other morals, **that the influential classes**, and those *who take upon themselves to be leaders of the people*,[2] **are fully liable to all the passionate error**[3] **that has ever characterized the maddest mob**.[4] Clergymen, judges, statesmen,—the wisest, calmest, holiest persons of their day,—stood in the inner circle round about the gallows, loudest to applaud the work of blood, latest to confess themselves miserably deceived. **If any one part of their proceedings can be said to deserve less blame than another**,[5] it was the singular indiscrimination **with which they persecuted**,[6] not merely the poor and aged, as in former judicial massacres, but people of all ranks; their own equals, brethren, and wives. Amid the disorder of such various ruin, it is not strange **that a man of inconsiderable note, like Maule, should have trodden the martyr's path to the hill of execution almost unremarked in the throng of his fellow-sufferers**.[7] But, in after days, **when the frenzy of that hideous epoch had subsided**,[8] it was remembered how loudly Colonel Pyncheon had joined in the general cry, to purge the land from witchcraft; nor did it fail to be whispered, **that there was an invidious acrimony in the zeal**[9] *with which he had sought the condemnation of Matthew Maule*.[10]"

⚙ **E8-19** → Identify the type and function of the dependent clauses in the following paragraph.

1. _____

   _____   _____

2. _____

   _____   _____

3. _____

   _____   _____

4. _____

   _____   _____

5. _____

   _____   _____

6. _____

_____   _____

7. _____

_____   _____

8. _____

_____   _____

9. _____

_____   _____

10. _____

_____   _____

"Patrick Floyd, secretary of the murdered man, testified that he had been in a position to overlook the whole garden from the time when Colonel Druce last appeared alive in the doorway to the time when he was found dead; as he, Floyd, had been on the top of a step-ladder clipping the garden hedge. Janet Druce, the dead man's daughter, confirmed this, and said that she had sat on the terrace of the house throughout that time and had seen Floyd at his work. Touching some part of the time, this is again supported by Donald Druce, her brother, who overlooked the garden standing at his bedroom window in his dressing-gown, since he had risen late. Lastly the account is consistent with the one that was given by Dr. Valentine, a neighbor, who called for a time to talk with Miss Druce on the terrace, and by the Colonel's solicitor, Mr. Aubrey Traill, who was apparently the last to see the murdered man alive—presumably with the exception of the murderer."

☼ E8-20 → Identify the type and function of the dependent clauses in the paragraph below.

1. _____

_____ _____

2. _____

_____ _____

3. _____

_____ _____

4. _____

_____ _____

5. _____

_____ _____

6. _____

_____ _____

7. _____

_____ _____

8. _____

_____ _____

9. _____

_____ _____

10. _____

_____ _____

11. _____

_____ _____

12. _____

_____ _____

13. _____

_____ _____

14. _____

_____ _____

15. _____

_____   _____

"Because religion cannot be organised, because God is everywhere and immediately accessible to every human being, it does not follow that religion cannot organise every other human affair. It is indeed essential to the idea that God is the Invisible King of this round world and all mankind, that we should see in every government, great and small, from the council of the world-state that is presently coming, down to the village assembly, the instrument of God's practical control. Religion which is free, speaking freely through whom it will, subject to a perpetual unlimited criticism, will be the life and driving power of the whole organised world. So that if you prefer not to say that there will be no church, if you choose rather to declare that the world-state is God's church, you may have it so if you will. Provided that you leave conscience and speech and writing and teaching about divine things absolutely free, and that you try to set no nets about God."

9 GRAMMATICAL POSITIONS

DEFINITIONS

⚙ **E9-1** → Match Part A with the correct definition in Part B.

Part A

1. Grammatical position marks . . . . _____
2. Constituents do not arbitrarily occupy . . . . _____
3. We identify four grammatical positions: . . . . _____
4. The nominal position is occupied by . . . . _____
5. The verbal position is occupied by . . . . _____
6. The adjectival position is occupied by . . . . _____
7. The adverbial position is occupied by . . . . _____
8. Functions that occupy the nominal position are . . . . _____
9. Functions that occupy the verbal position are . . . . _____
10. Functions that occupy the adjectival position are . . . . _____
11. Functions that occupy the adverbial position are . . . . _____
12. Adverbs or prepositional phrases in adverbial positions occur . . . . _____
13. Prepositional phrases can occupy . . . . _____
14. Participles can occupy adjectival and . . . . _____
15. Identifying grammatical positions is often a good way to distinguish . . . . _____
16. Nouns, infinitives, and gerunds can occupy . . . . _____
17. Infinitives can occur . . . . _____
18. Position is . . . . _____
19. A major problem solved by position . . . . _____
20. The least complicated position is . . . . _____

Part B

A. ... the nominal position.

B. ... is identifying modifiers.

C. ... predicates, primary auxiliaries, and modals.

D. ... the verbal position.

E. ... adjectival and adverbial positions.

F. ... word and phrase modifiers, and adverb complements.

G. ... word and phrase modifiers, subjective complements and determiners.

H. ... words and phrases by form and function.

I. ... nominal, verbal, adjectival and adverbial.

J. ... adverb words, phrases and clauses, as well as present and past participle, absolute and prepositional phrases.

K. ... adjective words, phrases and clauses, as well as present and past participle, and prepositional phrases.

L. ... where a sentence constituent GOES.

M. ... lexical verbs and also auxiliaries, which carry out verbal functions.

N. ... in nominal and adverbial positions.

O. ... subjects, direct and indirect objects, subjective and objective complements, appositives, objects of prepositions, and some connectors.

P. ... sentence constituents based on form and function.

Q. ... adverbial positions.

R. ... pre-nominally or post-nominally.

S. ... any position within a sentence.

T. ... noun words, phrases and clauses, as well as pronouns, gerunds, infinitives, and some conjunctions.

NOMINAL POSITIONS

✿ **E9-2** → Identify the word(s) in the nominal positions.

Example:

"Presently his father came along with the whirring machine."

NOMINALS
his father
whirring machine

1. "But middle-class Americans don't simply cast ballots for Republicans."

   _____   _____   _____

2. "All during the season he had worked at it in the coolness and peace of the evenings after supper."

   _____   _____   _____

   _____   _____   _____

   _____

3. "Even in the shadow of the cherry-trees the grass was strong and healthy."

   _____   _____   _____

4. "The doctor mused upon the situation, but he could make nothing of it."

   _____   _____   _____

   _____   _____

5. "'By all accounts,' replied the other, 'he wasn't half so angry as the secretary was.'"

   _____   _____   _____

   _____

6. "The favorite Democratic explanation is that the red staters are hicks who have been blinded by righteousness."

   _____   _____   _____

   _____   _____

7. "For the mainly Democratic audience—this was a crowd of Washington journalists and luminaries from Hollywood and Manhattan."

   _____   _____   _____

   _____   _____   _____

   _____

8. "Tillich reminded us that paintings are not simply photographs or photographic reproductions of events-reproductions."

   _____   _____   _____

   _____   _____   _____

9. "The doctor paused, and with the howl of the machine no longer occupying the sense, one could hear the robins in the cherry-trees arranging their affairs."

   _____   _____   _____

   _____   _____   _____

   _____   _____

10. "I remember the elder, whose name I think is Herbert Druce and who is an authority on horse-breeding, talked about nothing but a mare he had bought and the moral character of the man who sold her—while his brother Harry seemed to be brooding on his bad luck at Monte Carlo."

    _____   _____   _____

    _____   _____   _____

    _____   _____   _____

    _____   _____   _____

    _____   _____   _____

    _____

✿ E9-3 → Identify the clauses in nominal positions.

Example:

"Each was interested in what the other said."

CLAUSE
what the other said

1. "But Robert admitted quite frankly that he preferred to stay where he was and talk to Mrs. Pontellier."

   _____

2. "Robert was interested, and wanted to know what manner of girls the sisters were, what the father was like, and how long the mother had been dead."

_____

_____

_____

3. "And she begged that Robert would interest himself, and discover, if possible, whether she was entitled to the indulgence accompanying the remarkably curious Mexican prayer-beads."

_____

_____

_____

4. "From his trousers pockets he took a fistful of crumpled bank notes and a good deal of silver coin, which he piled on the bureau indiscriminately with keys, knife, handkerchief, and whatever else happened to be in his pockets."

_____

5. "She never knew precisely what to make of it; at that moment it was impossible for her to guess how much of it was jest and what proportion was earnest."

_____

_____

_____

6. "At the time of my brother's death the fact was frequently commented upon that, unlike most literary folk, he had never known what it was to be poor and to suffer the pangs of hunger and failure."

_____

_____

_____

7. "With all Mrs. Hale's other emotions came the fear now that maybe Harry wasn't dressed warm enough—they hadn't any of them realized how that north wind did bite."

_____

_____

8. "'Well, ladies,' said the county attorney, as one turning from serious things to little pleasantries, 'have you decided whether she was going to quilt it or knot it?'"

_____

9. "They acknowledge that there are other ways of studying human beings that also throw light on what policies should be pursued."

_____

_____

10. "The lady in black had once received a pair of prayer-beads of curious workmanship from Mexico, with very special indulgence attached to them, but she had never been able to ascertain whether the indulgence extended outside the Mexican border."

_____

VERBAL POSITIONS

☼ **E9-4** → Identify the word/phrases in verbal positions.

Example:

"'Perfectly sound!' said Holmes."

VERBAL
said

1. "If we are to criticize economists, it is to point out that they have been all too willing to agree that wealth is the supreme goal and that, therefore, they are the best counselors of national and global policy."

_____   _____

_____   _____

_____

2. "Holmes was sitting with his back to me, and I had given him no sign of my occupation."

_____

_____

3. "Since we have been so unfortunate as to miss him and have no notion of his errand, this accidental souvenir becomes of importance."

_____

_____

_____

4. "He had never said as much before, and I must admit that his words gave me keen pleasure, for I had often been piqued by his indifference to my admiration and to the attempts which I had made to give publicity to his methods."

_____

_____

_____

_____

5. "And I would have you believe, my sons, that the same Justice which punishes sin may also most graciously forgive it, and that no ban is so heavy but that by prayer and repentance it may be removed."

_____

_____

_____

_____

_____

6. "The paper man she was making would have had his leg injured, but for her habitual care of whatever she held in her hands."

_____

_____

_____

7. "Mr. Brooke again winced inwardly, for Dorothea's engagement had no sooner been decided, than he had thought of Mrs. Cadwallader's prospective taunts."

_____

_____

_____

8. "Sir James Chettam had returned from the short journey which had kept him absent for a couple of days, and had changed his dress, intending to ride over to Tipton Grange."

_____

_____

_____

9. "And the reason it seemed she couldn't cross it now was simply because she hadn't crossed it before."

_____

_____

_____

_____

10. "Those artists who would have been willing to go along might have added powerful visual propaganda to Hitler's own violent verbal expressionism."

_____

_____

ADJECTIVAL POSITIONS

⚙ E9-5 → Identify the words/phrases in adjectival positions. (For this exercise ignore prepositional phrase adjectival modifiers as units.)

Example:

"But he was a tight-fisted hand at the grindstone."

ADJECTIVAL
tight-fisted
at the grindstone

1. "Scrooge. A squeezing, wrenching, grasping, scraping, clutching, covetous old sinner!"

_____

2. "It was cold, bleak, biting weather: foggy withal: and he could hear the people in the court outside, go wheezing up and down, beating their hands upon their breasts, and stamping their feet upon the pavement stones to warm them."

_____   _____

_____   _____

_____   _____

3. "The Lord Mayor, in the stronghold of the mighty Mansion House, gave orders to his fifty cooks and butlers to keep Christmas as a Lord Mayor's household should."

_____   _____

_____

4. "If the good Saint Dunstan had but nipped the Evil Spirit's nose with a touch of such weather as that, instead of using his familiar weapons, then indeed he would have roared to lusty purpose."

_____   _____

_____   _____

_____

5. "It was ablaze with candles, and I caught glimpses of fine gentlemen and ladies in the rooms."

_____   _____

6. "And presently, winding through the trees, we were in sight of a long, brick mansion trimmed with white, and a velvet lawn before it all flecked with shadows."

_____   _____

7. "He was spotlessly neat, apparelled in immaculate white from shoes to hat, and in the various Eastern ports where he got his living as ship-chandler's water-clerk he was very popular."

_____   _____

_____   _____

_____

8. "He was a very tall, thin man, with a long nose like a beak, which jutted out between two keen, gray eyes, set closely together and sparkling brightly from behind a pair of gold-rimmed glasses."

_____   _____

_____   _____

9. "It was only then that I perceived that the pilgrim ship episode was a good starting-point for a free and wandering tale; that it was an event, too, which could conceivably colour the whole 'sentiment of existence' in a simple and sensitive character."

_____   _____

_____   _____

_____

10. "The driver was a young man of three- or four-and-twenty, with a cigar between his teeth; wearing a dandy cap, drab jacket, breeches of the same hue, white neckcloth, stick-up collar, and brown driving-gloves—in short, he was the handsome, horsey young buck who had visited Joan a week or two before to get her answer about Tess."

—————————————————   —————————————————

—————————————————   —————————————————

—————————————————   —————————————————

—————————————————   —————————————————

—————————————————

⚙ **E9-6** → Identify the clauses in adjectival positions.

Example:

"He who has not penetrated them deeply knows nothing of the past of this blooming region of Russia."

ADJECTIVAL
who has not penetrated them deeply

1. "As she looked at her children, from whom so speedy a separation was threatened, it is impossible to describe the full force of her speechless grief, which seemed to quiver in her eyes and on her lips convulsively pressed together."

—————————————————————————————————

—————————————————————————————————

2. "When the mother saw that her sons were also mounted, she rushed towards the younger, whose features expressed somewhat more gentleness than those of his brother."

—————————————————————————————————

3. "Before them still stretched the field by which they could recall the whole story of their lives, from the years when they rolled in its dewy grass down to the years when they awaited in it the dark-browed Cossack maiden, running timidly across it on quick young feet."

—————————————————————————————————

4. "Such are the deeds that are taking place in the Ukraine!"

—————————————————————————————————

5. "The poor orator who had called down destruction upon himself jumped out of the caftan, by which they had seized him, and in his scant parti-coloured under waistcoat clasped Bulba's legs, and cried, in piteous tones, 'Great lord! gracious noble! I knew your brother, the late Dóroscha.'"

_____

_____

6. "There was, in fact, nothing that could make us angry with the world or each other."

_____

7. "When I stood in the midst of the little circle, which promised to be the support of my declining age, I could not avoid repeating the famous story of Count Abensberg, who, in Henry the Second's progress through Germany, while other courtiers came with their treasures, brought his thirty-two children, and presented them to his sovereign as the most valuable offering he had to bestow."

_____

_____

_____

_____

8. "My second boy Moses, whom I designed for business, received a sort of miscellaneous education at home."

_____

9. "The merchant in town, in whose hands your money was lodged, has gone off, to avoid a statute of bankruptcy, and is thought not to have left a shilling in the pound."

_____

10. "Mr. Wilmot, who seemed before sufficiently inclined to break off the match, was by this blow soon determined: one virtue he had in perfection, which was prudence, too often the only one that is left us at seventy-two."

_____

_____

_____

ADVERBIAL POSITIONS

⚙ **E9-7** → Identify the words/phrases in adverbial positions. (For this exercise ignore prepositional phrase adverbial modifiers as units.)

Example:

"At sunset hour the forest was still, lonely, sweet with tang of fir and spruce."

ADVERBIALS
At sunset hour
with tang of fir and spruce

1. "This was the family of a very poor policeman in a Bavarian village, with extremely gifted children."

   _____   _____

2. "Indeed, it was very much more than they had ever owned before, because their mother, in her care for them and desire to have them look well in the eyes of this rich uncle, had spent money and pains to give them pretty and serviceable clothes."

   _____   _____

   _____   _____

   _____   _____

3. "Evidently he caught Bo's admiring gaze, for, with a word to his companions, he sauntered toward the window where the girls sat."

   _____   _____

   _____

4. "Then Beasley came forward to the fire, stretching his hands to the blaze."

   _____   _____

   _____   _____

5. "Anson's sudden action then seemed a leap of his whole frame; Wilson, likewise, bent forward eagerly."

   _____   _____

   _____   _____

6. "Morel crouched at the knees and showed his fist in an ugly, almost beast-like fashion. William was white with rage."

   _____   _____

7. "Then the children watched with joy as the metal sank suddenly molten, and was shoved about against the nose of the soldering-iron."

_____   _____

_____   _____

8. "When he got down to the New Inn, at Bretty, his father was not yet come."

_____   _____

_____

9. "The discovery was verified by noting that some of the rotting stumps were hacked all round, in a most unwoodmanlike way, while others were cut straight across, and the butt ends of the corresponding trunks had the blunt wedge-form given by the axe of a master."

_____   _____

_____   _____

_____

10. "They turned awkwardly hither and thither and seemed trying to escape, but unable to retrace their steps."

_____   _____

✿ **E9-8** → Identify the clauses in adverbial positions.

Example:

"Where the old land-surveyor had put down woods, lakes, and rivers, they marked out the cleared spaces."

ADVERBIAL
Where the old land-surveyor had put down woods, lakes, and rivers

1. "But, in after days, when the frenzy of that hideous epoch had subsided, it was remembered how loudly Colonel Pyncheon had joined in the general cry, to purge the land from witchcraft."

_____

2. "While the elderly gentleman stood looking at the Pyncheon-house, both the frown and the smile passed successively over his countenance."

_____

3. "The decision came after dark, more than six hours after the judges retired to deliberate."

   _____

4. "Mr. Yushchenko has urged hundreds of thousands of his supporters to continue their 13-day protest in Kiev's main square until the changes are passed."

   _____

5. "Why, I hardly thought myself younger than I am now, it seems so little while ago since I used to see you playing about the door of the old house, quite a small child!"

   _____

6. "'At the end of the meetings, we'll find out where we are and make a decision and evaluate where he'll end up,' Cuza said. 'But it could take longer than the weekend.'"

   _____

   _____

7. "And he can detach part of himself and treat it as if it were not himself, just as a man may beat his breast or, as Cranmer the martyr did, thrust his hand into the flames."

   _____

   _____

   _____

   _____

8. "Each time, the delay seemed to be without purpose, but rather from a forgetfulness of the purpose which had set him in motion, or as if the person's feet came involuntarily to a stand-still, because the motive power was too feeble to sustain his progress."

   _____

   _____

9. "He kneeled on the stones, however, in vain; they kept what they concealed; and if the face of the tomb did become a face for him it was because her two names became a pair of eyes that didn't know him."

   _____

   _____

10. "He could not be sad, because his son had died for America, died for freedom, and even though the unchristian politicians kept us from winning that war, as we should have, he knew in his heart that we had really won, because his boy had died for a good cause, and now although the work at home did not get done, he was prouder than ever to be an American, and only another true American could understand what he meant."

_____

_____

_____

_____

_____

_____

GRAMMATICAL POSITIONS

✿ **E9-9** → Identify the grammatical positions of the bolded words/phrases.

Example:

"In another moment **down went** Alice after it."

POSITION
verbal

1. "The rabbit-hole went straight on like a tunnel **for some way**, and then dipped suddenly down."

   ☐ NOMINAL   ☐ VERBAL   ☐ ADJECTIVAL   ☐ ADVERBIAL

2. "Either the well was **very deep**, or she fell very slowly, for she had plenty of time as she went down to look about her."

   ☐ NOMINAL   ☐ VERBAL   ☐ ADJECTIVAL   ☐ ADVERBIAL

3. "First, she tried to look down and make out what she **was coming to**, but it was too dark to see anything."

   ☐ NOMINAL   ☐ VERBAL   ☐ ADJECTIVAL   ☐ ADVERBIAL

4. "After such a fall as this, I shall think nothing of **tumbling** downstairs!"

   ☐ NOMINAL   ☐ VERBAL   ☐ ADJECTIVAL   ☐ ADVERBIAL

5. "Alice had learnt several things of this sort **in her lessons** in the schoolroom, and though this was not a very good opportunity for showing off her knowledge."

   ☐ NOMINAL   ☐ VERBAL   ☐ ADJECTIVAL   ☐ ADVERBIAL

6. "**In a general way**, I cannot remember that our life as boys differed in any essential from that of other boys."

☐ NOMINAL ☐ VERBAL ☐ ADJECTIVAL ☐ ADVERBIAL

7. "My brother went to the Episcopal Academy and **his weekly report** never failed to fill the whole house with an impenetrable gloom."

☐ NOMINAL ☐ VERBAL ☐ ADJECTIVAL ☐ ADVERBIAL

8. "As a schoolboy he was **aggressive, radical, outspoken, fearless**, usually of the opposition and, indeed, often the sole member of his own party."

☐ NOMINAL ☐ VERBAL ☐ ADJECTIVAL ☐ ADVERBIAL

9. "Richard **was** forever **leading** his little band over the pass while the band, wholly indifferent as to whether the road led to honor, glory, or total annihilation, meekly followed its leader."

☐ NOMINAL ☐ VERBAL ☐ ADJECTIVAL ☐ ADVERBIAL

10. "But the Point Pleasant **of that time** had very little in common with the present well-known summer resort."

☐ NOMINAL ☐ VERBAL ☐ ADJECTIVAL ☐ ADVERBIAL

✿ E9-10 → Identify the grammatical positions of the bolded clauses.

Example:

"An issue **upon which this book will be found particularly uncompromising** is the dogma of the Trinity."

POSITION
adjectival

1. "Nevertheless it is well to prepare the prospective reader for statements **that may jar harshly against deeply rooted mental habits**."

☐ NOMINAL ☐ VERBAL ☐ ADJECTIVAL ☐ ADVERBIAL

2. "He is quite unable to pretend any awe for **what he considers the spiritual monstrosities** established by that undignified gathering."

☐ NOMINAL ☐ VERBAL ☐ ADJECTIVAL ☐ ADVERBIAL

3. "But **when a religion has been interrogated** it has always had hitherto a tale of beginnings, the name and story of a founder."

☐ NOMINAL ☐ VERBAL ☐ ADJECTIVAL ☐ ADVERBIAL

4. "It has, as a matter of fact, a very fine and subtle theology, flatly opposed to any belief **that could, except by great stretching of charity and the imagination, be called Christianity**."

☐ NOMINAL   ☐ VERBAL   ☐ ADJECTIVAL   ☐ ADVERBIAL

5. "And even to-day it has to be noted that a large majority of those **who possess and repeat the Christian creeds** have come into the practice so insensibly from unthinking childhood."

☐ NOMINAL   ☐ VERBAL   ☐ ADJECTIVAL   ☐ ADVERBIAL

6. "We may speculate **whether it is not what the wiser among the Gnostics meant by the Demiurge**, but since the Christians destroyed all the Gnostic books that must remain a mere curious guess."

☐ NOMINAL   ☐ VERBAL   ☐ ADJECTIVAL   ☐ ADVERBIAL

7. "But **while most of Company E's work in fighting insurgents was on foot**, the biggest danger the men faced came in traveling to and from camp"

☐ NOMINAL   ☐ VERBAL   ☐ ADJECTIVAL   ☐ ADVERBIAL

8. "The spirit of God will not let the believer rest **until his life is readjusted** and as far as possible freed from the waste of these base diversions."

☐ NOMINAL   ☐ VERBAL   ☐ ADJECTIVAL   ☐ ADVERBIAL

9. "It includes all those heresies **which result from wrong-headed mental elaboration**, as distinguished from those which are the result of hasty and imperfect apprehension."

☐ NOMINAL   ☐ VERBAL   ☐ ADJECTIVAL   ☐ ADVERBIAL

10. "**Whatever claim Caesar may make to rule men's lives and direct their destinies outside the will of God** is a usurpation."

☐ NOMINAL   ☐ VERBAL   ☐ ADJECTIVAL   ☐ ADVERBIAL

MATCH EXERCISES

⚙ **E9-11** → Find examples for Part A in Part B, **USING EACH SENTENCE ONLY ONCE**.

Part A

1. Nominal position [SUBJECT/NOUN CLAUSE] _____

2. Verbal position [PAST TENSE/PROGRESSIVE ASPECT] _____

3. Adjectival position [SUBJECTIVE COMPLEMENT MODIFIER] _____

4. Adverbial position [PREDICATE MODIFIER] _____

5. Adverbial position [MODIFYING ANOTHER ADVERB] _____

Part B

A. "That as soon as a party has gain'd its general point, each member becomes intent upon his particular interest."

B. "He said this so lucidly and consistently that he could see it further impose itself."

C. "I was complaining once to a friend that though "Erewhon" had met with such a warm reception, my subsequent books had been all of them practically still-born."

D. "That he should turn around because his mood changed seems to me unthinkable."

E. "On every side, the seven gables pointed sharply towards the sky, and presented the aspect of a whole sisterhood of edifices, breathing through the spiracles of one great chimney."

⚙ **E9-12** → Find examples for Part A in Part B, **USING EACH SENTENCE ONLY ONCE**.

Part A

1. Nominal position [DIRECT OBJECT/GERUND] _____

2. Nominal position [INDIRECT OBJECT/PRONOUN] _____

3. Verbal position [FUTURE TENSE/PERFECT ASPECT] _____

4. Adjectival position [CLAUSE MODIFIER] _____

5. Adjectival position [PREPOSITIONAL PHRASE MODIFIER] _____

Part B

A. "New forms will have been more slowly formed, and old forms more slowly exterminated."

B. "Stop a minute; I believe I've got a cutting that will give you all the particulars."

C. "But when I questioned my father on these matters he would give me no answers."

D. "The women at the Cross-Roads, twelve miles away, were dressed in coarse butternut wool and huge sunbonnets."

E. "I remember once bringing back from the Cross-Roads a crumpled newspaper, which my father read again and again, and then folded up and put in his pocket."

✿ **E9-13** → Find examples for Part A in Part B, **USING EACH SENTENCE ONLY ONCE**.

Part A

1. Nominal position [NOUN CLAUSE/INDIRECT OBJECT]   _____

2. Verbal position [PAST TENSE/PERFECT PROGRESSIVE ASPECT]   _____

3. Adjectival position [APPOSITIVE]   _____

4. Adjectival position [MODIFYING AN INDIRECT OBJECT]   _____

5. Adverbial position [MODIFYING AN ADJECTIVE]   _____

Part B

A. "After that it was rather late in the season."

B. "However, when they had been running half an hour or so, and were quite dry again, the Dodo suddenly called out 'The race is over!'"

C. The generous old man threw whomever he met a few coins.[1]

D. "He gave the [old] cap a parting squeeze, in which his hand relaxed."

E. "The spoken word, born of the people, gave soul and wing to literature."

1 Contrived example.

✿ **E9-14** → Find examples for Part A in Part B, **USING EACH SENTENCE ONLY ONCE**.

Part A

1. Nominal position [GERUND/DIRECT OBJECT]   _____

2. Verbal position [PRESENT TENSE/SIMPLE ASPECT]   _____

3. Adjectival position [MODIFYING AN APPOSITIVE]   _____

4. Adjectival position [MODIFYING AN OBJECTIVE COMPLEMENT]   _____

5. Adverbial position [MODIFYING A SENTENCE]   _____

Part B

A. "They call it here 'the house' pre-eminently."

B. "This constant menace, this perpetual pressure of foes on all sides, acted at last like a fierce hammer shaping and hardening resistance against itself."

C. "Whereupon she found herself actually hungry, and while she ate she glanced out of the stage, first from one side and then from the other."

D. "Wherever I turned my eyes, that terrible picture was before me."

E. "'Do you know, I envy you that,' Sir James said, as they continued walking at the rather brisk pace set by Dorothea."

⚙ **E9-15** → Find examples for Part A in Part B, **USING EACH SENTENCE ONLY ONCE.**

Part A

1. Adverbial position [ADVERB CLAUSE/AS A COMPLEMENT]   _____

2. Verbal position [PRESENT TENSE/PERFECT PROGRESSIVE ASPECT]   _____

3. Nominal position [NOUN CLAUSE/AS A SUBJECTIVE COMPLEMENT]   _____

4. Adjectival position [CLAUSE MODIFYING A SUBJECT]   _____

5. Verbal position [FUTURE TENSE/PROGRESSIVE ASPECT]   _____

Part B

A. "The honour of being a journalist is that you are not only able to observe the times you live in, but influence them."

B. "Political leaders on both sides will be watching for disaffected members who might cross the floor and tip the balance of power."

C. "He and his aides said the protest should continue until the opposition-drafted electoral amendments become law."

D. "13 of the 21 men who were killed had been riding in Humvees that failed to deflect bullets or bombs."

E. "Baltovich, who was immediately granted $200,000 bail pending the retrial, appealed his March 1992 conviction for second-degree murder."

⚙ **E9-16** → Find examples for Part A in Part B, **USING EACH SENTENCE ONLY ONCE**.

Part A

1. Nominal position [NOUN PHRASE/APPOSITIVE] _____

2. Verbal position [PAST TENSE/PROGRESSIVE ASPECT] _____

3. Nominal position [NOUN CLAUSE/OBJECT OF THE PREPOSITION] _____

4. Adjectival position [RELATIVE CLAUSE/MODIFYING A DIRECT OBJECT] _____

5. Adverbial position [ADVERB CLAUSE/MODIFYING A SENTENCE] _____

Part B

A. "David changed our country's history through what his reporting revealed."

B. "Lt. Gen. James N. Mattis of Richland, Wash., commander of the First Marine Division, said he had taken every possible step to support Company E."

C. "Because there were two solid (training) runs and the course is in good shape, I'm not apprehensive at all."

D. "Authorities were still searching for others who may have been aboard, Lieut. Willis said."

E. "The class-action certified Friday by the Ontario court covers students who attended the Mohawk Institute from 1922 to 1969."

PARAGRAPH ANALYSIS

⚙ **E9-17** → Identify the grammatical functions of the bolded word(s) in the following paragraph.

1. ☐ NOMINAL ☐ VERBAL ☐ ADJECTIVAL ☐ ADVERBIAL

2. ☐ NOMINAL ☐ VERBAL ☐ ADJECTIVAL ☐ ADVERBIAL

3. ☐ NOMINAL ☐ VERBAL ☐ ADJECTIVAL ☐ ADVERBIAL

4. ☐ NOMINAL ☐ VERBAL ☐ ADJECTIVAL ☐ ADVERBIAL

5. ☐ NOMINAL ☐ VERBAL ☐ ADJECTIVAL ☐ ADVERBIAL

6. ☐ NOMINAL ☐ VERBAL ☐ ADJECTIVAL ☐ ADVERBIAL

7. ☐ NOMINAL ☐ VERBAL ☐ ADJECTIVAL ☐ ADVERBIAL

8. ☐ NOMINAL ☐ VERBAL ☐ ADJECTIVAL ☐ ADVERBIAL

9. ☐ NOMINAL ☐ VERBAL ☐ ADJECTIVAL ☐ ADVERBIAL

10. ☐ NOMINAL ☐ VERBAL ☐ ADJECTIVAL ☐ ADVERBIAL

"The man was **Halpin Frayser**.[1] He lived in St. Helena, but where he lives now is **uncertain**,[2] for he is dead. One who practises **sleeping**[3] in the woods with nothing under him but the dry leaves and the damp earth, and **nothing**[4] over him but the branches from which the leaves **have fallen**[5] and the sky from which the earth has fallen, can**not**[6] hope for great longevity, and Frayser had already attained the age of thirty-two. There are persons in this world, millions of persons, and **far and away**[7] the best persons, who regard that as a very advanced age. They are the children. To those who view the voyage of life from the port of departure the bark **that**[8] has accomplished any considerable distance appears already in close approach to the **farther**[9] shore. However, it is not certain that Halpin Frayser **came**[10] to his death by exposure."

☼ **E9-18** → Identify the grammatical functions of the bolded word(s) in the following paragraph.

1. ☐ NOMINAL	☐ VERBAL	☐ ADJECTIVAL	☐ ADVERBIAL
2. ☐ NOMINAL	☐ VERBAL	☐ ADJECTIVAL	☐ ADVERBIAL
3. ☐ NOMINAL	☐ VERBAL	☐ ADJECTIVAL	☐ ADVERBIAL
4. ☐ NOMINAL	☐ VERBAL	☐ ADJECTIVAL	☐ ADVERBIAL
5. ☐ NOMINAL	☐ VERBAL	☐ ADJECTIVAL	☐ ADVERBIAL
6. ☐ NOMINAL	☐ VERBAL	☐ ADJECTIVAL	☐ ADVERBIAL
7. ☐ NOMINAL	☐ VERBAL	☐ ADJECTIVAL	☐ ADVERBIAL
8. ☐ NOMINAL	☐ VERBAL	☐ ADJECTIVAL	☐ ADVERBIAL
9. ☐ NOMINAL	☐ VERBAL	☐ ADJECTIVAL	☐ ADVERBIAL
10. ☐ NOMINAL	☐ VERBAL	☐ ADJECTIVAL	☐ ADVERBIAL

"The power to become habituated to his surroundings is a **marked characteristic**[1] of mankind. Very few of us realise with conviction the intensely **unusual, unstable, complicated, unreliable**,[2] temporary nature of the economic organisation by which Western Europe **has lived**[3] for the last half century. We assume some of the **most peculiar and temporary**[4] of our late advantages as natural, permanent, and **to be depended on**,[5] and we lay our plans accordingly. On this sandy and false foundation we scheme for social improvement and dress our political platforms, pursue **our animosities and particular ambitions**,[6] and feel ourselves **with enough margin**[7] in hand to foster, not assuage, civil conflict in the European family. **Moved by insane delusion and reckless self-regard**,[8] the German people overturned the foundations on which we all **lived and built**.[9] But the spokesmen of the French and British peoples have run the risk of completing the ruin which Germany began, by a peace which, if it is carried into effect, must impair yet further, when it might have restored, the delicate, complicated organisation, already shaken and broken by war, through which alone **the European peoples**[10] can employ themselves and live."

⚙ **E9-19** → Identify the grammatical functions of the bolded word(s) in the following paragraph.

1. ☐ NOMINAL   ☐ VERBAL   ☐ ADJECTIVAL   ☐ ADVERBIAL
2. ☐ NOMINAL   ☐ VERBAL   ☐ ADJECTIVAL   ☐ ADVERBIAL
3. ☐ NOMINAL   ☐ VERBAL   ☐ ADJECTIVAL   ☐ ADVERBIAL
4. ☐ NOMINAL   ☐ VERBAL   ☐ ADJECTIVAL   ☐ ADVERBIAL
5. ☐ NOMINAL   ☐ VERBAL   ☐ ADJECTIVAL   ☐ ADVERBIAL
6. ☐ NOMINAL   ☐ VERBAL   ☐ ADJECTIVAL   ☐ ADVERBIAL
7. ☐ NOMINAL   ☐ VERBAL   ☐ ADJECTIVAL   ☐ ADVERBIAL
8. ☐ NOMINAL   ☐ VERBAL   ☐ ADJECTIVAL   ☐ ADVERBIAL
9. ☐ NOMINAL   ☐ VERBAL   ☐ ADJECTIVAL   ☐ ADVERBIAL
10. ☐ NOMINAL   ☐ VERBAL   ☐ ADJECTIVAL   ☐ ADVERBIAL

"Now, **when I say**[1] **that I am in the habit of going to sea**[2] **whenever I begin to grow hazy about the eyes**,[3] and begin to be over conscious of my lungs, I do not mean to have it inferred **that I ever go to sea as a passenger**.[4] For to go as a passenger you must needs have a purse, and a purse is but a rag unless you have something in it. Besides, passengers get sea-sick—grow quarrelsome—don't sleep of nights—do not enjoy themselves much, as a general thing;—no, I never go as a passenger; nor, though I am something of a salt, do I ever go to sea as a Commodore, or a Captain, or a Cook. I abandon the glory and distinction of such offices to those

who like them.[5] For my part, I abominate all honorable respectable toils, trials, and tribulations of every kind whatsoever. It is quite **as much as I can do to take care of myself**,[6] without taking care of ships, barques, brigs, schooners, and what not. And as for going as cook,—**though I confess there is considerable glory in that**,[7] a cook being a sort of officer on ship-board—yet, somehow, I never fancied broiling fowls;—though once broiled, judiciously buttered, and **judgmatically salted and peppered**,[8] there is no one **who will speak more respectfully**,[9] not to say reverentially, of a broiled fowl than I will. It is out of the idolatrous dotings of the old Egyptians upon broiled ibis and roasted river horse, **that you see the mummies of those creatures in their huge bake-houses the pyramids.**[10]"

⚙ **E9-20** → Find the following in the paragraph below.

1. Six clauses in nominal positions

    _____

    _____

    _____

    _____

    _____

    _____

2. Four clauses in adjectival positions

    _____

    _____

    _____

    _____

3. Three clauses in adverbial positions

    _____

    _____

    _____

"When we look to the individuals of the same variety or sub-variety of our older cultivated plants and animals, one of the first points which strikes us, is, that they generally differ much more from each other, than do the individuals of any one species or variety in a state of nature. When we reflect on the vast diversity of the plants and animals which have been cultivated, and which have varied during all ages under the most different climates and treatment, I think we are driven to conclude that this greater variability is simply due to our domestic productions having been raised under conditions of life not so uniform as, and somewhat different from, those to which the parent-species have been exposed under nature. There is, also, I think, some probability in the view propounded by Andrew Knight, that this variability may be partly connected with excess of food. It seems pretty clear that organic beings must be exposed during several generations to the new conditions of life to cause any appreciable amount of variation; and that when the organisation has once begun to vary, it generally continues to vary for many generations. No case is on record of a variable being ceasing to be variable under cultivation. Our oldest cultivated plants, such as wheat, still often yield new varieties: our oldest domesticated animals are still capable of rapid improvement or modification."

10 SENTENCES

DEFINITIONS

✿ E10-1 → Match Part A with the correct definition in Part B.

Part A

1. The sentence is the largest . . . . _____
2. Simple sentences consist of . . . . _____
3. Compound sentences consist of . . . . _____
4. Complex sentences consist of . . . . _____
5. Compound-complex sentences consist of . . . . _____
6. Sentences are also identified . . . . _____
7. A declarative sentence is . . . . _____
8. An imperative sentence expresses . . . . _____
9. Interrogative 'yes-no' questions . . . . _____
10. Wh-questions . . . . _____
11. English also has a tag question structure . . . . _____
12. Exclamatory sentences denote . . . . _____
13. All structures are based on verb type . . . . _____
14. Sentence constituents are identified . . . . _____
15. Sentence patterns focus on . . . . _____

Part B

A. ... two or more independent clauses and at least one dependent clause.

B. ... a command, request, or forbidding an action.

C. ... which is a transitive, intransitive or linking verb.

D. ... which is a combination of a declarative statement followed by an inverted question that is actually tagged on.

E. ... only one independent clause.

F. ... a simple statement, declaration or assertion.

G. ... the verb as their nucleus.

H. ... one independent clause and at least one dependent clause.

I. ... by form, by function and position.

J. ... are formed with interrogative pronouns.

K. ... expect a simple yes or no answer.

L. ... by type, that is, by form.

M. ... the speaker's attitude or opinion toward the subject.

N. ... two or more independent clauses linked by a coordinating conjunction.

O. ... syntactic structure in our language system.

SVO VARIATIONS

✿ **E10-2** → Identify the sentence structures as SVO variations.

Example:

"Everything seemed possible"

STRUCTURE
S-V-SC/pa

1. "Kidd appeared to be physically close to that in practice."

    _____

2. "He gave them an intriguing, if unusual, choice."

    _____

3. "Federal employees have always faced routine background checks."

    _____

4. "They were told that they had failed."

   _____

5. "Gucci, Louis Vuitton and Chanel, are prospering."

   _____

6. "It is called elder abuse, the polite rubric for crimes against the aged."

   _____

7. "That is why we cannot win the war on drugs."

   _____

8. "Ms. Couric made early detection her cause."

   _____

9. "He taught Breton detachment and sarcasm."

   _____

10. "His tongue was still red, his eyes not yet glazed."

    _____

SENTENCE STRUCTURE VARIATIONS

✪ **E10-3** → Identify the sentence structure as simple, compound, complex, or compound/complex.

Example:

"The gorgeous night has begun again."

TYPE
simple

1. "High winds, driving snow and poor visibility forced cancellation of Thursday's final training for the first women's World Cup downhill race of the season."

   _____

2. "We turn our faces to what the eternal evening brings."

   _____

3. "We hear him and take him among us, like a wind of music."

   _____

4. "This powerful tableau, haunting in its cruciform reflection, strikes and challenges Christian readers of Night."

   _____

5. "There, in the high bright window he dreams, and sees what we are blind to."

   _____

6. "No, miss; I've been in six scrimmages, and never got a scratch till this last one."

   _____

7. "The fancy seemed to tickle him mightily, for he laughed blithely."

   _____

8. "There they were! 'our brave boys,' as the papers justly call them, for cowards could hardly have been so riddled with shot and shell, so torn and shattered, nor have borne suffering for which we have no name."

   _____

9. "We may not have had a certain composer's experience, but we can recognize his or her attitude and relate it to our own."

   _____

10. "They were what true Christianity was really all about."

    _____

⚙ **E10-4** → Identify the sentence structure as simple, compound, complex, or compound/complex.

Example:

"Finally John Cavendish, finding his persuasions of no avail, went off to look up the trains."

TYPE
simple

1. "One, from his high bright window, looking down, peers like a dreamer over the rain-bright town."

   _____

2. "I am free to confess that I had a realizing sense of the fact that my hospital bed was not a bed of roses just then."

   _____

3. "One dark night in midsummer a man waking from a dreamless sleep in a forest lifted his head from the earth, and staring a few moments into the blackness, said: 'Catharine Larue.'"

   _____

4. "When he saw my horse's breast fairly pushing the barrier, he did put out his hand to unchain it, and then sullenly preceded me up the causeway, calling, as we entered the court, 'Joseph, take Mr. Lockwood's horse, and bring up some wine.'"

   _____

5. "With this hope I now publish my adventures; but I do so with great reluctance."

   _____

6. "After such a fall as this, I shall think nothing of tumbling downstairs!"

   _____

7. "Father Brown's friend and companion was a young man with a stream of ideas and stories, an enthusiastic young man named Fiennes, with eager blue eyes and blond hair."

   _____

8. "You are a clever, extraordinary man, you have made a brilliant career for yourself, and he is persuaded that you have turned out like this because he brought you up."

   _____

9. "Mr. Pontellier gave his wife half of the money which he had brought away from Klein's hotel the evening before."

   _____

10. "The heaviest rain, and snow, and hail, and sleet, could boast of the advantage over him in only one respect."

   _____

⚙ **E10-5** → Identify the sentence structure as simple, compound, complex, or compound/complex.

Example:

"He shut himself in, put his head down, said never a word."

TYPE
compound

1. "There were George Lambdin, Margaret Ruff, and Milne Ramsay, all painters of some note; a strange couple, Colonel Olcott and the afterward famous Madam Blavatsky, trying to start a Buddhist cult in this country; Mrs. Frances Hodgson Burnett, with her foot on the first rung of the ladder of fame, who at the time loved much millinery finery."

   _____

2. "He told of a land of wooded hill and pleasant vale, of clear water running over limestone down to the great river beyond, the Ohio—a land of glades, the fields of which were pied with flowers of wondrous beauty, where roamed the buffalo in countless thousands, where elk and deer abounded, and turkeys and feathered game, and bear in the tall brakes of cane."

   _____

3. "It was, in fact, a most remarkable exhibition of Russian strength, forced by dire necessity from the bosom of the people."

   _____

4. "Jimmie preserved a gloomy silence, and so Henry began to use seductive wiles in this affair of washing a wagon."

   _____

5. "So your grave, middle-aged family practitioner vanishes into thin air, my dear Watson, and there emerges a young fellow under thirty, amiable, unambitious, absent-minded, and the possessor of a favourite dog, which I should describe roughly as being larger than a terrier and smaller than a mastiff."

   _____

6. "She again opened the storm-door, and this time joined the three men and the one woman waiting for her in the big two-seated buggy."

   _____

7. "That he should be regarded as a suitor to herself would have seemed to her a ridiculous irrelevance."

   _____

8. "It is, therefore, of the highest importance to gain a clear insight into the means of modification and coadaptation."

   _____

9. "By taking the current a little farther up, the rest of the family got safely over, where we had an opportunity of joining our acknowledgments to hers."

   _____

10. "During my brother's confinement, which I resented a good deal, notwithstanding our private differences, I had the management of the paper; and I made bold to give our rulers some rubs in it, which my brother took very kindly, while others began to consider me in an unfavorable light, as a young genius that had a turn for libelling and satyr."

    _____

SENTENCE PATTERN VARIATIONS

✿ **E10-6** → Identify the sentence structure as declarative, imperative, interrogative, or exclamatory.

Example:

"Why not give us Sylvester Stallone as King Lear while we're at it?"

STRUCTURE
interrogative

1. "My God, everyone is going to think that this is the most hyped thing in the world!"

   _____

2. "Why must my integrity and intelligence be questioned?"

   _____

3. "Yet this is where the real challenge lies."

   _____

4. "The medical encounter is documented in a medical record."

   _____

5. "We won't be divided!"

   _____

6. "What were the lessons for progressives and fundamentalists of the decade-long battle during the 1970s?"

   _____

7. "'We have to boil the water!'"

   _____

8. "And if you think for a minute you will see that this must be so."

   _____

9. "Their first three opponents, Charlotte, Memphis and New Orleans, have a combined record of 10-34."

   _____

10. "Get hold of yourself, Popular Front! Help the heroic *Frente popular*!"

    _____

✿ **E10-7** → Identify the basic sentence pattern variations.

Example:

"Medicine is a branch of health science."

PATTERN
NP LV N + M

1. "Yet this is where the real challenge lies."

   _____

2. "Polly, give Mis' McChesney some salt."

   _____

3. "But most must become part of the wage labor force."

   _____

4. "Some of the deleted material is relevant."

   _____

5. "A person with a health problem or concern sees a doctor for help."

_____

6. "It had started at 7:00."

_____

7. "He saw that Marner's eyes were set like a dead man's."

_____

8. "In that sense, the remedy of a new trial appears reasonably capable of removing any prejudice suffered."

_____

9. "The daughter with the hearing problem turned her deaf ear to the box."

_____

10. "The sunshade continued to approach slowly."

_____

☼ **E10-8** → Identify the basic sentence pattern variations.

Example:

"You haven't any."

PATTERN

NP	TV	NP^2(Do)

1. "The afternoon appeared far advanced."

_____

2. "The young folk of the village, very smart in coats with otter collars, gave deferential greeting to old Nazaire Larouche."

_____

3. "A sudden commotion arose in the back of the room."

_____

4. "I have received your favor of the 23d."

_____

5. "Sometimes it seemed an ecstasy of delight and happiness."

_____

6. "I should think!"

_____

7. "But, like Odysseus, the President looked wiser."

_____

8. "One could walk all round, seeing little front gardens with auriculas and saxifrage in the shadow of the bottom block, sweet-williams and pinks in the sunny top block."

_____

9. "But the great thing was that he saw in this no vulgar reminder of any 'sweet' speech."

_____

10. "How beautiful are the noble children!"

_____

✿ **E10-9** → Identify the basic sentence pattern variations.

Example:

"I shall never forget my first sight of Mary Cavendish."

PATTERN

NP	TV	NP²	Prp-ph

1. "The increasing pace of Germany gave her neighbours an outlet for their products."

_____

2. "Mrs. Button, a viperous Londoner, yearned for noise."

_____

3. "Commencing his labours at Brockhurst during the closing years of the reign of Queen Elizabeth, Denzil Calmady completed them in 1611 with a royal house-warming."

_____

4. "Touching that monstrous bulk of the whale or ork we have received nothing certain."

_____

5. "Her face told it then."

_____

6. "But Mrs. Wessels, a lean, middle-aged little lady, with a flat, pointed nose, had no suggestions to offer."

_____

7. "His hands, slim, long, and with tapering fingers like a girl's, reached forward eagerly."

_____

8. "I give you my hand upon that."

_____

9. "He felt an irresistible desire to bathe in the pool."

_____

10. "But the tower showed us the old home in a new light."

_____

MATCH EXERCISES

✿ **E10-10** → Find examples for Part A in Part B, **USING EACH SENTENCE ONLY ONCE**.

1. These clauses may appear in any order within the sentence.

Part A[1]

1. Simple sentence [ONE INDEPENDENT CLAUSE] _____

2. Compound sentence [TWO INDEPENDENT CLAUSES] _____

3. Complex sentence [INDEPENDENT + DEPENDENT CLAUSES] _____

4. Compound sentence [FOUR INDEPENDENT CLAUSES] _____

5. Complex sentence [ONE INDEPENDENT + TWO DEPENDENT CLAUSES] _____

6. Complex sentence [TWO INDEPENDENT + ONE DEPENDENT CLAUSE] _____

7. Complex sentence [TWO INDEPENDENT + TWO DEPENDENT CLAUSES] _____

8. Compound/complex sentence [TWO INDEPENDENT + THREE DEPENDENT CLAUSES] _____

9. Compound/complex sentence [THREE INDEPENDENT + THREE DEPENDENT CLAUSES] _____

10. Compound/complex sentence [ONE INDEPENDENT + SIX DEPENDENT CLAUSES] _____

Part B

A. "However, this bottle was not marked 'poison,' so Alice ventured to taste it, and finding it very nice (it had, in fact, a sort of mixed flavour of cherry-tart, custard, pineapple, roast turkey, toffee, and hot buttered toast), she very soon finished it off."

B. "And when he showed his white teeth he seemed to lose a little of his dignity and there was something faintly fawning about him."

C. "I estimated that the winter of 1854–55 destroyed four-fifths of the birds in my own grounds; and this is a tremendous destruction, when we remember that ten per cent is an extraordinarily severe mortality from epidemics with man."

D. "NORTHWESTWARDLY from Indian Hill, about nine miles as the crow flies, is Macarger's Gulch."

E. "I regret to say that I did not deliver a moral sermon upon the duty of forgiving our enemies, and the sin of profanity, then and there; but, being a red-hot Abolitionist, stared fixedly at the tall rebel, who was a copperhead, in every sense of the word, and privately resolved to put soap in his eyes, rub his nose the wrong way, and excoriate his cuticle generally, if I had the washing of him."

F. "He told his wife the same story, and she seemed to believe him."

G. "Then away out in the woods I heard that kind of a sound that a ghost makes when it wants to tell about something that's on its mind and can't make itself understood, and so can't rest easy in its grave, and has to go about that way every night grieving."

H. "Was it possible that they might be the lost ten tribes of Israel?"

I. "If she marries and children come, she will have no time to think about the garden."

J. "Mrs. Pontellier reached over for a palm-leaf fan that lay on the porch and began to fan herself, while Robert sent between his lips light puffs from his cigarette."

✿ **E10-11** → Find examples for Part A in Part B, **USING EACH SENTENCE ONLY ONCE**.

Patterns are given only for the independent clauses.

Part A

1. NP LV C/av + NP ITV C   _____

2. NP TV NP^2 + NP LV C/av   _____

3. NP TV NP^2 + NP TV NP^2 P-ph   _____

4. NP ITV C/P-ph   _____

5. NP ITV C/P-Ph + NP TV NP^2 NP^2 _____

Part B

A. "He kept his cigar alight, and kindled every fresh one from the ashes."

B. "He will even speak well of the bishop, and I tell him it is unnatural in a beneficed clergyman."

C. "The Patna had a long bridge, and all the boats were up there."

D. "She seemed so far away from her girlhood, she wondered if it were the same person walking heavily up the back garden."

E. "The judge retreated to the cold manner of the bench."

⚙ **E10-12** → Find examples for Part A in Part B, **USING EACH SENTENCE ONLY ONCE**.

Patterns are given only for the independent clauses.

Part A

1. NP TV NP^2 _____

2. NP TV NP^2 I-ph _____

3. NP ITV C/av + NP ITV C/av _____

4. NP ITV C/P-Ph _____

5. NP LV SC/p-aj _____

Part B

A. "The thing will of itself appear natural."

B. "The subject therefore insensibly changed from the business of antiquity to that which brought us both to the fair."

C. "I shall hereafter have occasion to show that the exotic Lobelia fulgens."

D. "Manning came slowly and hesitatingly through the French window, and stood as near it as he could."

E. "I could understand anyone saying that the words were from a newspaper."

PARAGRAPH ANALYSIS

⚙ **E10-13** → Identify the bolded sentence structures as simple-compound-complex-compound/complex variations in the following paragraph.

1. _____
2. _____
3. _____
4. _____
5. _____
6. _____
7. _____
8. _____
9. _____
10. _____

"**I see few signs of sudden or dramatic developments anywhere.**[1] Riots and revolutions there may be, but not such, at present, as to have fundamental significance. Against political tyranny and injustice revolution is a weapon. **But what counsels of hope can revolution offer to sufferers from economic privation which does not arise out of the injustices of distribution but is general?**[2] **The only safeguard against revolution in Central Europe is indeed the fact that, even to the minds of men who are desperate, revolution offers no prospect of improvement whatever.**[3] There may, therefore, be ahead of us a long, silent process of semi-starvation, and of a gradual, steady lowering of the standards of life and comfort. **The bankruptcy and decay of Europe, if we allow it to proceed, will affect everyone in the long run, but perhaps not in a way that is striking or immediate.**[4]

"This has one fortunate side. **We may still have time to reconsider our courses and to view the world with new eyes.**[5] **For the immediate future events are taking charge, and the near destiny of Europe is no longer in the hands of any man.**[6] **The events of the coming year will not be shaped by the deliberate acts of statesmen, but by the hidden currents, flowing continually beneath the surface of political history, of which no one can predict the outcome.**[7] In one way only can we influence these hidden currents—by setting in motion those forces of instruction and imagination which change opinion. **The assertion of truth, the unveiling of illusion, the dissipation of hate, the enlargement and instruction of men's hearts and minds, must be the means.**[8]

"**In this autumn of 1919 in which I write, we are at the dead season of our fortunes.**[9] The reaction from the exertions, the fears, and the sufferings of the past five years is at its height. Our power of feeling or caring beyond the immediate questions of our own material well-being is temporarily eclipsed. **The greatest events outside our own direct experience and the most dreadful anticipations cannot move us.**[10]"

☼ **E10-14** → Identify the patterns of the bolded structures in the following paragraph.

I. _____

2. _____

3. _____

4. _____

5. _____

6. _____

7. _____

8. _____

9. _____

10. _____

"To the white men in the waterside business and to the captains of ships he was just Jim—nothing more. **He had, of course, another name,**[1] but **he was anxious**[2] that it should not be pronounced. His incognito, which had as many holes as a sieve, was not meant to hide a personality but a fact. When **the fact broke through the incognito**[3] **he would leave suddenly the seaport**[4] where he happened to be at the time and go to another—generally farther east. He kept to seaports because **he was a seaman in exile**[5] from the sea, and had Ability in the abstract, which is good for no other work but that of a water-clerk. **He retreated in good order**[6] towards the rising sun, and **the fact followed him casually**[7] but inevitably. Thus in the course of years he was known successively in Bombay, in Calcutta, in Rangoon, in Penang, in Batavia—and in each of these halting-places **[he] was just Jim the water-clerk**.[8] Afterwards, when **his keen perception of the Intolerable drove him away**[9] for good from seaports and white men, even into the virgin forest, the Malays of the jungle village, where he had elected to conceal his deplorable faculty, added a word to the monosyllable of his incognito. **They called him Tuan Jim—Lord Jim**.[10]"

SENTENCE ANALYSIS

✿ **E10-15** → Analyze the following sentences, using tree diagrams.

I. **Running for politics might be rewarding.**

2. **Bernard could have been travelling with her.**

answer key

CHAPTER ONE

Morphemes

E1-1

1. C
2. O
3. A
4. R
5. I
6. P
7. M
8. K
9. Q
10. D
11. G
12. J
13. F
14. E
15. S
16. H
17. T
18. B
19. L
20. N

E1-2

1. power
2. happy
3. guilt
4. authentic
5. ocean
6. can
7. annual
8. success
9. desire
10. person

E1-3

1. habit
2. canon
3. situat(e)
4. present
5. cast
6. regular
7. light
8. simila(r)
9. reciprocat(e)
10. ex(a)mpl(e)

E1-4

1. architect
2. labor
3. base + ball
4. perish
5. scribe
6. will
7. treat
8. observ(e)
9. gravit(y)
10. vent

E1-5

1. scope
2. close
3. form
4. firm
5. inter
6. myth
7. portion
8. continu(e)
9. perish
10. form

E1-6

1. -ing
2. re-
3. -s
4. be-
5. -ion
6. in-
7. -ness
8. -ed
9. -est
10. un-

E1-7

1. ten- + -ure
2. -(i/y)ze-(at)ion
3. mis- -ion -s
4. -(i/y) -est
5. em- -en -ed
6. ex- + -pense
7. -en -ing
8. un- -ing -ness
9. sub- + -ject
10. semi- -ed

E1-8

1. -y
2. -ness
3. -ize
4. -ism
5. -ent -cy
6. dis- -ment
7. non- -al
8. il- -ity
9. -(y/i) -ness
10. un- -able

E1-9

1. un- -ful -ly
2. non- ful(l)- -ment
3. un- -ate -ly
4. in- -(a/i)ble -ity
5. re- -(at)ion
6. de- ize- -(at)ion
7. -(ua)l -ize
8 re- -(at)ion -al
9. un- -ative -ly
10. -ive -ly

E1-10

1. {-ing pp}
2. {-s pl ps}
3. {-est sp}
4. {-en ptp}
5. {-s pl}
6. {-s 3 p sg}
7. {-ed pt}
8. {-ing pp}
9. {-ed ptp}
10. {-ed pt}

E1-11

1. {-s pl ps}
2. {-ed ptp}
3. {-s pl}
4. {-er cp}
5. {-ed ptp}
6. {-s sg ps}
7. {-est sp}
8. {3 p sg}
9. {-ing pp}
10. {-er cp}

E1-12

1. bound/inflectional/{-s pl}
2. bound/derivational
3. base/free
4. bound/inflectional/{-ed pt or ptp}
5. bound/derivational
6. bound/inflectional/{-ed pt}
7. bound/base
8. bound/derivational
9. bound/inflectional/{-s pl}
10. base/free

E1-13

1. bound/inflectional/{-ed ptp}
2. base/free
3. bound/derivational
4. bound/inflectional/{-s pl}
5. bound/inflectional/{-est sp}
6. free/base
7. bound/derivational/{-er cp}
8. bound/inflectional/{-ed pt or ptp}
9. bound/inflectional/{-er cp}
10. base/bound

E1-14

1. C   women**'s**
2. B   sub + **ject**
3. D   **de**institut**ionalization**
4. E   have f**ou**nd
5. A   **undis**closed

E1-15

1. D   mahogany
2. A   brilliancy
3. E   encounter or relationship
4. B   dirty
5. C   counterclockwise

E1-16
1. D
2. E
3. A
4. B
5. C

E1-17
1. C
2. E
3. D
4. A
5. B

E1-18
1. driven
2. attacker
3. mostly
4. increased/exploded
5. policemen/roadside

E1-19
1. attractive/international/ terrorist/basic
2. biggest
3. nation's/its
4. seen
5. dis + rupt

E1-20

1.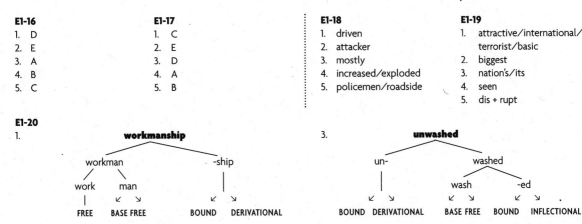

2.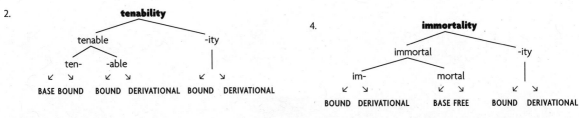

3. (see above)

4.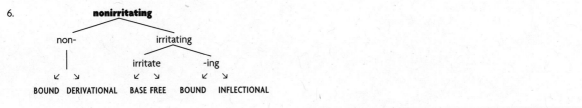

5.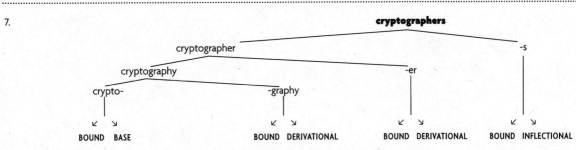

6.

7.

8.

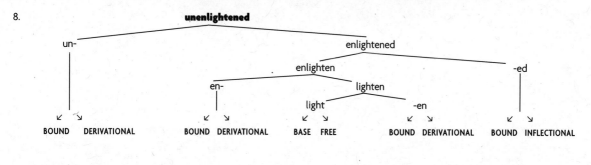

9.

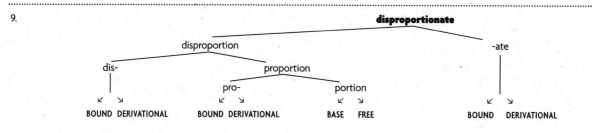

10.

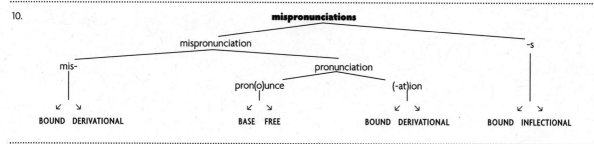

CHAPTER TWO
Words: Form Class

E2-1

1. R	6. T	11. P	16. D
2. O	7. C	12. B	17. L
3. H	8. S	13. Q	18. F
4. M	9. N	14. E	19. J
5. A	10. K	15. G	20. I

E2-2

	STEM	{-S PL}	{-S SG PS}	{-S PL PS}
1.	sun	suns	sun's	suns'
	flare	flares	flare's	flares'
	light	lights	light's	lights'
2.	practice	practices	n/a	n/a
	medicine	medicines	medicine's	medicines'
	science	sciences	science's	sciences'
	art	arts	art's	arts'
3.	clamor	clamors	n/a	n/a
	siren	sirens	siren's	sirens'
	night	nights	night's	nights'
4.	piano	pianos	piano's	pianos'
	youth	youths	youth's	youths'
5.	asker	askers	asker's	askers'
	answer	answers	answer's	answers'
	street	streets	street's	streets'
6.	year	year	year's	years'
	peace	n/a	n/a	n/a
	process	processes	n/a	n/a
	Ireland	n/a	Ireland's	n/a
7.	word	words	word's	words'
	bell	bells	bell's	bells'
	sorrow	sorrows	n/a	n/a
8.	defence	defences	defence's	n/a
	acquittal	acquittals	n/a	n/a
	retrial	retrials	n/a	n/a
9.	rock	rocks	rock's	rocks'
	root	roots	root's	roots'
	movement	movements	movement's	movements'
10.	court	courts	court's	courts'
	decision	decisions	decision's	decisions'
	point	points	point's	n/a

E2-3

	NOUN	TYPE
1.	days	common-abstract-countable
	experiences	common-abstract-countable
	death	common-abstract-countable
2.	Yankees	proper-concrete-countable
	storyline	common-concrete-countable
3.	Genomics	common-concrete-countable
	influence	common-abstract-countable
	practice	common-abstract-countable
4.	Michigander	proper-concrete-countable
	arm	common-concrete-countable
	shoulder	common-concrete-countable
5.	sort	common-abstract-countable
	fascination	common-abstract-non-countable
6.	Friday	proper-abstract-countable
	pressure	common-abstract-countable
	director	common-concrete-countable
7.	Bruins	proper-concrete-countable
	level	common-concrete-countable
8.	auditorium	common-concrete-countable
	floor	common-concrete-countable
	building	common-concrete-countable
9.	U.S.A.	proper-concrete-non-countable
	chaos	common-abstract-non-countable
	evil	common-abstract-countable
	world	common-concrete-countable
	Jesus	proper-concrete-non-countable
10.	critics	common-concrete-countable
	works	common-concrete-countable

E2-4

	WORD	DERIVATIONAL SUFFIX
1.	security	-ity
2.	stillness	-ness
3.	attention	-ion
4.	writer	-er
5.	government	-ment
6.	legislature	-ure
7.	subsidy	-y
8.	internships	-ship
9.	manager	-er
	specialist	-ist
10.	utterance	-ance
	conspiracy	-acy

E2-5

1. thrown — took
2. understood — looked
3. led — teach
4. standing — saw
5. suspect — have — tells — is
6. used — have — proved
7. is — feel
8. do — separated
9. claim — needed — is
   added — integrated
10. directed — turned

E2-6

	WORD		DERIVATIONAL AFFIX
1.	sympathize	→	-ize
2.	accustomed	→	ac-
3.	heighten	→	-en
4.	clothed	→	-e-
5.	exclaiming	→	ex-
6.	derail	→	de-
7.	invalidate	→	-ate or in-
8.	attest	→	at-
9.	postdate	→	post-
10.	strengthen	→	-en

E2-7

SOURCE VERB
1. propose
2. labour
3. impress
4. entertain   recite   applaud
5. dispense
6. detain
7. administer
8. forgive
9. repent   view
10. decide

E2-8

The bolded word is the one appearing in the exercise.

	STEM	(S 3 P SG)	(-ING PP)	(-ED PT)	(-ED PTP)
1.	push	pushes	pushing	**pushed**	pushed
2.	seem	seems	seeming	**seemed**	seemed
3.	be	**is**	being	was	been
	become	**becomes**	becoming	became	become
4.	see	sees	seeing	saw	**seen**
	be	is	being	was	**been**
5,	hint	hints	hinting	**hinted**	hinted
	feign	feigns	feigning	**feigned**	feigned
6.	make	**makes**	making	made	made
	tell	**tells**	telling	told	told
	go	goes	going	went	**gone**
7.	extend	extends	extending	**extended**	extended
8.	hear	hears	hearing	**heard**	heard
9.	rise	rises	rising	**rose**	risen
	begin	begins	beginning	**began**	begun
10.	come	comes	coming	**came**	come

E2-9

1. finite / non-finite
2. finite / finite
3. finite / non-finite / finite
4. finite / finite
5. finite / non-finite
6. finite / non-finite / finite
7. finite / non-finite / finite
8. non-finite / non-finite
9. finite / finite
10. non-finite / finite / finite

E2-10

1. linking — intransitive
2. transitive — intransitive
3. linking — intransitive
4. transitive — intransitive — linking
5. intransitive — linking
6. intransitive — transitive — intransitive
7. transitive — transitive
8. transitive — linking
9. transitive — linking
10. intransitive — transitive

E2-11

1. frosty — wiry
2. undocumented — family
3. opposition — government
4. powerful — car — Shiite — Adhamiya
5. patient-doctor — accurate — medical — treatment
6. major — world — male-dominant — gender
7. final — white — special — wayward
   pristine — capitalist
8. genre — contemporary — Christian — modern
   worship
9. class — cultural — language
10. Enlightenment — Medieval — organic — primary

E2-12

The bolded word is the one appearing in the exercise.

	STEM	{-ER CP}	{-EST SP}
1.	**green**	greener	greenest
	yellow	yellower	yellowest
2.	**narrow**	narrower	narrowest
3.	dark	**darker**	darkest
4.	good	better	**best**
5.	**white**	whiter	whitest
	full	fuller	fullest
	beautiful	more beautiful	most beautiful
	slender	**more slender**	most slender
6.	**large**	larger	largest
	amicable	more amicable	most amicable
7.	**profound**	more profound	most profound
8.	brief	briefer	**briefest**
9.	wise	**wiser**	wisest
10.	**few**	fewer	fewest
	good	better	best

E2-13

	BASE	SUFFIX			BASE	SUFFIX
1.	glory	-ous	7.		appreciate	-ive
2.	character	-istic			humour	-ous
3.	enigma	-(t)ical	8.		ghoul	-ish
4.	moment	-ary	9.		sun(n)	-y
5.	sensation	-al			delight	-ful
6.	rascal	-ly	10.		person	-al

E2-14

1. upward
2. instantly   again
3. likewise
4. again   very   near
5. sometimes   loudly   there   again
6. chiefly   soon
7. still   violently   backward
8. boy-like
9. along   now   then
10. here   there   by   once   so   cheerfully

E2-15

	POSITIVE	{-ER CP}	{-EST SP}
1.	spotlessly	more spotlessly	most spotlessly
2.	quickly	more quickly	most quickly
	kindly	more kindly	most kindly
3.	slowly	more slowly	most slowly
4.	suddenly	more suddenly	most suddenly
5.	gently	more gently	most gently
6.	swiftly	more swiftly	most swiftly
7.	faintly	more faintly	most faintly
8.	exactly	more exactly	most exactly
9.	strangely	more strangely	most strangely
10.	secretly	more secretly	most secretly

E2-16

1. D
2. A
3. E.
4. B
5. C

E2-17

1. D
2. C
3. A
4. E
5. B

E2-18

1. music
2. bought
3. extremely/seriously
4. more substantial
5. center

E2-19

1. physician's
2. home/health
3. have/include
4. Primary healthcare medical
5. therefore

E2-20

1. present participle
2. proper noun
3. transitive verb {-ed ptp} (passive voice)
4. past participle as an adjective modifier
5. regular adjective
6. regular adverb
7. noun {-s pl ps}
8. infinitive
9. linking verb
10. adverb

CHAPTER THREE

Words: Structure Class

E3-1

1.	O	6.	T	11.	B	16.	I
2.	G	7.	P	12.	J	17.	E
3.	R	8.	A	13.	H	18.	K
4.	C	9.	Q	14.	D	19.	L
5.	F	10.	S	15.	M	20.	N

E3-2

These pronouns are identified by form only. If the form does not identify the gender and case, then n/a meaning non-applicable is given.

	PRONOUN	PERSON	NUMBER	GENDER	CASE
1.	we	1st	plural	n/a*	subjective
	our	1st	plural	n/a	possessive
2.	me	1st	singular	n/a	objective
	he	3rd	singular	masculine	subjective
	it	3rd	singular	neuter	objective
3.	I	1st	singular	n/a	subjective
	they	3rd	plural	n/a	subjective
	him	3rd	singular	masculine	objective
4.	his	3rd	singular	masculine	possessive
	mine	1st	singular	n/a	possessive
5.	them	3rd	plural	n/a	objective
	her	3rd	singular	feminine	objective
	they	3rd	plural	n/a	subjective
	she	3rd	singular	feminine	subjective
6.	I	1st	singular	n/a	subjective
	my	1st	singular	n/a	possessive
	your	2nd	singular/ plural	n/a	possessive
7.	it	3rd	singular	neuter	objective
	its	3rd	singular	neuter	possessive
8.	you	2nd	singular/ plural	n/a	objective
	they	3rd	plural	n/a	subjective
9.	it	3rd	singular	neuter	subjective
	us	1st	plural	n/a	objective
	I	1st	singular	n/a	subjective
10.	my	1st	singular	n/a	possessive
	I	1st	singular	n/a	subjective
	they	3rd	plural	n/a	subjective
	their	3rd	plural	n/a	possessive
	they	3rd	plural	n/a	subjective

*In the gender column, "n/a" frequently means "not clear from the sentence." The actual context would often make the gender obvious, although gender is relevant only for third person singular.

E3-3

	PRONOUN	PERSON	NUMBER	GENDER	REFERENCE
1.	itself	3rd	singular	n/a	Point Pleasant
2.	herself	3rd	singular	feminine	She
3.	yourselves	2nd	plural	n/a	you
4.	myself	1st	singular	n/a	I
5.	ourselves	1st	plural	n/a	we both
6.	himself	3rd	singular	masculine	He
7.	yourself	2nd	singular	n/a	you
8.	himself	3rd	singular	masculine	Richard
	themselves	3rd	plural	n/a	these friends and Richard
9.	oneself	3rd	singular	n/a	one
10.	yourselves	2nd	plural	n/a	you

E3-4

	PRONOUN	TYPE	CASE
1.	what	interrogative	n/a
2.	who	relative	subjective
	whose	relative	possessive
3.	which	relative	subjective
4.	whose	interrogative	possessive
5.	that	relative	subjective
6.	which	interrogative	n/a
7.	whom	interrogative	objective
8.	whom	relative	objective
9.	whose	relative	possessive
10.	who	interrogative	subjective

E3-5

	PRONOUN	TYPE	REFERENT/PROXIMITY
1.	one another's	reciprocal	Hamas, Islamic Jihad, and Fatah
2.	this	demonstrative	nearby
3.	each other	reciprocal	faces
	each other's	reciprocal	faces
4.	that	demonstrative	far away
5.	these	demonstrative	nearby
6.	one another	reciprocal	church-bells
7.	those	demonstrative	far away
8.	that	demonstrative	far away
9.	one another	reciprocal	they
10.	these	demonstrative	nearby

E3-6

	PRONOUN	SPECIFIER/QUANTIFIER
1.	no one	specifier
2.	nothing	specifier
3.	enough	quantifier
4.	no one	specifier
5.	some	quantifier
6.	many	quantifier
	everyone	specifier
7.	everything	specifier
	all	specifier
8.	something	specifier
9.	anything	specifier
10.	several	quantifier

E3-7

	PRONOUN	TYPE
1.	which	interrogative
	her	personal/objective
2.	nobody	indefinite
	himself	reflexive
	such a	indefinite
	that	demonstrative
3.	who	relative
	they	personal/subjective
4.	many	indefinite
	them	personal/objective
	they	personal/subjective
	it	personal/objective
5.	you	personal/subjective
	such a	indefinite
	you	personal/subjective
	each other	reciprocal
6.	whose	relative/possessive
	his	personal/possessive
7.	much	indefinite
	its	personal/possessive
8.	they	personal/subjective
	themselves	intensive
	that	relative
9.	he	personal/subjective
	their	personal/possessive
	which	relative
	one another's	reciprocal
10.	what	interrogative
	all	indefinite
	those	demonstrative
	he	personal/subjective
	his	personal/possessive
	that	demonstrative

E3-8

	DETERMINER	TYPE
1.	your	personal/possessive
	the	definite article
2.	its	personal/possessive
	the	definite article
	few	indefinite
3.	which	interrogative
	the	definite article
4.	their	personal/possessive
	the	definite article
5.	the	definite article
	president's	possessive of names
	some	indefinite
6.	the	definite article
	first	numbers
	two	numbers
	the	definite article
	both	indefinite

7.	a	indefinite article
	two	numbers
	a	indefinite article
	this	demonstrative
8.	whose	relative possessive
	the	definite article
	another	indefinite
9.	a	indefinite article
	the	definite article
	the	definite article
	what a	intensifier
10.	the	definite article
	eight	numbers
	double	multipliers/fractions
	the	definite article
	second	numbers

E3-9

	AUXILIARY	FORM	TENSE
1.	is	3rd p sg	present
2.	has	3rd p sg	past
	been	-ed ptp	n/d
3.	be	stem	n/d
	were	plural	past
4.	had	n/d	past
5.	have	stem	n/d
	been	-ed ptp	n/d
6.	were	plural	past
	being	-ing pp	n/d
7.	are	plural	present
8.	was	3rd p sg	past
9.	was	3rd p sg	past
10.	is	3rd p sg	present
	being	-ing pp	n/d

E3-10

	AUXILIARY	MOOD/ATTITUDE
1.	may	possibility
	might	possibility
2.	should	condition
	would	condition
	might	possibility
3.	shall	futurity
	can	ability (or lack of)
4.	must	obligation
	should	obligation
5.	should	obligation
	can	ability (or lack of)
6.	should	condition
	could	ability
7.	will	probability
	ought to	obligation
8.	must	obligation
	could	ability
9.	would	condition/futurity
10.	may	possibility
	must	obligation

E3-11

	AUXILIARY	TYPE
1.	might	modal
	have	primary 1
	been	primary 2
2.	have	primary 1
	did	stand-in do
3.	can	modal
	might	modal
4.	can	modal
	ought to	modal
5.	could	modal
	have	primary 1
	been	primary 2
6.	must	modal
	be	primary 2
7.	does	stand-in do
	will	modal
8.	would	modal
	should	modal
9.	are	primary 2
	may	modal
10.	had	primary 1
	would	modal

E3-12

	PREPOSITION	TYPE
1.	to	simple
	about	simple
	in	simple
	to	simple
2.	concerning	-ing
	in	simple
3.	in	simple
	instead of	phrasal
	out of	phrasal
	for	simple
4.	from	simple
	with	simple
5.	like	simple
	ahead of	phrasal
	like	simple
	along with	phrasal
	like	simple
6.	of	simple
	in	simple
	during	-ing
	in	simple
7.	of	simple
	in addition to	phrasal
8.	of	simple
	with	simple
	up to	phrasal
	about	simple
9.	to	simple
	from	simple
	for	simple
	with regard to	phrasal

10. following — -ing
    of — simple
    to — simple
    in — simple
    throughout — simple

E3-13

	CONJUNCTION	TYPE	CLASS
1.	as long as	subordinating	conjunction
	which	subordinating	relative pronoun
2.	that	subordinating	relative pronoun
	but	coordinating	conjunction
	and	coordinating	conjunction
3.	neither-nor	correlative	indefinite pronoun
	whom	subordinating	relative pronoun
	that	subordinating	relative pronoun
4.	who	subordinating	relative pronoun
	and	coordinating	conjunction
	when	subordinating	relative adverb
5.	however	conjunctive	adverb
	as	subordinating	conjunction
	and	coordinating	conjunction
6.	whatever	subordinating	indefinite relative
	that	subordinating	relative pronoun
7.	meanwhile	conjunctive	adverb
	for	coordinating	conjunction
	whom	subordinating	relative pronoun
8.	but	coordinating	conjunction
	why	subordinating	relative adverb
9.	since	subordinating	conjunction
	and	coordinating	conjunction
10.	whose	subordinating	relative pronoun
	and	coordinating	conjunction
	while	subordinating	conjunction
	and	coordinating	conjunction

E3-14

	WORD	TYPE
1.	preposition	phrasal
2.	auxiliary	primary
	subordinating	conjunction
3.	auxiliary	modal
4.	preposition	-ing
5.	adverb	conjunction
	subordinating	conjunction
	coordinating	conjunction
6.	auxiliary	stand-in 'do'
	reciprocal	pronoun
7.	subordinating	conjunction
	determiner	proper name
8.	auxiliary	modal
	preposition	phrasal
9.	determiner	numbers
	reciprocal	pronoun
10.	auxiliary	primary
	preposition	phrasal

E3-15
1. D
2. A
3. E
4. B
5. C

E3-16
1. E
2. C
3. B
4. A
5. D

E3-17
1. was
2. where
3. the single
4. and
5. all

E3-18
1. do
2. these two
3. who
4. either-or
5. although

E3-19
1. Determiner plus post-determiner
2. Primary auxiliary 2
3. Relative adverb conjunction
4. Primary auxiliary 1
5. Personal pronoun/possessive
6. Subordinating conjunction/time
7. Personal pronoun/subjective
8. Simple preposition
9. Relative pronoun conjunction
10. Personal pronoun/possessive

E3-20
Word Analysis:
1. Nouns

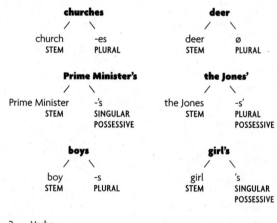

2. Verbs

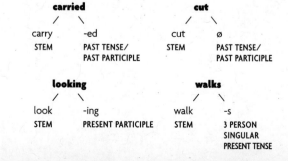

3. Adjectives

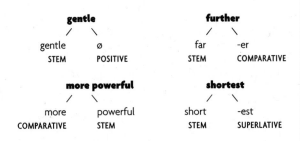

4. Adverbs

5. Pronouns

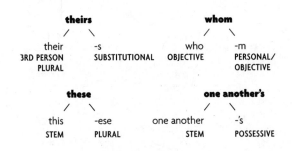

CHAPTER FOUR
Phrases

E4-1

1. J	6. O	11. A	16. P
2. R	7. K	12. H	17. F
3. C	8. G	13. Q	18. M
4. L	9. N	14. S	19. B
5. E	10. T	15. D	20. I

E4-2

1. The new rich
   the nineteenth century
   large expenditures
2. these thoughts
   my present purpose
3. The delicate organisation
   these peoples
   factors internal
   the system
4. the good
   our children
5. this remarkable system
   its growth
   a double bluff or deception

6. Entertainment Weekly
   15 rising stars
   its annual "Breakouts" issue
7. a legend
   the business
   'The Apprentice' 3-hour finale
8. the greater part
   the money interest
   these foreign investments
   a reserve
9. Bridges TV
   the first American Muslim TV network
   the Arab-population-rich metro Detroit area
10. His walk, his hand, and his voice
    the attempt
    the aspect
    a very old man
    his strength
    important occasions

E4-3

1. would have been
   could have been taken
2. was really almost reaching out
   would do
3. had told
   had ... been
4. had made
   must have been much soothed
5. 've mentioned
   never really intended
6. has been working
   has been frustrated
7. will most probably sift
   would make
   would have made
8. was conducted
   was also calculated
9. could have done
   would simply have stretched
10. does not control
    will probably lead

E4-4

1. had swept through	past
was only pushing	past
2. do ... go	present
3. shall be passing	future
goes out	present
4. are seen	present
5. had swept	past
was only pushing	past
6. will be	future
have been	present
7. are ... saying	present
are buried	present
8. shall set	future
shall have	future

9. did ... picture — past
    have found — present
10. would have — past
    are ... playing — present
    have ... been caught — present
    have ... been caught — present

E4-5

1. may be — simple
2. have been — perfect
    haven't been caught — perfect
3. is ... having — progressive
    have ... been linked — perfect
4. has been discussing — perfect progressive
5. is ... returning — progressive
    had planned — perfect
6. didn't make — simple
    would have [made] — perfect
    had been — perfect
7. would instruct — simple
    could be — simple
8. has been working — perfect progressive
    has been frustrated — perfect
9. might meet — simple
    are based — simple
10. have been feeling — perfect progressive
    have shaken — perfect

E4-6

1. will face — future — simple
    is succeeding — present — progressive
2. were returning — past — progressive
    had rigged — past — perfect
3. was being discussed — past — progressive
    had crept — past — perfect
    was awaiting — past — progressive
4. had been asked — past — perfect
5. may have been expecting — present — perfect progressive
    had ... counted — past — perfect
6. is shining — present — progressive
    must be shining — present — progressive
    has haunted — present — perfect
7. must leave — present — simple
    had been forgetting — past — perfect progressive
8. had gone out — past — perfect
    was shining — past — progressive
    had been — past — perfect
9. will have crept in — future — perfect
    have ... been — present — perfect
10. doesn't want — present — simple
    will be — future — simple

E4-7

1. the most distinctive and innovative — adjective
2. now too late — adverb
    directly homewards — adverb

as fast as possible — adverb
3. the various statutory — adjective
4. The most highly developed — adjective
    the Western or Hippocratic — adjective
    traditional Chinese — adjective
5. The patient-doctor — adjective
    an accurate medical — adjective
6. so basely, so ungratefully — adverb
7. very carefully — adverb
8. a handsome young — adjective
    five hundred — adjective
9. more obliquely — adverb
10. a little further off — adverb
    five or six — adjective

E4-8

1. Moxon's expounding — gerund
2. shocking intelligence — present participle
3. comparatively inexperienced — past participle
    killing his fellow men — gerund
4. a low humming or buzzing — gerund
5. strongly defined — past participle
    half obscured — past participle
6. a whirring of wheels — gerund
7. failed initiatives — past participle
    facing the government — present participle
    trying to juggle the demands — present participle
    restoring devolution to Northern Ireland — present participle
    giving constitutional guarantees to unionists — present participle
    delivering some sort of power arrangements — present participle
8. a singularly good-natured man — past participle
9. half thinking — present participle
    the stranger's uncommon greeting — gerund
    the historic surroundings — gerund
10. upturned collar — past participle
    quietly smoking — present participle

E4-9

1. on television — prepositional
    of a network anchor — prepositional
    for hours on end — prepositional
    to the ego — prepositional
    than almost any other kind — prepositional
    of public performance — prepositional
2. in a Baghdad courtroom — prepositional
    to hear — infinitive
    to trial — prepositional
    as a war criminal — prepositional
3. for me to get — infinitive
    without a guide — prepositional
4. to refrain — infinitive
    from provoking me — prepositional
    as a special favour — prepositional
5. to hire — infinitive

for to walk	infinitive
without a gun	prepositional
in his hand	prepositional
along an ordinary road	prepositional
out of the question	prepositional
to him	prepositional
to other spririted young men	prepositional
of his kind	prepositional
6. to be	infinitive
for the bed	prepositional
7. by the prominent role	prepositional
to have played	infinitive
at the Second Vatican Council	prepositional
by Pope John XXIII	prepositional
in 1962	prepositional
to formulate	infinitive
for the church	prepositional
in the modern world	prepositional
8. to forsake	infinitive
for her to take leave	infinitive
9. to bring	infinitive
to Washington	prepositional
to make	infinitive
10. for parents to make	infinitive
for their children	prepositional
to a social service agency	prepositional
to assume	infinitive
for a child	prepositional

E4-10

1. present participle
2. gerund
6. infinitive
7. verb

3. past participle
4. noun
5. gerund
8. absolute
9. prepositional
10. past participle

E4-11

1. adverb
2. past participle
3. infinitive
4. present participle
5. gerund
6. adjective
7. verb
8. present participle
9. noun
10. prepositional

E4-12	E4-13	E4-14	E4-15	E4-16	E4-17
1. C	1. D	1. D	1. C	1. E	1. B
2. E	2. C	2. E	2. D	2. C	2. C
3. A	3. B	3. B	3. A	3. B	3. E
4. B	4. E	4. A	4. E	4. A	4. A
5. D	5. A	5. C	5. B	5. D	5. D

E4-18

1. planted so close
2. to be called/to be observed
3. during the crucial time
4. The central garden
5. no straying

E4-19

1. adverb phrase
2. infinitive
3. gerund phrase
4. prepositional phrase
5. present participle phrase
6. verb phrase
7. noun phrase
8. gerund phrase
9. absolute phrase
10. adjective phrase

E4-20

NOUN

1a.

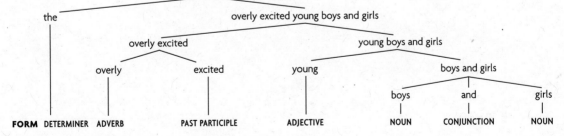

1b.

ADJECTIVE

2a.

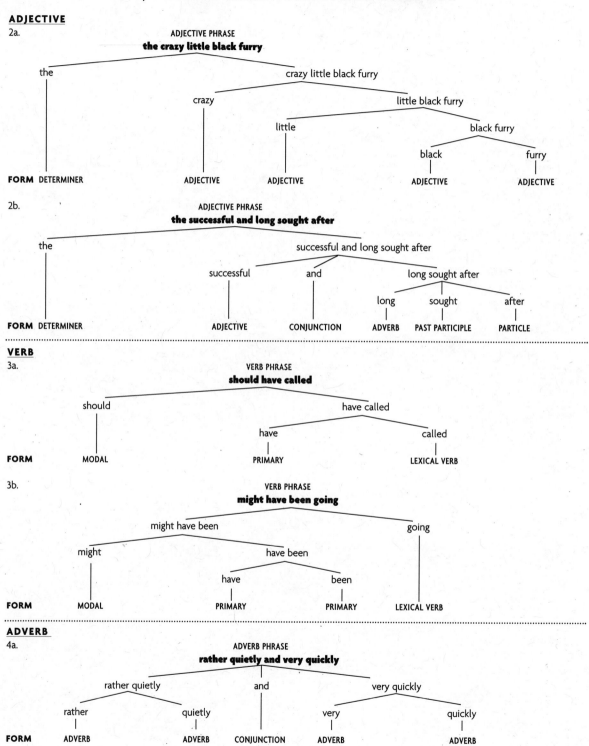

ADJECTIVE PHRASE
the crazy little black furry

- the
- crazy little black furry
  - crazy
  - little black furry
    - little
    - black furry
      - black
      - furry

FORM DETERMINER | ADJECTIVE | ADJECTIVE | ADJECTIVE | ADJECTIVE

2b.

ADJECTIVE PHRASE
the successful and long sought after

- the
- successful and long sought after
  - successful
  - and
  - long sought after
    - long
    - sought
    - after

FORM DETERMINER | ADJECTIVE | CONJUNCTION | ADVERB | PAST PARTICIPLE | PARTICLE

VERB

3a.

VERB PHRASE
should have called

- should
- have called
  - have
  - called

FORM MODAL | PRIMARY | LEXICAL VERB

3b.

VERB PHRASE
might have been going

- might have been
  - might
  - have been
    - have
    - been
- going

FORM MODAL | PRIMARY | PRIMARY | LEXICAL VERB

ADVERB

4a.

ADVERB PHRASE
rather quietly and very quickly

- rather quietly
  - rather
  - quietly
- and
- very quickly
  - very
  - quickly

FORM ADVERB | ADVERB | CONJUNCTION | ADVERB | ADVERB

4b.

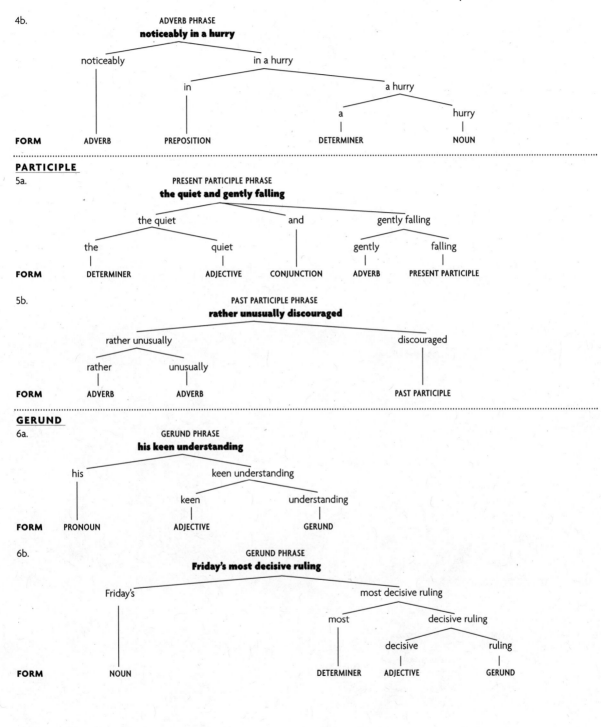

ADVERB PHRASE
noticeably in a hurry

	noticeably	in a hurry			a hurry			
		in				a		hurry
FORM	ADVERB	PREPOSITION				DETERMINER		NOUN

PARTICIPLE

5a.

PRESENT PARTICIPLE PHRASE
the quiet and gently falling

	the quiet		and	gently falling	
	the	quiet		gently	falling
FORM	DETERMINER	ADJECTIVE	CONJUNCTION	ADVERB	PRESENT PARTICIPLE

5b.

PAST PARTICIPLE PHRASE
rather unusually discouraged

	rather unusually		discouraged
	rather	unusually	
FORM	ADVERB	ADVERB	PAST PARTICIPLE

GERUND

6a.

GERUND PHRASE
his keen understanding

	his	keen understanding	
		keen	understanding
FORM	PRONOUN	ADJECTIVE	GERUND

6b.

GERUND PHRASE
Friday's most decisive ruling

	Friday's	most decisive ruling		
		most	decisive ruling	
			decisive	ruling
FORM	NOUN	DETERMINER	ADJECTIVE	GERUND

INFINITIVE

7a.

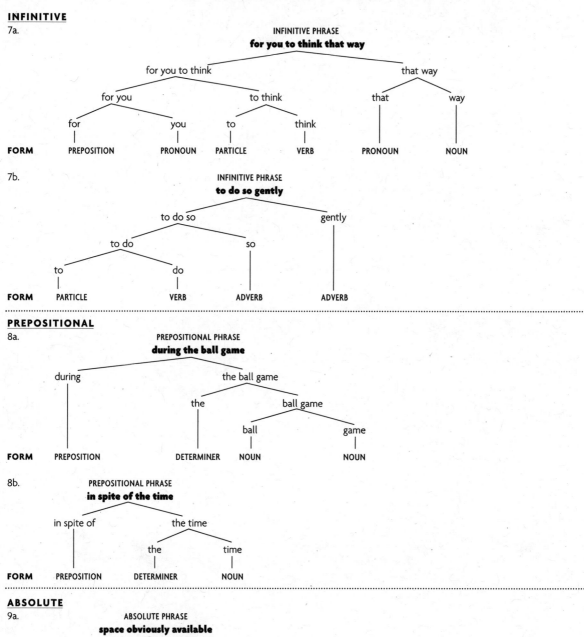

INFINITIVE PHRASE
for you to think that way

for you to think — that way

for you — to think

for — you — to — think

that — way

FORM: PREPOSITION — PRONOUN — PARTICLE — VERB — PRONOUN — NOUN

7b.

INFINITIVE PHRASE
to do so gently

to do so — gently

to do — so

to — do

FORM: PARTICLE — VERB — ADVERB — ADVERB

PREPOSITIONAL

8a.

PREPOSITIONAL PHRASE
during the ball game

during — the ball game

the — ball game

ball — game

FORM: PREPOSITION — DETERMINER — NOUN — NOUN

8b.

PREPOSITIONAL PHRASE
in spite of the time

in spite of — the time

the — time

FORM: PREPOSITION — DETERMINER — NOUN

ABSOLUTE

9a.

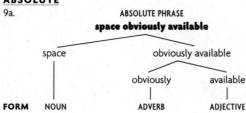

ABSOLUTE PHRASE
space obviously available

space — obviously available

obviously — available

FORM: NOUN — ADVERB — ADJECTIVE

9b.

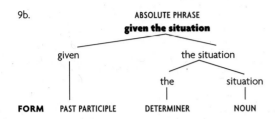

CHAPTER FIVE

Clauses

E5-1

1.	M	6.	C	11.	G	16.	H
2.	J	7.	S	12.	R	17.	L
3.	T	8.	I	13.	P	18.	N
4.	O	9.	A	14.	B	19.	D
5.	K	10.	Q	15.	F	20.	E

E5-2

	CLAUSE	TYPE
1.	I am free to confess	independent
	that I had a realizing sense of the fact	dependent
	that my hospital bed was not a bed of roses just then.	dependent
2.	Bioethics is a field of study	independent
	which concerns the relationship between biology, science, medicine and ethics, philosophy and theology.	dependent
3.	when I peeped into the dusky street lined	dependent
	with what I at first had innocently called market carts,	dependent
	I recalled sundry reminiscences	independent
	I had heard from nurses of longer standing.	dependent
4.	I progressed by slow stages up stairs and down,	independent
	till the main hall was reached,	dependent
	I paused to take breath and a survey.	independent
5.	Tell them to take off socks, coats and shirts,	independent
	scrub them well,	independent
	put on clean shirts,	independent
	the attendants will finish them off,	independent
	lay them in bed.	independent
6.	He thought it odd,	independent
	with a little perfunctory shiver,... he lay down again	independent
	(and) went to sleep.	independent
	as if in deference to a seasonal presumption that the night was chill,	dependent
7.	He thought	independent
	(that) he was walking along a dusty road	dependent
	that showed white in the gathering darkness of a summer night.	dependent

8.	Their children had the social and educational opportunities of their time and place,	independent
	(they) had responded to good associations and instruction with agreeable manners and cultivated minds.	independent
9.	As he grew to such manhood	dependent
	as is attainable by a Southerner	dependent
	who does not care	dependent
	which way elections go,	dependent
	the attachment between him and his beautiful mother ... became yearly stronger and more tender.	independent
	—whom from early childhood he had called Katy—	dependent
10.	The dust in the road was laid;	independent
	trees were adrip with moisture;	independent
	birds sat silent in their coverts;	independent
	the morning light was wan and ghastly, with neither colour nor fire.	independent

E5-3

1. whether the DUP would agree to participate in such a forum with Sinn Fein members
2. whoever else might benefit by Mrs. Inglethorp's death
3. that he was too old to work,
   (that) his only son had been killed in Vietnam
4. he wanted everyone to know
   how important their support was in his final battle
5. whatever decision is taken
6. [that] the emotional impacts are huge
7. what they prefer to call "partnership" government
8. that the current bill would endanger troops by interfering with the Pentagon's ability to share intelligence with battlefield commanders
9. the basis that it was undemocratic
   [the basis] that the government was surreptitiously setting this agenda
10. that in the Bible itself maxims can be found
    whether they are reasonable and just

E5-4

1. which are not for sale in the market
2. none of whom would make the splash
   that Meyer would have made
3. who has nothing
   that she need be personally ashamed of
   that passed up to the time
4. who had warned me so earnestly
   to whose warning I had, alas, paid no heed
5. that brought a boost of optimism to the Yushchenko
      supporters
   who have been in the streets of Kiev since the original vote
6. that may surface
   whom White knows from his Pac-10 days as the athletic
      director at Arizona State
   who has led the Broncos on a 22-game-winning streak
7. that had planted these vegetables
   [that had] kept the soil so clean and orderly
8. for whom this opera night had been an event
   who had lived for twenty-two years in a second-class town
      of central Massachusetts
9. that was ushered in that December morning
   that vied with each other
10. that work in these medical laboratory departments
    each of whom usually hold a medical technology degree
    who actually perform the tests, assays, and procedures
       needed for providing the specific services

E5-5

1. where unionists have a slim hold on the largest party title
2. why the children persisted in playing in the sun
   when they might be under the trees
3. where skills in a speciality of medicine are learned
4. why he sat alone
   when the farm work needed to be done
5. Where the Bible was opened
6. when they're caught
7. where he said security has improved significantly
8. when the water went bad in May, 2000
9. why they were unable to give accurate answers
10. where he had left me
    why I should loiter there

E5-6

1. in that ... chances of a successful partnership are high
   if the ideological gap between the sharing parties is narrow
2. as long as he could
   till he suddenly sank down in a heap
3. as soon as this view of the world is adopted
   (as soon as) the other (is) discarded
4. unless it suited his purpose to turn at you with a
      devouring glare
   before he let loose a torrent of foamy, abusive jargon that
      came like a gush from a sewer
5. If we are to criticize economists
6. because he could not swim

7. while the profession of medicine refers to the social
      structure of the group of people formally trained to
      apply that knowledge to treat disease
8. while another 337 have been detained on shore
9. so that he could return to Rome
10. As soon as he was warm
    before he drew out his guineas
    as he ate his unwonted feast

E5-7

1. that there was a range still farther back	noun
2. who had the smallest idea	relative adjective
who were themselves on the other side of it	relative adjective
if, indeed, there was any one at all	adverb
3. when I spoke to him	relative adverb
which gratified him greatly	relative adjective
4. that I would begin exploring	noun
as soon as shearing was over	adverb
(that) it would be a good thing to take Chowbok with me	noun
that I meant going to the nearer ranges for a few days' prospecting	noun
that he was to come too	noun
5. why this should be so	relative adverb
of which with my imperfect knowledge of the language I could make nothing whatever	relative adjective
that it was a very heinous offence	noun
6. that she had never before seen a rabbit with either a waist-coat pocket or a watch to take out of it	noun
7. (that) she knew	relative adjective
that were of the same age as herself	relative adjective
if she could have been changed for any of them	noun
8. While she was looking at the place	adverb
where it had been	relative adverb
9. whom she sentenced	relative adjective
who of course had to leave off being arches to do this	relative adjective
10. If the Israelis stop their agression against our people	adverb
(that) we can reach a final agreement	noun

E5-8

1. that the people ... were very loath to leave
   the villages   noun
   (that) they worked with   relative adjective
   in which they lived   relative adjective
2. that Kiefer is a modern German artist   noun
   that he is an expressionist,   noun
3. which I have collected on this curious
   subject   relative adjective
   which determine the reproduction of
   animals under confinement   relative adjective
   that carnivorous animals, even from the
   tropics, breed in this country pretty
   freely under confinement   noun
   whereas, carnivorous birds, with the rarest
   exceptions, hardly ever lay fertile eggs   adverb
4. When we look to the hereditary varieties
   or races of our domestic animals and
   plants   adverb
   (when we) compare them with species
   closely allied together   adverb
5. the breeds of which differ considerably
   from each other in structure   relative adjective
   that they all have descended from the
   common wild duck and rabbit   noun
6. that all the breeders of the various
   domestic animals and the cultivators
   of plants ... are firmly convinced   noun
   with whom I have ever conversed   relative adjective
   whose treatises I have read   relative adjective
   that the several breeds ... are descended from
   so many aboriginally distinct species   noun
   to which each has attended   relative adjective
7. if we look at each species as a special
   act of creation   adverb
   why more varieties should occur in a
   group having many species, than in
   one having few   relative adverb
8. if varieties be looked at as incipient species   adverb
   that ... the species of that genus present
   a number of varieties,   noun
   wherever many species of a genus have
   been formed   adverb
9. as every one knows   adverb
   (that) near villages and small towns I have
   found the nests of bumble-bees more
   numerous than elsewhere   noun
   which I attribute to the number of cats   relative adjective
   that destroy the mice   relative adjective
10. If we assume from the start   adverb
    that we cannot learn anything from others   noun
    because our own position has no room
    for growth   adverb

E5-9

1. C
2. D
3. A
4. E
5. B

E5-10

1. E
2. D
3. A
4. C
5. B

E5-11

1. because Dr. P. ... fell to work with a vigor
2. whose mysteries he understood so well
3. that I was a weaker vessel
4. though nothing would have induced me to confess it then
5. which soon convinced me

E5-12

1. who, ... , hummed a wandering tune
2. as he rode
3. where his thumb came in taking it off
4. though he was not thinking of anything in particular
5. which inclined him somewhat to the left of a straight line **or**
   that carried him

E5-13

1. [Noun]
2. [Adverb/ concession]
3. [Noun]
4. [Noun]
5. [Relative-adverb/place]
6. [Adverb/time]
7. [Adverb/time]
8. [Relative-adjective/non-personal]
9. [Adverb/time]
10. [Relative-adjective/personal]

E5-14

1. [Adverb/reason]
2. [Noun]
3. [Adverb/time]
4. [Adverb/comparison]
5. [Noun]
6. [Relative-adjective/non-personal]
7. [Relative-adjective/non-personal]
8. [Adverb/time]
9. [Relative-adjective/non-personal]
10. [Relative-adjective/non-personal]

E5-15

Clause analysis:

1. Noun clause

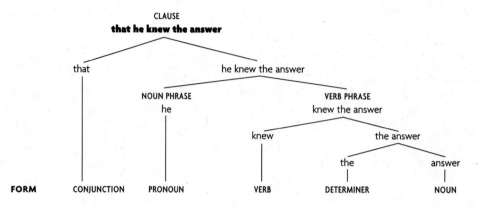

2. Relative adjective clause

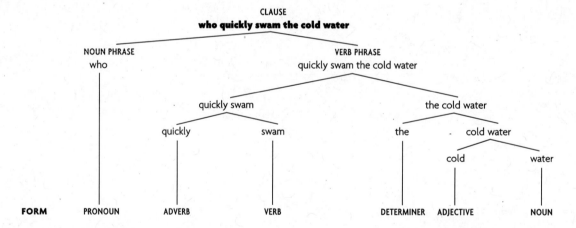

3. Adverbial clause

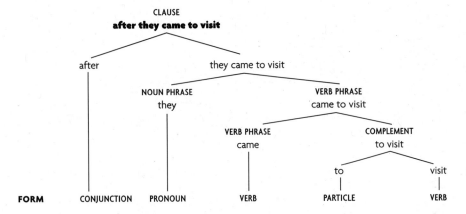

CHAPTER SIX

Major Grammatical Functions

E6-1

1. Q	6. G	11. I	16. H
2. T	7. L	12. B	17. K
3. M	8. N	13. O	18. E
4. P	9. A	14. D	19. J
5. C	10. S	15. F	20. R

E6-2

1. it [to practice medicine without a proper degree in that field]
   doctors
2. Notre Dame
   White
3. a large number of alternative approaches to health
   many
4. Procedural disputes between the British Government and
      Sinn Fein
   the recent resumption of IRA bombings in London
5. The village of Styles St. Mary
   Styles Court
6. Joseph Ratzinger
   he
7. The prime minister
   the government
8. Justices Michael Moldaver, Robert Sharpe and Eileen Gillese
   a new trial
9. Government lawyer Sylvain Lussier
   Gomery
   that
10. he
   [he]

E6-3

1. would ... sit
   dream
   lay
2. (a)re
   (a)re going
   said
3. will be watching
   might cross
   tip
4. did ... test
   did ... penalize
5. have been
   are
   give
6. had let go
   folded
   Come on
   ran
   was going
   caught hold
   pulled ... up
7. would invite
   could ... be used
   said
8. seems
   (a)re
   ought to get
9. had ... determined
   should go
   would have been
10. had run off
   was

E6-4

1. had — indicative
   were — subjunctive
2. was forcing — indicative
   be — subjunctive
3. be — subjunctive
   am — indicative
4. clothe — subjunctive
   freeze — subjunctive
5. screwed up — indicative
   blow — imperative
6. is known — indicative
   can be gathered — indicative
7. come — imperative
   come and be refreshed — imperative
8. be — subjunctive
   would ... think — indicative
9. had — subjunctive (conditional)
   would be — indicative
10. can be given — indicative

E6-5

1. active — A hand of each of the children was taken by Catherine.
2. passive — The arrival of the Gimmerton band increased our pleasure.
3. passive — About the middle of the night Mrs. Linton wakened me from my first nap.
4. passive — (Someone) was sacrificing his health and strength.
5. active — A little may have done by him in all these vocations.
6. active — The hearth was being swept by me.
7. passive — (Someone) did not shoot the bird.
8. active — Next time intelligence may be gathered by you for yourself.
9. passive — The young brigands, soon beginning to mingle in the sports, pillaged the latter most ruthlessly.
10. passive — [Someone] has declared Supplemental Security Income (SSI) ineligible.

E6-6

	VOICE	TRANSITION
1.	passive	The wide embrace of this conception altogether captivated Dorothea.
2.	active	A far wider range of possibilities than gladness and enjoyment is presented to them by pain and mishap.
3.	active	A remarkable feat of bodily exertion was being undertaken by him.
4.	active	The gentilities of a profession may be pursued by him.
5.	passive	And I do not see that Dorothea's opinions should bind me now we are going into society.
6.	passive	Threats secured the practical unanimity of Nicaea.
7.	passive	The fact that a fuller life was opening before her possessed her whole soul.

8. active — The company's first mine at Spinney Park, on the edge of Sherwood Forest was formally opened by Lord Palmerston.
9. active — Life is being made jolly difficult for us (by it).
10. active — A new will is suddenly and hurriedly made by your mother.

E6-7

1.	present	simple	indicative	active
	past	simple	indicative	active
2.	past	progressive	indicative	passive
	past	simple	indicative	active
3.	past	perfect	indicative	passive
4.	present*	simple	imperative	active
	present	simple	indicative	active
5.	present	simple	subjunctive	active
	future	simple	indicative	active
6.	present	simple	imperative	active
	past	simple	indicative	passive
7.	future	perfect	indicative	active
8.	future	progressive	indicative	active
9.	present	simple	subjunctive	active
10.	present	simple	indicative	passive

E6-8

1. a one-on-one competition
2. a major step forward
3. the assertion
   prominence
4. his meeting
   these people
   what (they have done)
5. us
   the personal dimension
6. some ring boxes
   a bright gleam
7. his books
   that he writes at the highest level of theology
8. [that] they leave *time* for parents to make arrangements for their children
   time
   arrangements
   [that they] refer *them* to a social service agency if necessary
   them
9. its way
   Adam
   dishonor
10. the judge
    no one
    [that] he would embrace *the option* mercifully permitted him by his lordship
    the option
    the sum

---

*Imperatives really have future rather than present intention.

E6-9

1. them
2. Europe
3. themselves
4. your question
5. Breton
6. papa
7. him
8. them
9. Yegor Semyonitch
10. Kovrin

E6-10

1. predicate   past   simple
   subject
2. direct object
   indirect object
3. predicate   present   progressive
   direct object
4. indirect object
   predicate   past   simple
5. indirect object
   direct object
6. direct object
   subject
7. subject
   predicate   past   perfect
8. subject
   direct object
9. predicate   past   progressive
   subject
10. subject [delayed]

E6-11

1. predicate   present   simple
   direct object
2. predicate   present   simple
   indirect object
3. subject
   indirect object
4. subject
   predicate   past   simple
5. subject
6. subject [delayed]
   predicate   present   simple
7. indirect object
8. predicate   past   perfect progressive
9. direct object
   direct object
10. direct object

E6-12

1. C
2. D
3. B
4. E
5. A

E6-13

1. E
2. C
3. D
4. B
5. A

E6-14

1. B
2. E
3. D
4. A
5. C

E6-15

1. B
2. D
3. A
4. E
5. C

E6-16

1. E
2. A
3. D
4. C
5. B

E6-17

1. D
2. C
3. E
4. B
5. A

E6-18

1. that we can spend hundreds of millions
2. have ... learnt
3. them
4. the outward aspect of life
5. are ... picking

E6-19

1. subject
2. direct object
3. indirect object
4. predicate [present perfect]
5. direct object
6. subject [delayed]
7. predicate [present perfect]
8. direct object
9. subject
10. predicate [past simple]

E6-20

1. subject
2. predicate [past perfect]
3. indirect object
4. direct object
5. direct object
6. indirect object
7. predicate [past perfect]
8. predicate [past simple]
9. direct object
10. subject

CHAPTER SEVEN

Minor Grammatical Functions

E7-1

1. T	6. N	11. E	16. H
2. Q	7. C	12. K	17. O
3. L	8. S	13. P	18. F
4. D	9. I	14. G	19. B
5. J	10. A	15. R	20. M

E7-2

	PREPOSITION	OBJECT
1.	into	the consciousness
	of	the Roman world
2.	upon	these matters
	during	the last half century
3.	outside	the will
	of	God
4.	from	the grip
	of	the blind powers
	beneath	the threshold

5.	because of	the Greeks
	of	Christ
	because of	the Jews
6.	without	significance
	for or against	God
	to	him
7.	for	statements
	against	deeply rooted mental habits
8.	of	other states
	of	penalties
	including	jail time
	for	such actions
9.	from	its very opening proposition
	of	the old Arminian teachings
	of	Wesleyans and Methodists
10.	regarding	sexual things

E7-3

	MODIFIER	TYPE
1.	The industrious	adjective phrase modifier
	among the carved images	prepositional phrase/adverb modifier
2.	once	adverb modifier
	outside of the water	prepositional phrase/adverb modifier
	gradually	adverb modifier
	more and more	adverb phrase modifier
	to life	prepositional phrase/adverb modifier
	on land	prepositional phrase/adverb modifier
3.	enormous open	adjective phrase modifier
	with heavy iron bars	prepositional phrase/adjective modifier
	high and barren	adjective phrase modifier
	the roosting	adjective phrase modifier
	of hundreds	prepositional phrase/adjective modifier
	of pigeons	prepositional phrase/adjective modifier
4.	originally	adverb modifier
	into the rocks	prepositional phrase/adverb modifier
	of the western mountains	prepositional phrase/adjective modifier
	northward	adverb modifier
	in the desert	prepositional phrase/adverb modifier
5.	a kind	adjective phrase modifier
	occasionally	adverb modifier
	a hard	adjective phrase modifier
6.	meanwhile	adverb modifier
	a certain	adjective phrase modifier
	by the name	prepositional phrase/adjective modifier
	of Barbero	prepositional phrase/adjective modifier

	of western Asia	prepositional phrase/adjective modifier
	of a most curious language	prepositional phrase/adjective modifier
7.	a thousand years later	adverb phrase modifier
	to the rule	prepositional phrase/adverb modifier
	of the Amorites	prepositional phrase/adjective modifier
8.	of the many divinities	prepositional phrase/adjective modifier
	widely	adverb modifier
	in western Asia	prepositional phrase/adverb modifier
9.	one day	adverb phrase modifier
	from the camp	prepositional phrase/adverb modifier
	of the Jews	prepositional phrase/adjective modifier
10.	unfortunately	adverb modifier
	already	adverb modifier
	by another Semitic	prepositional phrase/adjective modifier
	called the Canaanites	past participle phrase/adjective modifier

E7-4

	PHRASE	FUNCTION
1.	the story of Winifried and the Thunder-Oak	appositive
2.	James Lockyer	appositive
	an innocent man	objective complement
3.	frustrated	subjective complement/p-aj
	to be a large part of your appeal	subjective complement/p-n
4.	the city	subjective complement/p-n
	Forsaken	appositive
5.	to an outpouring	adverb complement
6.	of the water	adverb complement
	green	objective complement
7.	a delay	appositive
8.	working	subjective complement/p-aj
	talking	subjective complement/p-aj
9.	the River Clarita	objective complement
	no more Ablis, but Saloma	subjective complement/p-n
10.	into a quiet haven	adverb complement
	to his own country and his father's house	adverb complement
	onward	adverb complement

E7-5

	CONNECTOR	TYPE
1.	Yet	coordinating conjunction
	where	subordinating conjunction/relative adverb
2.	But	coordinating conjunction
	even though	subordinating conjunction/adverb concession
	and	coordinating conjunction
3.	that	subordinating conjunction/relative pronoun
	as well as	subordinating conjunction/adverb comparison
	and	coordinating conjunction
	who	subordinating conjunction/relative pronoun
	that	subordinating conjunction/noun clause
4.	who	subordinating conjunction/relative pronoun
	or	coordinating conjunction
	whose	subordinating conjunction/relative pronoun
5.	however	conjunctive adverb/concession
	not only ... but also	correlative conjunction
	because	subordinating conjunction/reason
	because	subordinating conjunction/reason
6.	Whatever	subordinating conjunction/indefinite relative pronoun
	whether ... or	correlative conjunction
	what	subordinating conjunction/noun clause
7.	that	subordinating conjunction/noun clause
	not only ... but also	correlative conjunction
	who	subordinating conjunction/relative pronoun
8.	which	subordinating conjunction/relative pronoun
	and	coordinating conjunction
9.	whichever	subordinating conjunction/indefinite relative pronoun
	and	coordinating conjunction
	if	subordinating conjunction/adverb concession
	or	coordinating conjunction
10.	why	subordinating conjunction/relative adverb
	which	subordinating conjunction/relative pronoun
	when	subordinating conjunction/relative adverb

E7-6

1. appositive
2. objective complement
3. appositive
4. adjective modifier/prepositional phrase
5. object of the preposition
6. subjective complement/predicate adjective
7. objective complement
8. object of the preposition
9. adverb modifier/prepositional phrase
10. subjective complement/predicate noun

E7-7

	STRUCTURE	FUNCTION
1.	prepositional phrase	adjective modifier
2.	noun phrase	subject
3.	participle phrase	adverb sentence modifier
4.	adverb phrase	adverb modifier
5.	verb phrase	predicate
6.	gerund phrase	object of preposition
7.	infinitive phrase	subject extra-posed
8.	participle phrase	adjective modifier
9.	noun phrase	direct object
10.	adjective phrase	objective complement

E7-8

1. appositive
   adjective modifier
2. subjective complement/predicate noun
   object of the preposition
3. predicate
   objective complement
4. adjective modifier/prepositional phrase
   subjective complement/predicate adjective
5. adverb sentence modifier
   direct object
6. subject
   connector/correlative conjunction
7. direct object
   indirect object
8. objective complement
   direct object extra-posed
9. adjective modifier/prepositional phrase
   appositive
10. connector/conjunctive adverb
    predicate

E7-9

1. objective complement
   subjective complement/(prepositional phrase) predicate adjective
2. direct object
   adjective modifier
3. adverb modifier
   adverb modifier
4. subject
   adverb modifier
5. subjective complement/predicate adjective
   direct object
6. appositive
   indirect object
7. connector/conjunctive adverb
   subjective complement/predicate adjective
8. subject

direct object
9. appositive
   adjective modifier
10. appositive
    adverb complement

E7-10
1. subject [extra-posed (delayed)]
2. subject
3. modifier/relative adjective
4. modifier/relative adverb
5. modifier/adverb/comparison
6. modifier/relative adjective
7. modifier/adverb/reason
8. modifier/relative adjective
9. objective complement
10. modifier/relative adjective

E7-11
1. modifier/adverb sentence/time
2. direct object
3. object of the preposition
4. modifier/relative adjective
5. modifier/relative adverb
6. subjective complement/predicate noun
7. subject
8. appositive
9. modifier/relative adjective
10. modifier/adverb/reason

E7-12
1. C
2. D
3. A
4. E
5. B

E7-13
1. E
2. C
3. A
4. B
5. D

E7-14
1. C
2. E
3. B
4. A
5. D

E7-15
1. B
2. C
3. A
4. E
5. D

E7-16
1. E
2. C
3. D
4. A
5. B

E7-17
1. C
2. D
3. B
4. E
5. A

E7-18
1. commonly known as Carolus Magnus or Charlemagne
2. what a Frankish chieftain of those early days meant
3. this occasion
4. when he promised to be faithful to his King

5. to retire/to be faithful

E7-19
1. subject
2. subjective complement/predicate adjective
3. adverb complement
4. indirect object
5. object of the preposition
6. predicate
7. adjective modifier
8. direct object
9. appositive
10. adverb modifier

E7-20
1. adverb modifier
2. connector
3. direct object
4. adjective modifier
5. subjective complement/predicate noun
6. adverb complement
7. appositive
8. appositive
9. adverb modifier
10. object of the preposition

CHAPTER EIGHT
Clause Functions

E8-1

1. J	6. T	11. B	16. R
2. Q	7. E	12. I	17. P
3. G	8. O	13. L	18. N
4. M	9. C	14. D	19. K
5. A	10. H	15. S	20. F

E8-2

CLAUSE	FUNCTION
1. that such arrangements may be rewarded with increased powers to local government	direct object
2. whatever is popular at the time	object of preposition
3. Whether or not Winstanley was intentionally dialectical	subject
4. that he had often spoken words of love to Madame Ratignolle	subject (extra-posed)
5. what she herself called very fond of music	subjective complement/p-n
6. that he had kept up with everything said about him in his absence	objective complement
7. that the ultimate decision on governing Northern Ireland would be made by the majority of its citizens	objective complement

8. whatever it was   appositive
9. that local government in Northern
    Ireland has now become the focus
    of research in power sharing   subject (extra-posed)
10. what the Rebels is fighting for   object of preposition

E8-3

	PRONOUN	FUNCTION
1.	that	subject
2.	whose	modifier/adjective
3.	where	modifier/adverb
	which	object of preposition
4.	that	direct object
5.	who	subject
	whom	object of preposition
6.	where	modifier/adverb
7.	when	modifier/adverb
8.	whose	modifier/adjective
	whom	object of preposition
	whom	direct object
9.	who	subject
	whose	modifier/adjective
10.	why	modifier/adverb

E8-4

	RELATIVE CLAUSE	FUNCTION MODIFIED
1.	who was crossing the courtyard and	direct object
	(who) stopped me	direct object
2.	whose indebtedness to Nietzsche and his spiritual kinship with the expressionists were obvious	subject complement/ predicate noun
3.	that had landed with him	subject
4.	that emerged on Friday	subject
	whom an agent in college football said	subject complement/ predicate noun
5.	to whom it was addressed	object of the preposition
	which might be put to him	direct object
6.	where he would plant his fist	direct object
7.	whose people were of my own race	appositive
8.	who has more than once made use of my knowledge of London crime	appositive
9.	who deigned, at this second interview, to move the extreme tip of her tail, in token of owning my acquaintance	direct object
10.	that has ever come to a human being	object of the preposition
	that he brings to God	object of the preposition
	why a knowledge of evil ways should not determine the path of duty	subjective complement

E8-5

	CLAUSE	TYPE
1.	who tasted the wines being auctioned	non-restrictive
2.	when he named Pennington to start	non-restrictive
3.	which involved a gift of prominence to the bass horn	restrictive
4.	where I had one before	restrictive
5.	who was pregnant at the time	non-restrictive
6.	whose policies they oppose	restrictive
7.	when the United States and other governments started to experiment with anthrax as a weapon	non-restrictive
8.	of whom so few enjoyed the comforts of life	non-restrictive
9.	why Cabot would have followed the coast on his east	restrictive
10.	which may and must produce good or evil fruit, in a far distant time	restrictive

E8-6

	CLAUSE	FUNCTION
1.	largely because of the work's persistent overall theme of death	adverb clause as an adverb modifier/cause and effect
2.	Although compromises were now necessary,	adverb clause as a sentence modifier/ cause and effect
3.	cannot go ahead unless the parliament passes a slate of laws allowing another election	adverb clause as a complement/ condition
4.	could not be sad because his son had died for America, died for freedom	adverb clause modifying a predicate/ cause and effect
5.	even if it's not likely	adverb clause as a sentence modifier/ concession
6.	responded as well as we reasonably could given the unique and demanding circumstances	adverb clause as a complement/ comparison
7.	as if he had been the fiction editor	adverb clause as a complement/ comparison
8.	Since this article was written	adverb clause as a sentence modifier/time

9. as shaken parents try to shield
young children from the reality
of deportation — adverb clause as a
complement/time

10. would have to sue because their
complaints are different — adverb clause
modifying a predicate/
reason

E8-7

1. TYPE   noun
   FUNCTION   direct object   (knew)

2. TYPE   relative adverb/restrictive
   FUNCTION   modifier   (picking up)

   TYPE   noun
   FUNCTION   appositive   (difference)

3. TYPE   adverb/time
   FUNCTION   modifier/predicate   (told)

   TYPE   noun
   FUNCTION   direct object   (to explain)

4. TYPE   noun
   FUNCTION   direct object   (remember)

5. TYPE   relative adjective/non-restrictive
   FUNCTION   modifier   (Curia)

   TYPE   relative adjective/restrictive
   FUNCTION   modifier   (everything)

6. TYPE   noun
   FUNCTION   subject

7. TYPE   adverb/contrast
   FUNCTION   modifier/sentence

8. TYPE   noun
   FUNCTION   subjective complement   ('s)

9. TYPE   adverb/comparison
   FUNCTION   adverb complement   (seemed)

10. TYPE   noun
    FUNCTION   complement of an adjective (fearful)

E8-8

CLAUSE

1. that the position of the chair would be rotated
   TYPE   noun
   FUNCTION   subject   (extra-posed)

   who deplore violence and seek to pursue political progress
   by political means

TYPE   relative adjective/restrictive
FUNCTION   modifier   (members)

2. because the doctor has been given a monopoly on access to
   the prescription pad
   TYPE   adverb/reason
   FUNCTION   modifier   (important)

3. before the plant and the skilled labour could be developed
   within France
   TYPE   adverb/time
   FUNCTION   complement   (elapse)

   unless she could rely on receiving the coal from Germany
   TYPE   adverb/condition
   FUNCTION   complement   (deal)

4. that will help the child to remember not to steal in the future
   TYPE   relative adjective/restrictive
   FUNCTION   modifier   (action)

5. why Day seems to have used both
   TYPE   relative adverb/restrictive
   FUNCTION   complement   (is)

6. that there are other ways of studying human beings
   TYPE   noun
   FUNCTION   direct object   (acknowledge)

   that also throw light on
   TYPE   relative adjective/restrictive
   FUNCTION   modifier   (human beings)

   what policies should be pursued
   TYPE   noun
   FUNCTION   object of the preposition (on)

7. Since the world operates mechanically
   TYPE   adverb
   FUNCTION   modifier/sentence

8. which in turn adds endlessly to the stress upon the
   environment
   TYPE   relative adjective/non-restrictive
   FUNCTION   modifier   (consumption)

9. that Detroit is the first cable market to carry Bridges TV
   TYPE   noun
   FUNCTION   subject   (extra-posed)

   since it is here
   TYPE   adverb/reason
   FUNCTION   modifier   (fitting)

where the idea was born and initial research was done
TYPE   relative adverb
FUNCTION   modifier   (here)

10. that the annual grants were given out based on applications
    submitted by individual ports
    TYPE   noun
    FUNCTION   subjective completion/
                predicate noun   (is)

    [that the annual grants were ...] then awarded
    TYPE   noun
    FUNCTION   subjective completion/
                predicate noun   (is)

    even when department staff members found
    TYPE   adverb/concession
    FUNCTION   complement   (awarded)

    that many of the submissions lacked merit
    TYPE   noun
    FUNCTION   direct object   (found)

E8-9
    CLAUSE
1. If we do so
    TYPE   adverb/condition
    FUNCTION   sentence modifier

    before market prices reflect them
    TYPE   adverb/time
    FUNCTION   modifier   (predicate)

2. whatever you are
    TYPE   noun
    FUNCTION   appositive   (you)

3. which sometimes only over the course of many generations
   establishes clearly the constraints
    TYPE   relative adjective/restrictive
    FUNCTION   modifier   (process)

    within which they assume distinctive shapes
    TYPE   relative adjective/restrictive
    FUNCTION   modifier   (constraints)

4. when her name was announced in the library
    TYPE   adverb
    FUNCTION   modifier   (winced)

    where he was sitting alone
    TYPE   relative adverb/non-restrictive
    FUNCTION   modifier   (library)

5. that Mrs. Gold is a very polite, quiet woman
    TYPE   noun
    FUNCTION   direct object   (know)

who never raises her voice
TYPE   relative adjective/restrictive
FUNCTION   modifier   (woman)

6. [that] Mrs. Inglethorp took the coffee after dinner about
   eight o'clock
    TYPE   noun
    FUNCTION   direct object   (presume)

    whereas the symptoms did not manifest themselves until the
    early hours of the morning
    TYPE   adverb/contrast
    FUNCTION   sentence modifier

    which, on the face of it, points to the drug having been taken
    much later in the evening
    TYPE   relative adjective/non-restrictive
    FUNCTION   modifier   (it)

7. until our visitor had left us
    TYPE   adverb/time
    FUNCTION   modifier   (preserved)

    although it was easy for me ... to see
    TYPE   adverb/concession
    FUNCTION   modifier   (preserved)

    who knew him so well
    TYPE   relative adjective/non-restrictive
    FUNCTION   modifier   (me)

    that he was profoundly excited
    TYPE   noun
    FUNCTION   direct object   (see)

8. who could understand the higher inward life
    TYPE   relative adjective/restrictive
    FUNCTION   modifier   (man)

    with whom there could be some spiritual communion
    TYPE   relative adjective/restrictive
    FUNCTION   modifier   (man)

    who could illuminate principle with the widest knowledge
    a man
    TYPE   relative adjective/restrictive
    FUNCTION   modifier   (man)

    whose learning almost amounted to a proof
    TYPE   relative adjective/restrictive
    FUNCTION   modifier   (man)

    whatever he believed
    TYPE   noun
    FUNCTION   object of the preposition   (of)

9. which deal with spirit, purpose, and intention
   TYPE   relative adjective/restrictive
   FUNCTION   modifier   (*passages*)

   whether, in view of them, deception or hypocrisy has been practised
   TYPE   noun
   FUNCTION   direct object   (*judge*)

10. when I was seized again with those indescribable sensations
    TYPE   relative adverb/restrictive
    FUNCTION   complement   (*stepping*)

    that heralded the change
    TYPE   relative adjective/restrictive
    FUNCTION   modifier   (*sensations*)

    before I was once again raging and freezing with the passions of Hyde
    TYPE   adverb
    FUNCTION   modifier   (*had*)

E8-10
1. B
2. E
3. A
4. C
5. D

E8-11
1. E
2. C
3. B
4. A
5. D

E8-12
1. B
2. D
3. C
4. A
5. E

E8-13
1. C
2. A
3. E
4. B
5. D

E8-14
1. B
2. A
3. E
4. D
5. C

E8-15
1. B
2. D
3. C
4. E
5 A

E8-16
1. D
2. C
3. A
4. E
5. B

E8-17
1. D
2. B
3. A
4. E
5. C

E8-18

1. TYPE   relative adjective/non-restrictive
   FUNCTION   modifier   (*delusion*)

2. TYPE   relative adjective/restrictive
   FUNCTION   modifier   (*those*)

3. TYPE   noun
   FUNCTION   direct object   (*teach*)

4. TYPE   relative adjective/restrictive
   FUNCTION   modifier   (*error*)

5. TYPE   adverb
   FUNCTION   sentence modifier

6. TYPE   relative adjective/restrictive
   FUNCTION   modifier   (*indiscrimination*)

7. TYPE   noun
   FUNCTION   subject/extra-posed

8. TYPE   adverb
   FUNCTION   modifier   (*days*)

9. TYPE   noun
   FUNCTION   subject/extra-posed

10. TYPE   relative adjective/restrictive
    FUNCTION   modifier   (*zeal*)

E8-19
1. that he had been in a position to overlook the whole garden from the time
   TYPE   noun
   FUNCTION   direct object   (*testified*)

2. when Colonel Druce last appeared alive in the doorway to the time
   TYPE   relative adverb/restrictive
   FUNCTION   modifier   (*time*)

3. when he was found dead
   TYPE   relative adverb/restrictive
   FUNCTION   modifier   (*time*)

4. as he, Floyd, had been on the top of a step-ladder clipping the garden hedge
   TYPE   adverb/reason
   FUNCTION   sentence modifier

5. that she had sat on the terrace of the house throughout that time and had seen Floyd at his work
   TYPE   noun/compound noun clause
   FUNCTION   direct object   (*said*)

6. who overlooked the garden standing at his bedroom window in his dressing-gown
   TYPE   relative adjective/non-restrictive
   FUNCTION   modifier   (Druce/brother)

7. since he had risen late
   TYPE   adverb/reason
   FUNCTION   sentence modifier

8. that was given by Dr. Valentine
   TYPE   relative adjective/non-restrictive
   FUNCTION   modifier   (one)

9. who called for a time to talk with Miss Druce on the terrace
   TYPE   relative adjective/non-restrictive
   FUNCTION   modifier   (neighbor)

10. who was apparently the last to see the murdered man alive
    TYPE   relative adjective/non-restrictive
    FUNCTION   modifier   (Traill)

E8-20

1. Because religion cannot be organised
   TYPE   adverb/reason
   FUNCTION   sentence modifier

2. because God is everywhere and immediately accessible to every human being
   TYPE   adverb/reason
   FUNCTION   sentence modifier

3. that religion cannot organise every other human affair
   TYPE   noun
   FUNCTION   subject/extra-posed

4. that God is the Invisible King of this round world and all mankind
   TYPE   noun
   FUNCTION   appositive   (idea)

5. that we should see in every government ... the instrument of God's practical control
   TYPE   noun
   FUNCTION   subject (extra-posed)

6. that is presently coming
   TYPE   relative adjective/restrictive
   FUNCTION   modifier   (world-state)

7. which is free
   TYPE   relative adjective/restrictive
   FUNCTION   modifier   (religion)

8. whom it will (whoever it will)
   TYPE   noun
   FUNCTION   object of preposition   (through)

9. if you prefer not to say
   TYPE   adverb/condition
   FUNCTION   sentence modifier

10. that there will be no church
    TYPE   noun
    FUNCTION   direct object   (prefer)

11. if you choose rather to declare
    TYPE   adverb/condition
    FUNCTION   sentence modifier

12. that the world-state is God's church
    TYPE   noun
    FUNCTION   direct object   (choose)

13. if you will
    TYPE   adverb/condition
    FUNCTION   modifier   (have)

14. provided that you leave conscience and speech and writing and teaching about divine things absolutely free
    TYPE   adverb/condition
    FUNCTION   modifier (of previous sentence)

15. [provided] that you try to set no nets about God
    TYPE   adverb/condition
    FUNCTION   modifier (of previous sentence)

Paragraph structures are difficult contexts in which to identify grammatical functions, especially for clauses.

CHAPTER NINE

Grammatical Positions

E9-1

1. P	6. K	11. F	16. A
2. S	7. J	12. R	17. N
3. I	8. O	13. E	18. L
4. T	9. C	14. Q	19. B
5. M	10. G	15. H	20. D

E9-2

1. Americans	ballots	Republicans	
2. season	he	it	
coolness	peace	evenings	supper
3. shadow	cherry-trees	grass	
4. doctor	situation	he	nothing
it			
5. accounts	other	he	secretary

6. explanation   staters   hicks   who
   righteousness
7. audience   this   crowd   journalists
   luminaries   Hollywood   Manhattan
8. Tillich   us   paintings   photographs
   reproductions   events-reproductions
9. doctor   howl   machine   sense
   one   robins   cherry-trees   affairs
10. I   elder   name   I
    Herbert Druce   who   authority   horse-breeding
    nothing   mare   he   character
    man   who   her   brother
    Harry   luck   Monte Carlo

E9-3

1. that he preferred to stay
2. what manner of girls the sisters were
   what the father was like
   how long the mother had been dead
3. that Robert would interest himself
   and [that Robert would] discover
   whether she was entitled to the indulgence accompanying the
      remarkably curious Mexican prayer-beads
4. whatever else happened to be in his pockets
5. what to make of it
   how much of it was jest
   what proportion was earnest
6. that ... he had never known
   what it was to be poor
   [what it was] to suffer the pangs of hunger and failure
7. that maybe Harry wasn't dressed warm enough
   how that north wind did bite
8. whether she was going to quilt it or knot it
9. that there are other ways of studying human beings
   what policies should be pursued
10. whether the indulgence extended outside the Mexican
    border

E9-4

1. are   is   have been   is   are
2. was sitting   had given
3. have been   have   becomes
4. had ... said   must admit   gave
   had ... been piqued   had made
5. would have ... believe   punishes   may ... forgive
   is   may be removed
6. was making   would have had   held
7. winced   had ... been decided   had thought
8. had returned   had kept   had changed
9. seemed   couldn't cross   was
   had ... crossed
10. would have been   might have added

E9-5

1. a squeezing, wrenching, grasping, scraping, clutching,
      covetous old
2. cold, bleak, biting
   foggy
   their
   their
   their
   the pavement
3. the mighty
   his fifty
   a Lord Mayor's
4. the good
   the Evil Spirit's
   such
   his familiar
   lusty
5. ablaze
   fine
6. a long, brick
   a velvet
7. neat
   immaculate
   the various Eastern
   ship-chandler's
   popular
8. a ... tall, thin
   a long
   two keen, gray
   gold-rimmed
9. the pilgrim ship
   a good
   a free and wandering
   the whole
   a simple and sensitive
10. a young
    his
    a dandy
    drab
    the same
    white
    stick-up
    brown
    the handsome, horsey young

E9-6

1. from whom so speedy a separation was threatened
   which seemed to quiver in her eyes and on her lips
      convulsively pressed together
2. whose features expressed somewhat more gentleness than
      those of his brother
3. by which they could recall the whole story of their lives
4. that are taking place in the Ukraine
5. who had called down destruction upon himself
   by which they had seized him
6. that could make us angry with the world or each other

7. which promised to be the support of my declining age
   who ... brought his thirty-two children
   and [who] presented them to his sovereign as the most
       valuable offering
   [that] he had to bestow
8. whom I designed for business
9. in whose hands your money was lodged
10. who seemed before sufficiently inclined to break off
       the match
    which was prudence
    that is left us at seventy-two

E9-7
1. very
   extremely
2. Indeed
   ever
   before
   well
   in the eyes of this rich uncle
   to give them pretty and serviceable clothes
3. Evidently
   with a word to his companions
   toward the window
4. Then
   forward
   to the fire
   stretching his hands to the blaze
5. then
   likewise
   forward
   eagerly
6. at the knees
   in an ugly, almost beast-like fashion
7. Then
   with joy
   suddenly
   against the nose
8. to the New Inn
   at Bretty
   not yet
9. by noting ...
   all round
   in a most unwoodmanlike way
   straight across
   by the axe of a master
10. awkwardly
    hither and thither

E9-8
1. when the frenzy of that hideous epoch had subsided
2. while the elderly gentleman stood looking at the Pyncheon-
       house
3. after the judges retired to deliberate
4. until the changes are passed
5. since I used to see you playing about the door of the old
       house, quite a small child

6. where we are
   where he'll end up
7. as if it were not himself
   just as a man may beat his breast
   as Cranmer the martyr did
   [just as a man may] thrust his hand into the flames
8. as if the person's feet came involuntarily to a stand-still
   because the motive power was too feeble to sustain his
       progress
9. if the face of the tomb did become a face for him
   because her two names became a pair of eyes that didn't
       know him
10. because his son had died for America
    [because his son] died for freedom
    even though the unchristian politicians kept us from winning
        that war
    as we should have
    because his boy had died for a good cause
    although the work at home did not get done

E9-9
1. adverbial
2. adjectival
3. verbal
4. nominal
5. adverbial
6. adverbial
7. nominal
8. adjectival
9. verbal
10. adjectival

E9-10
1. adjectival
2. nominal
3. adverbial
4. adjectival
5. adjectival
6. nominal
7. adverbial
8. adverbial
9. adjectival
10. nominal

E9-11
1 D
2. C
3. A
4. E
5. B

E9-12
1. B
2. C
3. A
4. E
5. D

E9-13
1 C
2. B
3. E
4. D
5. A

E9-14
1. E
2. A
3. B
4. C
5. D

E9-15
1. C
2. D
3. A
4. E
5. B

E9-16
1. B
2. D
3. A
4. E
5. C

E9-17
1. nominal
2. adjectival
3. nominal
4. nominal
5. verbal
6. adverbial
7. adverbial
8. nominal
9. adjectival
10. verbal

E9-18
1. nominal
2. adjectival
3. verbal
4. adjectival
5. adjectival
6. nominal
7. adverbial
8. adjectival
9. verbal
10. nominal

E9-19
1. adverbial
2. nominal
3. adverbial
4. nominal
5. adjectival
6. adverbial
7. adverbial
8. adverbial
9. adjectival
10. nominal

E9-20

NOMINALS
1. that they generally differ much more from each other, than do the individuals of any one species or variety in a state of nature
2. [that] we are driven to conclude
3. that this greater variability is simply due to our domestic productions having been raised under conditions of life not so uniform as, and somewhat different from, those
4. that this variability may be partly connected with excess of food
5. that organic beings must be exposed during several

generations to the new conditions of life to cause any appreciable amount of variation
6. that … it generally continues to vary for many generations

ADJECTIVALS
1. which strikes us
2. which have been cultivated
3. which have varied during all ages under the most different climates and treatment
4. to which the parent-species have been exposed under nature

ADVERBIALS
1. When we look to the individuals of the same variety or sub-variety of our older cultivated plants and animals
2. When we reflect on the vast diversity of the plants and animals
3. when the organisation has once begun to vary

CHAPTER TEN

Sentences

E10-1
1. O
2. E
3. N
4. H
5. A
6. L
7. F
8. B
9. K
10. J
11. D
12. M
13. C
14. I
15. G

E10-2
1. S-V-SC/pn
2. S-V-IDO-DO
3. S-V-DO
4. S-V-IDO-DO
5. S-V
6. S-V-DO-C
7. S-V-C
8. S-V-DO-C
9. S-V-IDO-DO
10. S-V-SC/pa

E10-3
1. simple
2. complex
3. compound
4. simple
5. compound-complex
6. compound
7. compound
8. compound-complex
9. compound
10. complex

E10-4
1. simple
2. complex
3. compound
4. compound-complex
5. compound
6. simple
7. simple
8. compound-complex
9. complex
10. simple

E10-5
1. complex
2. complex
3. simple
4. compound
5. compound-complex
6. compound
7. complex
8. simple
9. complex
10. compound-complex

E10-6
1. exclamatory
2. interrogative
3. declarative
4. declarative
5. exclamatory
6. interrogative
7. exclamatory
8. declarative
9. declarative
10. imperative

E10-7

1. NP	LV	SC(av)
2. NP	TV	NP^2/NP^3
3. NP	LV	SC/pn
4. NP	LV	SC/paj
5. NP	TV	NP^2
6. NP	ITV	C/prp-ph
7. NP	TV	NP^2/n-cl
8. NP	LV	SC/paj
9. NP	TV	NP^2
10. NP	ITV	C/inf

E10-8

1. NP	LV	SC/paj
2. NP	TV	NP^2(Do)
3. NP	ITV	C(av)
4. NP	TV	NP^2(Do)
5. NP	LV	SC/pn
6. NP	ITV	
7. NP	LV	SC/paj
8. NP	ITV	C(av)
9. NP	LV	SC/pn
10. NP	LV	SC/paj

E10-9

1. NP	TV	NP^2	+	NP^3	+	Pp-ph
2. NP	ITV	C				
3. NP	TV	NP^2	+	Prp-ph		
4. NP	TV	NP^2				
5. NP	TV	NP^2	+	av		
6. NP	TV	NP^2	+	I-ph		
7. NP	ITV	C(av)				
8. NP	TV	NP^2	+	NP^3	+	Pp-ph
9. NP	TV	NP^2	+	I-ph		
10. NP	TV	NP^2	+	NP^3	+	Prp-ph

E10-10

1 D		6. B
2. F		7. J
3. H		8. C
4. A		9. E
5. I		10. G

E10-11
1 D
2. C
3. A
4. E
5. B

E10-12
1. E
2. C
3. D
4. B
5. A

E10-13
1. simple
2. compound-complex
3. complex
4. compound-complex
5. simple
6. compound
7. complex
8. simple
9. complex
10. simple

E10-14

1. NP	TV	NP^2	
2. NP	LV	C	
3. NP	TV	NP^2	
4. NP	TV	NP^2	Av
5. NP	LV	C	
6. NP	ITV	C	
7. NP	TV	NP^2	Av
8. NP	LV	C	
9. NP	TV	NP^2	Av
10. NP	TV	NP^2	NP^2

E10-15

Sentence analysis

1. Focus on gerund phrase:

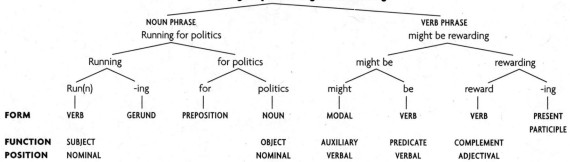

2. Focus on verb phrase:

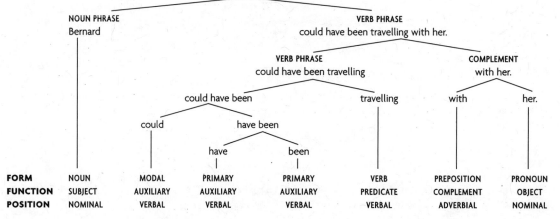

Using 529 lb. of Rolland Enviro100 Print instead
of virgin fibres paper reduces your ecological footprint of:

Trees: 4 ; 0.1 American football field
Solid waste: 286lb
Water: 2,697gal ; a shower of 0.6 day
Air emissions: 627lb ; emissions of 0.1 car per year